The
WITCHES
OF Hertfordshire

The WITCHES OF HERTFORDSHIRE

Simon Walker

TEMPUS

First published 2004

Tempus Publishing Limited
The Mill, Brimscombe Port,
Stroud, Gloucestershire, GL5 2QG

© Simon Walker, 2004

The right of Simon Walker to be identified as the Author
of this work has been asserted in accordance with the
Copyrights, Designs and Patents Act 1988.

All rights reserved. No part of this book may be reprinted
or reproduced or utilised in any form or by any electronic,
mechanical or other means, now known or hereafter invented,
including photocopying and recording, or in any information
storage or retrieval system, without the permission in writing
from the Publishers.

British Library Cataloguing in Publication Data.
A catalogue record for this book is available from the British Library.

ISBN 0 7524 3203 6

Typesetting and origination by Tempus Publishing Limited
Printed in Great Britain by Midway Colour Print, Wiltshire

Contents

Acknowledegments 7
Introduction 9
Prologue 11

Part One: History
1 The Development of Witchcraft and Magic 13
2 The Witch Hunt in Continental Europe 25
3 Witches in England: 1500-1736 40
4 The Reality of Witchcraft 88

Part Two: Hertfordshire Cases
Note on the Sources 95
5 Maleficium 97
6 Cunning Folk and Fortune Tellers 111
7 Possession and Bewitchment 117
8 Jane Wenham of Walkern: 1711-1712 135
9 Unofficial Action 155
10 Appearances of the Devil 163
11 The Physical Evidence of Witchcraft 173
12 Miscellany 179

Conclusion 183
Appendix A: Table of Prosecutions in Herts 185
Appendix B: Statistics for Hertfordshire 194
Glossary 199
Bibliography 202
Notes 204
Index 216

ACKNOWLEDGEMENTS

I would like to acknowledge the work of other researchers whose efforts have made life so much easier for me. C.L. Ewen, whose trawl through Assize and other records was extensive; the work of Her Majesty's Stationery Office (as it then was) in publishing indictments for Hertfordshire during the reigns of Elizabeth I and James I; W. Le Hardy's *Quarter Session Rolls* (*Hertfordshire County Session Rolls, 1581-1698*) provides information from the Quarter Sessions records. W. B. Gerish, collector of Hertfordshire folklore in the early twentieth century, published some of the pamphlets included in this book, although on at least one occasion he chose to censor the original[1]; Alan Macfarlane, whose analysis of witchcraft cases in Essex has become a standard work on the subject. Ralph Merrifield's *The Archaeology of Ritual and Magic* is difficult to put down. Owen Davies's *Witchcraft, Magic and Culture 1736-1951* falls into the same category, as does *Religion and the Decline of Magic* by Keith Thomas. Barbara Rosen's *Witchcraft in England 1558-1618* is an extremely valuable work and not to be missed. Wallace Notestein and George Lymen Kittredge, though originally published before Ewen's work appeared, nonetheless both contain a wealth of detail and useful sources. W.C. Hazlitt's *Dictionary of Faiths and Folklore* is a delightful antiquarian compendium that includes numerous quotations from early works; where I have been able to verify these I have found no errors, and I am inclined to believe that he, his colleagues and his predecessors were painstaking in their work. Robert Thurston and Jeffrey Russell's books give very readable and thought-provoking overviews of international witchcraft. Publication details of these and many other books consulted are in the bibliography. A number of works from the fifteenth to eighteenth centuries have been reprinted over the years, though some are not easy to get hold of. Others I have been fortunate enough to consult in original form.

To provide a full list of those who deserve acknowledgement would be impossible, but here are some of them, in no particular order: Brian Hoggard; Bridget Howlett; Pauline Humphries; Bryn and Julie Lerwill; Gerry Tidy; Brendan King; Jenny Gibbons; Richard Walker; Lily Bradford; Janet Newman; Alan Millard; Claire Thornton and Alison Turner-Rugg of St Albans Museum; Ros Allwood, Gillian Riding and Caroline Frith of North Hertfordshire Museums Service; Liz Howe of the Museum of London Archaeological Service; the staff at Hertfordshire Archives and Local Studies (Hertfordshire County Record Office); and the staff of the British Library. To those not mentioned by name, I offer my apologies and thanks nonetheless.

On a more personal level, I want to thank all those around me, who have put up with me being a 'witchcraft bore' for far longer than I had any right to expect.

Note on Gender

I have been rather liberal with gender. In order to avoid the ponderous 'his or her...' I have used 'he/him/his' throughout. I am fully aware of the preponderance of women amongst the accused, and I have discussed the causes in the relevant place. I ask the reader to forgive me for placing ease of reading before political correctness in the instance.

Note on Spelling

Spelling was, in the past, a rather hit and miss affair. I considered modernizing spellings, but in the decided to leave them as they were written in most cases. Hence, for example, 'Stansted' appears as 'Stanstead'.

Copyright

Every effort has been made to trace original copyright holders. I apologize to any who may have been missed.

INTRODUCTION

We all think we know about witches. We know that they met in covens of thirteen, they flew on broomsticks, and, when caught, they were ducked or 'swum', in which case, to prove their innocence, they had to drown. If they floated, they were pronounced guilty, dried off and burned alive. Their power was considerable, their attitude malignant. Male witches were called warlocks. Many thousands lost their lives in England alone. Witchcraft was a surviving pagan religion, handed down through the generations, and practised in secret, only to be ruthlessly suppressed by the Christian Church as a dangerous rival.

The truth is often somewhat different, and it was one of those differences that prompted this book. For many years it had seemed to me quite illogical that a method of proving a suspect's innocence should result in death. I was not greatly surprised, therefore, to find that fact was at variance with the popular notion. That got me wondering. What else was fiction? What was the truth about witchcraft in England? More specifically, what about Hertfordshire, my home county?

Great Britain and Ireland comprise a group of islands off the coast of Continental Europe, and this physical separation has had a major impact on our history. As a result, some authors have treated British witchcraft, along with other facets of British history, as though it developed in isolation. But that isolation, though real, was not total. Witchcraft, magic and superstition in the British Isles did not develop on its own; the beliefs and practices of its people were introduced or influenced by outsiders, both violent and peaceful. In order to understand what happened here, we need some understanding of the development of occult beliefs in Europe too.

But this is a book about Hertfordshire, so it is upon Hertfordshire cases we shall concentrate. If necessary, we will stray across the borders from time to time into neighbouring counties in order to illustrate a point; there is no alternative. The physical evidence of witchcraft and magic is sometimes fleeting – curses and charms written on scraps of paper only rarely survive. Michael Dalton in 1618 rightly stated that we cannot expect too much direct evidence, 'seeing that all their [the witches'] works are the works of darknesse, and no witnesses present with them to accuse them...'[1] Fortunately, as beliefs do not stop at county boundaries, it is not unreasonable to suppose that those held in bordering counties such as Bedfordshire, Cambridgeshire and Essex were also to be found in Hertfordshire.

Little evidence has come down to us from the condemned witches themselves. Many witch suspects confessed, but often under duress. Though torture in England was against Common Law[2], some of the methods used against suspects fell little short of it. What is recorded of their statements was usually written by hostile authors, convinced of the prisoner's guilt.

Some, perhaps, believed themselves guilty. Other confessions must have been made by that strange group who confess to anything and everything under the sun. Were they all innocent, or were some of them really guilty of maleficent or heretical magical practices?

Prologue

On 21 March 1610, seven people appeared before William Cade, Justice of the Peace, and swore depositions against Margery Raye for the crime of witchcraft. Some of those present also laid accusations against Margery's daughter, Elizabeth. The accusers included Henry Beaman, a labourer; Elizabeth Nashe, a widow; Stephen Standly, a tailor; and Bernard Peddleton, a carpenter. They all came from Berkhamsted in south Hertfordshire. Yeoman John Howe of Littleheath in Northchurch, no more than a stone's throw away, also made allegations against the two women. Perhaps the most shocking feature of the case was that Margery's husband Ralph Raye, who was a sawyer, also gave evidence against her. So did Tobias Raye, another family member. Such was their belief of Margery's guilt that the witnesses all gave recognisances[1] for their appearance in court to give evidence against the accused if necessary. Two days later, Agnes Humphry entered into a similar recognisance. In the event, only Tobias Raye and Agnes Humphry were called to the box.

At the same time, Ralph Raye and Henry Shermantine entered into recognisances for the appearance of Elizabeth Raye at the Lent Sessions of the assizes, soon to be held at Hertford. The Clerk of Assize drew up indictments against the two women, and on 23 March their cases came to trial. The first hearing was before the Grand Jury, whose task was to decide whether there was indeed a case to answer, or whether the accusations were without foundation. According to the indictments, Margery and Elizabeth Raye had, on 1 October the previous year, bewitched Elizabeth Humphry. She had languished for some months, finally dying on 14 February 1610. Exactly what happened next is not certain, but it seems likely that the Grand Jury decided that, whilst

Margery Raye probably had indeed murdered Elizabeth Humphry by witchcraft, Elizabeth Raye did not have a case to answer.[2]

The Justices of Assize at the Lent hearings were Sir Thomas Walmesley and Sir John Croke. Both men were senior judges with considerable experience. We do not know which of the two heard Margery's case, but we do know that the jury found her guilty. Her indictment is endorsed with a short Latin abbreviation: '*Po se cul ca null Judm S*'. The full version would have read '*Ponit se super patriam de bono et malo, culpabilis, catalla nulla, judicium secundum formam statuti, suspendatur per collum*', which means 'places herself before the country for good or ill, found guilty, has no goods, judgement according to the form of the statute, let her be hanged by the neck.'[3]

How could it be that family members could turn against one another in such a way, with the result that a wife and mother lost her life at the end of a rope?[4]

PART ONE
HISTORY

I

THE DEVELOPMENT OF WITCHCRAFT AND MAGIC

What is a witch? A selection of definitions from dictionaries might help:

> A female magician, sorceress; in later use esp. a woman supposed to have dealings with the Devil or evil spirits and to be able with their cooperation to perform supernatural acts.[1]

> A person, usually female, who practises or professes to practise magic or sorcery, esp. black magic, or is believed to have dealings with the Devil.[2]

> Woman (or, archaically, man) using magic; old hag...[3]

There is some agreement; the witch was usually female, and magic was involved. The first two definitions refer to dealings with the Devil, and have strong implications of evil. The third is less dogmatic concerning the right and wrongs of witchcraft, but raises the stereotype of the aged and ugly witch. One authority defines a witch as someone who was persecuted either by the Church or the State under witchcraft laws; this is perhaps too narrow a definition – it omits most 'white' witches, who, as a benign force in society,[4] were rarely prosecuted, even though the Witchcraft Statute of 1563 made the persistent practice of magic, good or bad, a felony. Some contemporary authors' viewpoints included:

> In estimation of the vulgar people, a supernatural work between a corporal old woman and a spiritual devil. (1584)[5]

> Witchcraft is a wicked Art, serving for the working of wonders, by the assistance of the Devil, so farre forth as God shall in justice permit. (1608)[6]

> The chief thing that makes a witch, is a solemn bargain and covenant with infernal spirits. (1668)[7]

The diabolic element is present in all of them. This is interesting, because as we shall see, for the most part witches in England were convicted for the harm they did rather than the means they used to do it; and the concept of a pact with Satan is far less frequently encountered than in Continental Europe.

The word 'witch' is derived from the Old English *wiccan*, meaning to cast a spell, to work sorcery. Derivatives are *wicca*, a male witch, and *wicce*, a female one. The term 'witch' was, from early days, applied to practitioners of the craft of either sex. Contrary to popular belief, and to the claims of some of those professing to practise witchcraft today, there is no evidence of any connection with the Anglo-Saxon word *witan*, meaning wise. The only word associated with the magic arts that can claim to mean 'wise' is the Middle English 'wizard'. In time, a 'wissard' became a highly-skilled practitioner of magic; the top of the enchanters' tree, as it were.

Other words that need to be defined are 'warlock', 'sorcery' and 'magic'. A 'warlock' was not a male witch, as is often thought today. This Old English word originally referred to a traitor or a scoundrel. Not until the fifteenth century did it take on any flavour of magic, when it became associated with witches of both sexes. Only later did it assume its current meaning.

'Sorcery' is from the Old French, *sorcier*, and means the harnessing of occult powers to produce an effect on the temporal world. Its roots are in divination, or attempting to foretell events. Sorcery nowadays bears an implication of evil, but in the past it took no sides; it could be used for good or evil, according to the inclination of the practitioner.

'Magic' is from the Greek *magos*, a magician. The Latin form was *magus*. The key element of magic is coercion. Supernatural laws are harnessed to force a result, whether for good or evil.

Ritual and Prehistory

Belief in magic and the supernatural is much older than any of these definitions. It is prehistoric. Evidence includes the horned man at Trois Frères cave in the French Pyrenees, perhaps 10-15,000 years old, and the masks found at Star Carr in Yorkshire, dating from 7500 BC.[8]

Many pre-Roman sites are believed to have a ritual component – stone circles and barrows for example, and though we know little or nothing of the ceremonies associated with them, it seems highly likely that a

The horned man from Trois Frères cave. The figure's legs are unmistakably human. (Author, after a drawing by Abbé Breuil)

'magical' element did indeed exist. Alignments with celestial events also occur, but it would be unreasonable to suggest that, because a stone circle seems to have been a calendar, no ritual could have been attached to its use.

Many human bodies dating from the Iron Age have been found in bogs in northern Europe, some of them bearing signs of ritual sacrifice. A typical example was discovered in 1984 at Lindow End, Cheshire. Strangulation seems to be a common cause of death, and in the case of the Lindow man his skull was fractured, his jaw broken and his neck dislocated, injuries consistent with having been hanged.[9] His throat had been cut as well. In some cases, traces of ergot have been found in the contents of the stomach.[10] Whether the victims of such executions were criminals or sacrificial victims no one knows, but this excessive violence frequently used against these unfortunate people strongly suggests a ritual element to their deaths.[11]

There have been Bronze and Iron Age weapons found in a state that may imply a ritual or magical purpose. They are often bent or broken, perhaps 'killed', in order that their essence may travel to a spirit world. The numbers found, often within a small area, suggest that we may rule

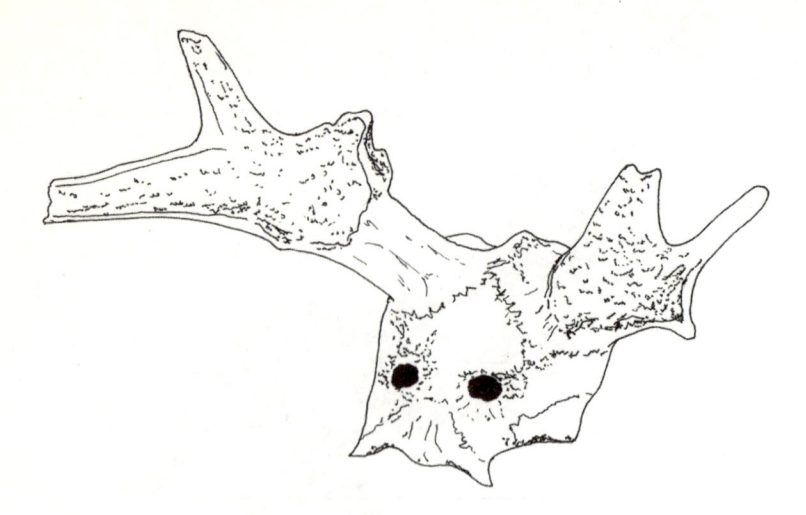

A mask from Star Carr in Yorkshire, made from a deer skull. The holes for the eyes are artificial – the animal's orbits are in a different position. Small holes at the back of the mask, not visible in this view, are thought to have been used to attach it to the wearer. (Author)

out the theory that they were discarded after being damaged; in any case, bronze and iron were valuable raw materials, much more likely to have been melted down and re-used than merely thrown away when damaged. A particularly large collection has been found at Flag Fen, near Peterborough in Cambridgeshire; others have been found in the River Thames.

Though nothing as specific as the paintings at Trois Frères or the Star Carr masks have come to light in Hertfordshire, there is little doubt that ritual activity in the county was as commonplace here as it was elsewhere. There are numerous examples of ritual burial – for example the Neolithic and Bronze Age long barrow and round barrows on Therfield Heath, to the south-west of Royston.

The Romans

There exist many examples of Greek and Roman curses scratched upon lead sheets found across Europe and North Africa. Sometimes the curse was buried with the dead at a funeral, or smuggled into the inhumation; on other occasions the curse was 'activated' by nailing it up in a particular god's shrine. The thinking behind the interment of curses may have been that the dead person will take the substance of the curse to the world beyond with them.

The authors were often passionate in the expression of their feelings, though in the example below the target of the curse seems uncertain; presumably the supernatural force appealed to is expected to know, and select the correct victim:

> May he who carried off Vilbia from me become as liquid as water. May she who devoured her become dumb, whether the culprit be Velvinna, Exsupereus, Severinus, Augustalis, Comitianus, Catusminianus, Germanilla or Jovina.[12]

The text is reversed, though the letters themselves are as normal; for example, 'JOVINA' is written 'ANIVOJ', and 'CATVSMINIANVS' becomes 'SVNAINIMSVAC', a practice that was, as we shall see, to prove remarkably persistent. This curse was found at the spring of Sulis Minerva at Bath, and was presumably addressed to that goddess.

A more local, though less complete, example dating from the second century AD came to light near Baldock, Hertfordshire.[13] Found in a grave, its context has been taken to indicate that the object of the curse should not long survive the person with whom it was buried.

The Baldock curse, like many other examples, has been pierced by nails. Like the bent or broken weapons and tools associated with earlier

The Baldock lead curse. 'TACITV' is clearly visible, reversed, bottom right. (Courtesy Letchworth Museum)

periods, the intention may be to 'kill' the curse for its trip to the underworld. The text probably reads: '*Viitiis Qvomodo… Iiss Significativr Tacitv Diificta*'. The latter part translates as 'in this fashion… Tacita is identified as the victim of this curse.' Like the Bath example, it is written in reverse.[14]

Another example, found in the City of London, is most intriguing. It reads:

> I curse Tretia Maria and her life and mind and liver and lungs all mixed up together, and her words, thoughts and memory; thus may she be unable to speak the things that are secret nor be able… nor …[15]

Unfortunately it is incomplete, but it seems that its originator was anxious that Tretia Maria should not reveal some damaging secret. It may have been a case of blackmail.

Curses were often written on lead, possibly because it lasts a long time: almost certainly longer than the intended victim, if it is hidden carefully.

Not all examples of Roman magic are malevolent; indeed some appear to be protective, for example, the magic square. Such was the fascination of the square that it remained in use until the twentieth century. It can be read backwards or forwards, horizontally or vertically:

R	O	T	A	S
O	P	E	R	A
T	E	N	E	T
A	R	E	P	O
S	A	T	O	R

The sentence produced (reversed, of course) is '*Sator Arepo Tenet Opera Rotas*,' which has been translated as 'The sower Arepo holds steady the wheels,'[16] though quite what that means is open to speculation. 'Arepo' is thought not to be a genuine name, but one invented to make the square work.

There have been claims that the square is a Christian cryptogram, but as an example survives from a pre-Christian context in the middle Danube this seems unlikely. The square crops up all over the Roman world, from Portugal and Pompeii, and from the Euphrates to England.

The square survived in magic and sorcery for centuries after the Romans left. An example of the square, dating from 1614, may be found in the parish church of Great Giddings in Cambridgeshire (see plate 1). In Somerset a late nineteenth/early twentieth-century charm used the same words.[17]

That magical practices disappeared with the adoption of Christianity by the Roman Empire is highly unlikely. Indeed, it is unlikely that paganism itself disappeared entirely. As was to happen later with the conversion of the Anglo-Saxons, earlier pagan rites and customs continued, sometimes side by side, and, following the collapse of Roman domination of Britain, may even have re-emerged as a full-blown religion.

The Anglo-Saxons

With the coming of the tribes loosely grouped under the name 'Saxons' paganism was reintroduced to Britain.[18] It was not the paganism the Romans had found amongst the Celts several hundred years before, but the paganism of the Germanic culture.
A Saxon curse ran:

> May you be consumed as coal upon the hearth,
> May you shrink as dung upon a wall,
> May you dry up as water in a pail
> May you become as small as a linseed grain,
> And much smaller than the hipbone of an itchmite,
> And may you become so small that you become nothing.[19]

Curses continued to be vehement, personal and prepared with considerable malice. But not all magical activity was of the malevolent kind. Charms for healing or for the removal of unsightly blemishes were also the stock-in-trade of the Saxon magician:

> For warts. Take hounds mie [urine] and a mouse's blood, mingle together, smear the warts therewith; they will soon depart away'[20]

This sort of charm appears repeatedly down the centuries, though the ingredients vary. In Hitchin in the 1960s I was told that the best cure for warts was to smear them with a piece of meat, which must then be buried in the garden. As the meat decomposed, the wart would disappear.[21]

In the mid-eighteenth century, William Ellis of Little Gaddesden in Hertfordshire described another magical cure:

A girl at Gaddesden, having the Evil in her feet from her infancy, at eleven years old lost one of her toes by it, and was so bad that she could hardly walk, therefore was to be sent to a London Hospital in a little time: but a beggar woman coming to the door, and hearing of it, said, that if they would cut off the hind leg, and the foreleg on the contrary side of that, of a toad, and wear them in a silken bag about her neck, it would certainly cure her; but it was to be observed, that on the toad's losing its legs, it was to be turned loose abroad, and as it pin'd wasted, and dy'd, the Distemper would likewise waste and die; which happened accordingly, for the girl was intirely cured by it, never having had the evil afterwards.[22]

Toads were widely believed to be powerful creatures, though whether for good or evil varied according to the superstition.

The reintroduction of Christianity into England began at the end of the sixth century, after 150 years of Saxon paganism. The Church followed its normal procedure of absorbing the pagan practices and sites of worship rather than confrontation. Pope Gregory I wrote to Saint Augustine in June of AD 601, instructing him not to destroy any well-built pagan places of worship, but to remove any idols and replace them with relics of the saints. Further, he told him that

> The people will not need to change their places of concourse, where of old they were wont to sacrifice cattle to demons, thither let them continue to resort on the day of the saint to whom the church is dedicated, and slay their beasts no longer as a sacrifice, but for a social meal in honour of Him whom they now worship.[23]

Less than a hundred years later the attitude of tolerance had changed. Theodore, the Archbishop of Canterbury who presided over synods in Hertford (AD 673), and Hatfield (AD 684), forbade a number of pagan practices in the *Liber Pœnitentialis* (*Book of Penitentials*). In addition to a prohibition on sacrifices to spirits, divination, and raising of storms,

> if anyone at the Kalends of January[24] goeth about as a stag or a bull-calf, that is, making himself into a wild animal, and dressing in the skins of a herd animal, and putting on the heads of beasts; those that in such wise transform themselves into the appearance of a wild animal, let them do penance for three years, because this is devilish.[25]

Theodore also forbade folk medicine:

> If any woman puts her daughter upon a roof or into an oven for the cure of a fever, she shall do penance for seven years.[26]

By the late ninth century the stance of Church and State had hardened even further. The dooms of Alfred decreed death for enchanters, magicians, wizards and witches; Edward the Elder and Guthrum pronounced that;

> If witches or diviners... be found anywhere in the land; let them be driven from the country... or let them totally perish within the country, unless they desist, and the more deeply make bot.[27]

Prosecutions took place, though records are scarce; one of the few examples is to be found in an Anglo-Saxon charter from about AD 963, which mentions the forfeiture of land in Northamptonshire as a result of image magic on the part of a mother and son. They were accused of making an effigy of Aelsi, father of Wulfstan, and driving iron nails into it. The mother was drowned at London Bridge and the son outlawed and forced to flee for his life.[28]

A few years later Aethelstan decreed death for witchcraft if it resulted in the death of the victim. In 1018 Canute's Charter ruled that his people should 'eschew all unrighteousness; that is, slaying of kinsmen, and murder, and perjury, and witchcraft and enchantment...'[29]

The Doom of Canute forbade:

> every heathenship; heathenship is that a man reverence idols; that is, that a man reverence heathen gods, and the sun or moon, fire or flood, water-wylls [wells?] or stones, or trees of the wood of any sort; or love witchcraft, or perform bad underhand work any wise; either by way of sacrifice or divining, or perform any act of such delusions.[30]

In the pre-Christian era, magic had been viewed as a tool, evil only when used for evil purposes. Now the tool itself became evil. In the eyes of the church it was an appeal to a power other than that of God. Nonetheless, charms with a distinctly magical tone continued in regular use:

> Against every evil rune lay [heathen charm], and one full of elvish tricks, write this writing in Greek letters: ++ Alpha ++ Omega + IESUM BERONIKH.[31]

The concept of a cult of witches, active in the skies after dark, was denied by the ecclesiastical authorities. However; the *Canon Episcopi* of about AD 900 referred to women being led astray by the Devil, and denied the reality of their flight:

…some wicked women perverted by the Devil, seduced by illusions and phantasms of demons, believe and profess themselves, in the hours of night, to ride upon certain beasts with Diana, the goddess of the pagans, and an innumerable multitude of women, and in the silence of the dead of night to traverse great spaces of earth, and to obey her commands as of their mistress, and to be summoned to her service on certain nights. But I wish it were they alone who perished in their faithlessness and did not draw many with them into their destruction of infidelity. For an innumerable multitude, deceived by this false opinion, believe this to be true, and so believing, wander from the right faith… such phantasms are imposed upon the minds of infidels and not by the divine but by the malignant spirit. Thus Satan himself, who transfigures himself into an angel of light, when he has captured the mind of a miserable woman and has subjugated her to himself by infidelity and incredulity, immediately transforms himself into the species and similitudes of different personages… the faithless mind thinks these things happen not in the spirit but in the body.

The *Canon* delayed the persecution of witches with its scepticism regarding the possibility of flight, but its very denial brought the subject to ecclesiastical and secular attention. Nonetheless its influence was felt to the end of the witch-hunts, even amongst Protestants, and its importance can scarcely be overestimated. But it took more than an edict from on high to change the beliefs of the ordinary man. Both the serf and his master carried on as they had always done, if less openly than before.

In addition to folk tales of Diana's hordes that affected the development of witch beliefs was the Wild Hunt. Of Teutonic origin, this folk tale held that a procession of malicious spirits roamed the untamed expanses of the countryside. Other stories told of groups of wild men and women living in the forests. These legends became associated with the stories of Diana and her cohorts, and developed into the witch 'Sabbats' of later years.

The Middle Ages

At the end of the first millennium those who practised magic were, for the most part, judged as much on the crimes they committed as for the use of the supernatural itself, though attitudes within the Church were hardening. But records of prosecutions are rare, and unless the crime was a particularly serious one, or involved the great and the mighty, an attitude of *laissez faire* seems to have prevailed. In England, this was to some extent due to the antipathy on the part of the monarchy towards the ambitions of the Church of Rome. William I resented interference in secular affairs, and his descendants, with one or two exceptions, felt much the same way. Though he specifically legislated against killing *veneno*, meaning by poison or sorcery, it did not stop him enlisting the aid of a female magician against the Saxons during the siege of the Isle of Ely in the year 1071. Her success was questionable to say the least – the Normans were routed in the attack, and the witch was killed.[32]

Belief in the power of witches was widespread. For example in the twelfth century, John of Salisbury, one-time secretary and supporter of Thomas Becket in his disputes with Henry II, claimed that witches could, with the help of devils, 'shake the elements together, and change the true nature of things.'[33]

An early record of prosecution is from Norfolk in the year 1209, when Agnes, wife of Odo, accused Gaiena of sorcery.[34] The defendant was acquitted after undergoing ordeal by iron.[35]

Under Edward I in the late thirteenth century the punishment for sorcerers was death, with hanging, ear-cropping or the pillory for enchanters, though there seems to have been little in the way of enforcement. The most prominent case of the era was the accusation made that Walter Langton, the bishop of Coventry, was a sorcerer who had made a pact with the Devil. Langton was forced to go to Rome to defend himself, and incurred considerable expense before finally being acquitted in 1303. His case is of particular interest insofar as he was accused of kissing the Devil's behind as an act of homage; an accusation that was later to be made against many alleged heretics and witches, especially in Continental Europe.

The level of commitment of much of the population to Christianity in England (as elsewhere in Europe) was less than total. The majority of the population could not read, even if books had been readily available. The source of religious knowledge was, for the masses, the Church. Walls were frequently painted with scenes or interpretations from the Bible. Popular themes were the Last Supper, the Crucifixion, and episodes from the life of the saint to whom the church was dedicated. Perhaps the theme most likely to make an impact on the congregation was the Last Judgement, a fine example of which can be seen in the church of Saint Mary the Virgin in Great Shelford, just over the Hertfordshire border in Cambridgeshire (see plate 2). At the centre sits Jesus Christ, with Mary on one side and John the Baptist on the other. To the left, the dead rise from their graves and ascend to heaven, whilst on the right they are dragged by devils into hell, which is depicted as the mouth of an enormous demon.[36] Here was a motif that all could understand.

Sermons were preached by a clergy that was sometimes almost as uneducated as its congregation. 'The ignorance of the clergy casteth the people into the ditch of error,' said the Archbishop Peckham in 1281.[37]

If the clergy became more knowledgeable in the following centuries, its congregations seem not to have done so. Three hundred years later a Norfolk parson bemoaned the fact that his flock knew more about Robin Hood than they did about religious matters. Certainly there were enough prosecutions of Hertfordshire folk in the seventeenth century for working during the period of divine service, demonstrating that, at least for many people, the material world was as important as the spiritual one. John Phipp of Stondon was summoned for grinding malt on a Sunday, and Richard Barnard of Datchworth for travelling with his horse and cart. In 1653 George Oswell 'did sit and drink with divers [sic] persons unknown in the dwelling house of Thomas Porter.' Four years later Cuthbert Peacock of Hitchin, a barber, 'did trim [the hair of] divers persons unknown on the Lord's Day, during divine service.' There were many more.[38]

2

THE WITCH HUNT IN CONTINENTAL EUROPE

Although this is a book about Hertfordshire, we cannot ignore events in Continental Europe, for although the British Isles were isolated geographically, that isolation was not cultural. British roots were European, and magical beliefs and practices were in many ways similar. Before the sixteenth century, prosecutions for witchcraft in England were rare. Across the Channel, the witch-hunts had already begun. The law of most of Continental Europe was based on the Roman system, which permitted torture. Witchcraft was a *crimen exceptum*, an exceptional crime, and safeguards against false confessions and accusations often went by the board. The justices worked from lists of questions called interrogatories, which often included such questions as, 'who were your accomplices?' Under torture, names were often forthcoming.

The persecution was fuelled by such books as Johan Nider's *Formicarius* (*Anthill*). Originally written in about 1435, this important and influential work was published posthumously in 1475.

Just a few years later, in 1486, Heinrich Institoris and Jacob Sprenger produced the *Malleus Maleficarum* (*The Hammer of Witches*). This witch-hunters' manual is studded with examples of witchcraft and earlier judgements; it is a treasure trove of European witch lore of the fifteenth century. At the same time it is a chilling document. The attitudes of the authors are misogynistic and narrow minded; and their absolute certainty that they are doing God's work is perhaps the most frightening of all.

Supported as it was by a papal bull of Pope Innocent VIII dated 9 December 1484, the book had great influence. The bull says that

> It has indeed lately come to our ears... that in some parts of Northern Germany, as well as in the provinces, townships, territories, districts, and

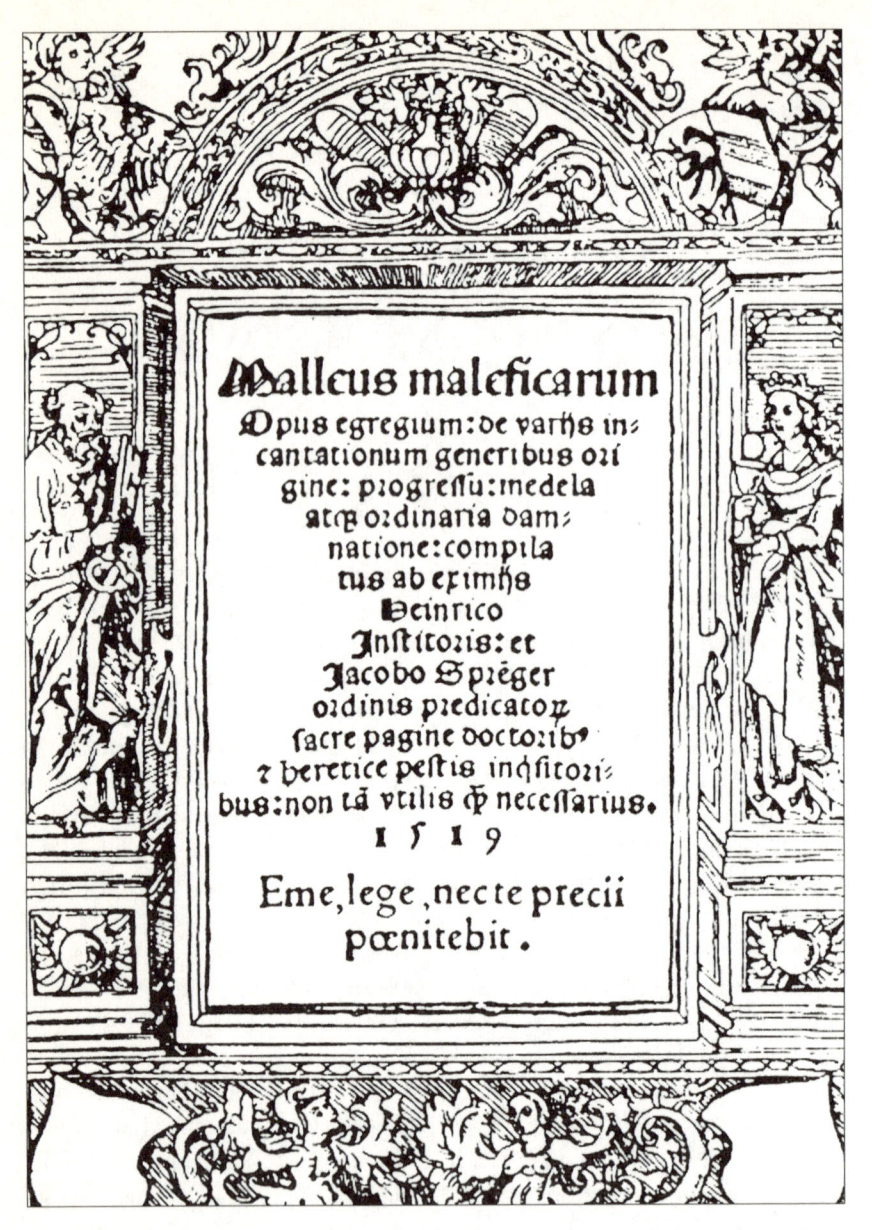

The Malleus Maleficarum, an edition published in 1519. An innocuous-looking title page for such an infamous book.

dioceses of Mainz, Cologne, Trèves, Salzburg, and Bremen, many persons of both sexes... have abandoned themselves to devils, incubi and succubi, and by their incantations, spells, conjurations, and other accursed charms and crafts, enormities and horrid offences, have slain infants yet in the mother's womb, as also the offspring of cattle, have blasted the produce of the earth, the grapes of the vine, the fruits of trees, nay, men and women, beasts of burthen, herd-beasts, as well as animals of other kinds, vineyards, orchards, meadows, pasture-land, corn, wheat, and all other cereals; these wretches furthermore afflict and torment men and women, beasts of burthen, herd-beasts, as well as animals of other kinds, with terrible and piteous pains and sore diseases, both internal and external; they hinder men from performing the sexual act and women from conceiving, whence husbands cannot know their wives nor wives receive their husbands; over and above this, they blasphemously renounce that Faith which is theirs by the Sacrament of Baptism, and at the instigation of the Enemy of Mankind they do not shrink from committing and perpetrating the foulest abominations and filthiest excesses to the deadly peril of their own souls, whereby they outrage the Divine Majesty and are a cause of scandal and danger to very many.

Not a few clerics and lay folk of those countries... are not ashamed to contend with the most unblushing effrontery that these enormities are not practised in those provinces, and consequently the aforesaid Inquisitors have no legal right to exercise their powers of inquisition... Wherefore we... decree and enjoin that the aforesaid Inquisitors be empowered to proceed to the just correction, imprisonment, and punishment of any persons, without let or hindrance, in every way...

Institoris and Sprenger were thus given exceptional powers in their campaign against witchcraft. The *Hammer of Witches* concludes that it is heresy to doubt the existence of witches, as is the belief that the effects ascribed to magic are natural phenomena. Any unorthodoxy was effectively stifled: to openly express disagreement required either great courage or great secular power.

The *Hammer* considers why it is that witches are more frequently female than male. Women were, said its authors, more credulous and more impressionable than men; they were intellectually like children. They were more carnal than men, and liars by nature. The book shows a clear contempt of women, though it should be borne in mind that such views were commonly held at that time. Midwives are accused of often being witches, and killing children in the womb, or during their birth:

For in the diocese of Basel at the town of Dann, a witch who was burned confessed that she had killed more than forty children, by sticking a needle

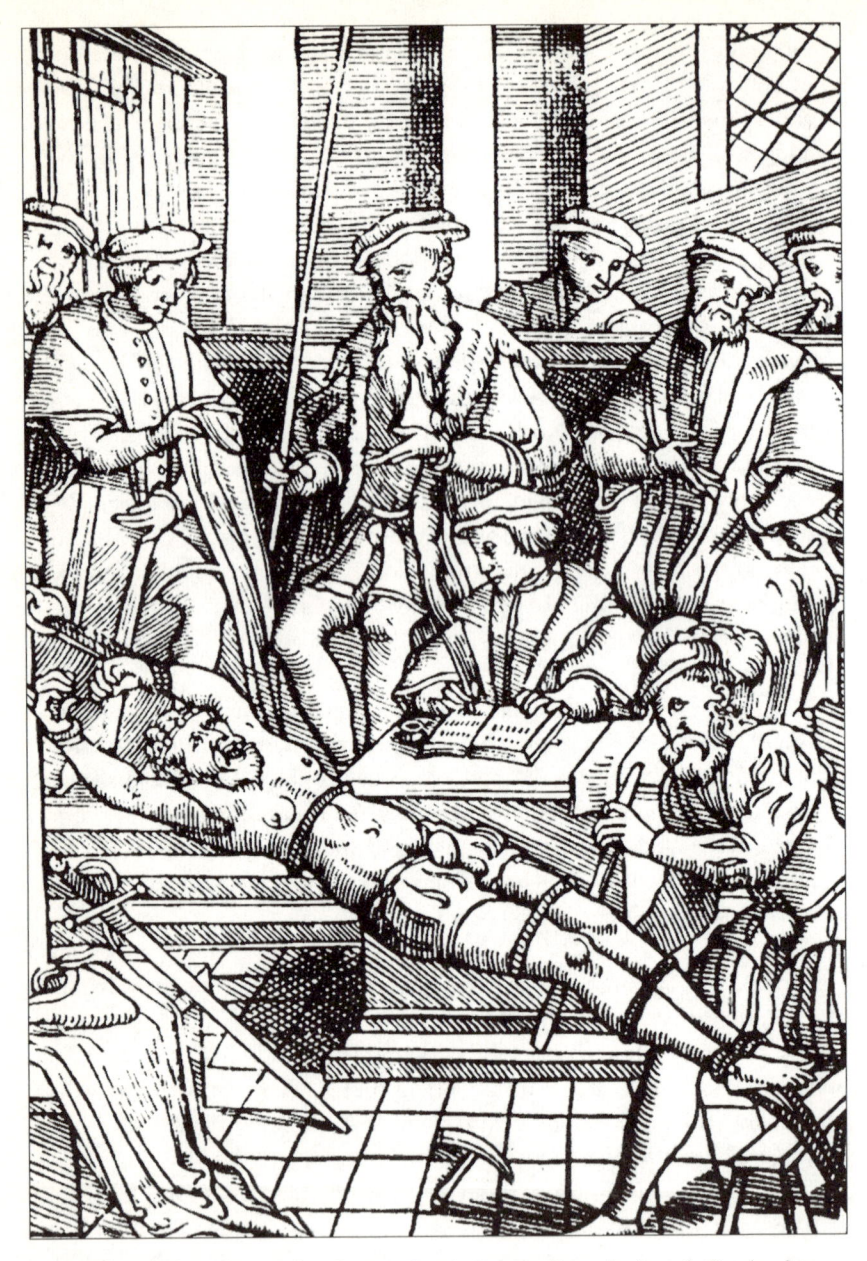

Torture is applied to a suspect, from Rerum Praxis Criminalium, *by Josse de Damhouder, a Flemish jurisconsult. The victim is being stretched, whilst at the same time a rope around his thighs is being tightened. A scribe records the questions and replies in his ledger.*

through the crowns of their heads into their brains, as they came out of the womb.[1]

The *Canon Episcopi* is attacked with some vehemence. Part of the section dealing with women imagining their flight with Diana is quoted, and refuted:

> But this opinion... leaves out of account the Divine permission with regard to the Devil's power, which extends to even greater things than this: and it is contrary to the meaning of Sacred Scripture, and has caused intolerable damage to Holy Church, since now for many years, thanks to this pestiferous doctrine, witches have remained unpunished, because the secular courts have lost their power to punish them.[2]

Part III is dedicated to procedures to be used in the capture, trial and punishment of witches. Who are appropriate judges? Which witnesses may give evidence? What are the 'points to be observed by the judge before the formal examination in the place of detention and torture'?

The suspect was to be stripped and searched. Every effort should be made to induce her to confess voluntarily. If she refused, the judge should

> order the officers to bind her with cords, and apply her to some engine of torture; and then let them obey at once but not joyfully, rather appearing to be disturbed by their duty. Then let her be released again at someone's earnest request, and taken to one side, and let her again be persuaded; and in persuading her, let her be told she can escape the death penalty.

Institoris and Sprenger go on to provide a number of excuses for making false offers of clemency. The judge may, for example, disclaim any responsibility by deputing another judge to sentence the witch to death in his stead. That suspects confessed is not a surprise — rather, it would be a surprise if they had not.

Next came sentencing. The sentences depended upon the persistence of the heresy. There were three degrees of suspicion: light, strong and grave. Complete acquittals were exceedingly rare. Those condemned on light suspicion were not to be convicted as heretics, but must nonetheless abjure the heresy of which they were suspected. A record of the sentence was made, and the suspect warned of dire consequences should he or she relapse. Strong suspicion might lead to a period of imprisonment in addition to the abjuration. Grave suspicion led to imprisonment, further torture or death by burning.

Suspects that confessed to heresy were in an even more perilous situation. At best they could expect a life of imprisonment, and a diet of bread and water; at worst, if they are impenitent, death by burning.

The *Malleus Maleficarum* was a runaway success; first published in Cologne, there were at least fourteen editions over the next twenty-five years, in Germany, Switzerland and France. It became a witch-hunter's handbook throughout Continental Europe, and it was the starting point for a rash of anti-witch writers to come.[3] Reginald Scot, an extreme sceptic on all matters magical, and writing a hundred years later, referred to

> James Sprenger and Henrie Insitor… from whom Bodin,[4] and all the writers that ever I have read, doo receive their light, authorities and arguments…[5]

The *Malleus Maleficarum* was followed by a number of works on witchcraft, for example the *Neuer Layenspiegel* (*New Mirror for Lay Persons*), published in Strasbourg in 1510 and 1511. The author, Ulrich Tenngler, used a good deal of material from the *Malleus Maleficarum*. The book became a second manual for prosecutors, and it too went through numerous editions. Later writers such as Francesco Maria Guazzo,[6] Jean Bodin,[7] Pierre de Lancre,[8] Nicholas Rémy[9] and Henri Boguet[10] produced books, each feeding upon earlier works, and stoking the fires of the witch-hunts. They all quote the *Malleus Maleficarum*.

However, the witch-hunters did not have it all their own way. Johan Weyer, a doctor, was bold enough to publish his *De praestigiis doemonum* (*On the Deception of Demons*) in 1563. Weyer maintained that witches suffered from delusions, and that the phenomena they were held responsible for had natural causes. He did not doubt that the Devil was active, but argued that some of the activities attributed to witches were beyond 'nature and reason itself.' Influenced by his teacher, Cornelius Agrippa,[11] Weyer insisted that the quality of evidence presented at many witchcraft trials was appalling. In his opinion, the typical witch was 'usually old, melancholic by nature, feeble-minded, easily given to despondency, and with little trust in God.' Jean Bodin promptly accused Weyer, amongst others, of the heresy of witchcraft himself.

It should not be thought that the witch-hunts in Europe were widespread; they were not. The areas most affected were Switzerland, Germany and southeastern France. Italy and Spain had relatively few trials. Once an outbreak began, however, it could become terrifying.

It is a common misconception that the witch-hunts were conducted exclusively by the Inquisition. Before the persecutions reached their height the secular courts had, in most instances, taken over prosecutions, though the Inquisition has to bear responsibility for many deaths, directly or indirectly. But whilst it was the secular courts that condemned the majority of witches, it was the Church that provided the theology behind the prosecutions. Nonetheless, where Inquisitions were involved, the

Witches raise a storm to wreck a ship at sea. The sorceress on the right holds a kettle with holes in the bottom, through which pours its contents – pure sympathetic magic. From Olaus Magnus, Historia de gentibus septentrionalibus, *1555.*

sentences handed down tended to be relatively light, ranging from penance or excommunication to imprisonment; but they could hand over an offender for punishment by the secular authorities.[12]

There were two views of witches: that of the common folk, and that of the elite. Ordinary people feared 'black' witches for the harm they could do. They believed a witch could control the weather and cause storms; she could harm men and animals, even kill them; she could cause butter to fail; she could steal crops by magic.[13] A white witch however, though viewed with caution, was a good person. She could break a bewitchment; protect against black witches and evil spirits; find lost or stolen goods; predict the future; provide love magic to attract or retain a mate; and cure man or beast from natural disease. Whilst the common man was happy to inform the authorities about black witches, he was less likely to do the same against the white.

The elite view was different. They believed that black witches did indeed carry out the offences that the ordinary folk feared. In addition they comprised a pan-European cult, the aim of which was the destruction of society in general and the Church in particular. Witches met in groups at meetings called sabbats, where they worshipped the Devil. They indulged in orgies, giving themselves sexually to demons; they murdered children and boiled them down to manufacture their evil ointments. To the educated man it was not just the black witch that was evil – her white sister was equally as bad, because she too worked with Satan. Even if the white witch seemed good, she was not. Whatever was not natural was done with the aid of

The witches' sabbat. The witches dine with demons. According to standard descriptions, an orgy usually followed. From the Compendium Maleficarum, *by Francesco Guazzo, 1608.*

Witches cook babies. The fat is caught in a trivet for use in ointments. The child in the background is to be boiled. From the Compendium Maleficarum, *by Francesco Guazzo, 1608.*

demons. In some ways the white was worse than the black, because whilst her deeds did not endanger the physical wellbeing of her clients, she put their immortal souls at risk. The *Malleus Maleficarum* put it succinctly:

> Again it is pointed out that the common method in practice of taking off a bewitchment, although it is quite unlawful, is for the bewitched persons to resort to wise women, by whom they are very frequently cured, and not by priests and exorcists. So experience shows that such cures are effected by the help of devils, which is unlawful to seek; therefore it cannot be lawful thus to cure a bewitchment, but it must be patiently borne.[14]

White witches were common. They could be found almost everywhere, and even allowing for exaggeration, there seem to have been a lot of them: 'There are very many such witches, for they are always to be found at intervals of one or two German miles,[15] and these seem to be able to cure any who have been bewitched by another witch in their own district'.[16]

Werewolves and Shapeshifters

Witches and magicians were not the only terrors the population had to face: a number of accusations of lycanthropy (the mythical transformation of a person into a wolf) appeared in the courts between the fifteenth and seventeenth centuries. In Bedburg in Germany, for example, Stubb Peter confessed without torture to being a werewolf, to raping and murdering girls, drinking their blood and eating their hearts.[17] His sentence was to be tied to a wheel and have his flesh torn off with red-hot pincers; he was then beheaded, burned, and his ashes scattered in the wind.

There was a direct link between lycanthropy and witchcraft: witches were said to be able to change their shape at will. But, like the werewolf, if wounded in their animal form, they bore the mark of their wound when they changed back into their human shape. Indeed, some witches were accused of being werewolves too. Gilles Garnier, who was condemned to be burned on 18 January 1573 at Dole near Lyons, had, witnesses claimed, attacked and killed children, eating their flesh raw; he was convicted of witchcraft and lycanthropy.[18] The connection was not doubted by Institoris and Sprenger:

> There is incidentally a question concerning wolves, which sometimes snatch men and children out of their houses and eat them, and run about with such astuteness that by no skill or strength can they be hurt or

The devil carries off a surprisingly young-looking witch, emphasising the dangers of witchcraft to the witches themselves. From Olaus Magnus, Historia de gentibus septentrionalibus, *1555.*

captured. It is to be said that this sometimes has a natural cause, but it is sometimes due to a glamour, when it is effected by witches.[19]

The *Canon Episcopi* had rejected the possibility of shape changing, but it had been weakened by the argument that the *Canon* referred only to matters in the past – it did not apply to the witches of the fifteenth century, an argument supported by Jean Bodin, Paul Grilland[20] and Henri Boguet, amongst others.

In Britain, werewolf accusations were uncommon, in part due to the scarcity of the real animal from the fifteenth century.[21] In the thirteenth century though, Gervasius of Tilbury recorded that 'in England we often see men changed into wolves at the changes of the moon, which kind of men the French call *Gerulfos*, but the English 'werewulf.'[22]

Witches, unlike werewolves, were believed to be able to adopt many different forms. The shape they selected might depend upon their intentions. Whether the shape change was real, or an illusion created by the Devil, was a matter for dispute. Many held that the observer was deceived by the Devil – it was all an illusion. Others believed that witches really changed their shape; how else could they enter houses and wreak their mischief?

The Gender of Witches

A good deal has been written in the last thirty years about witchcraft and gender. There is no doubt that the majority of witches prosecuted were women, though percentages varied from region to region. Various explanations have been advanced to explain the imbalance; it has for example been claimed that the witch-hunts were a deliberate persecution of women, or that the medical profession was behind the brutality in order to suppress midwives, who were seen as competition for male doctors.

From antiquity, women in the Judeo-Christian culture have been viewed as inferior to men. They were thought to have inherited the original sin of Eve, and were therefore easy victims for corruption by Satan; they, if anyone, were likely to become witches. This attitude was prevalent throughout Europe, and was reflected in the figures: 75-80 per cent of prosecutions were of women. But was it a deliberate strategy by the male elite to persecute women because of their sex? There are two major difficulties with this theory. As we have already noted, prosecutions were patchy.

Two settlements geographically close to each other might have very different experiences of witch trials. If the prosecutions were the result of a coordinated attack upon women as a whole, one would expect to see better organisation.

Witches take the form of small creatures in order to enter the house on the left and perform their mischief. From the Compendium Maleficarum, *Francesco Guazzo, 1608. In the text, Guazzo denies the reality of shape-shifting, and attributes it to a 'glamour' by the Devil.*

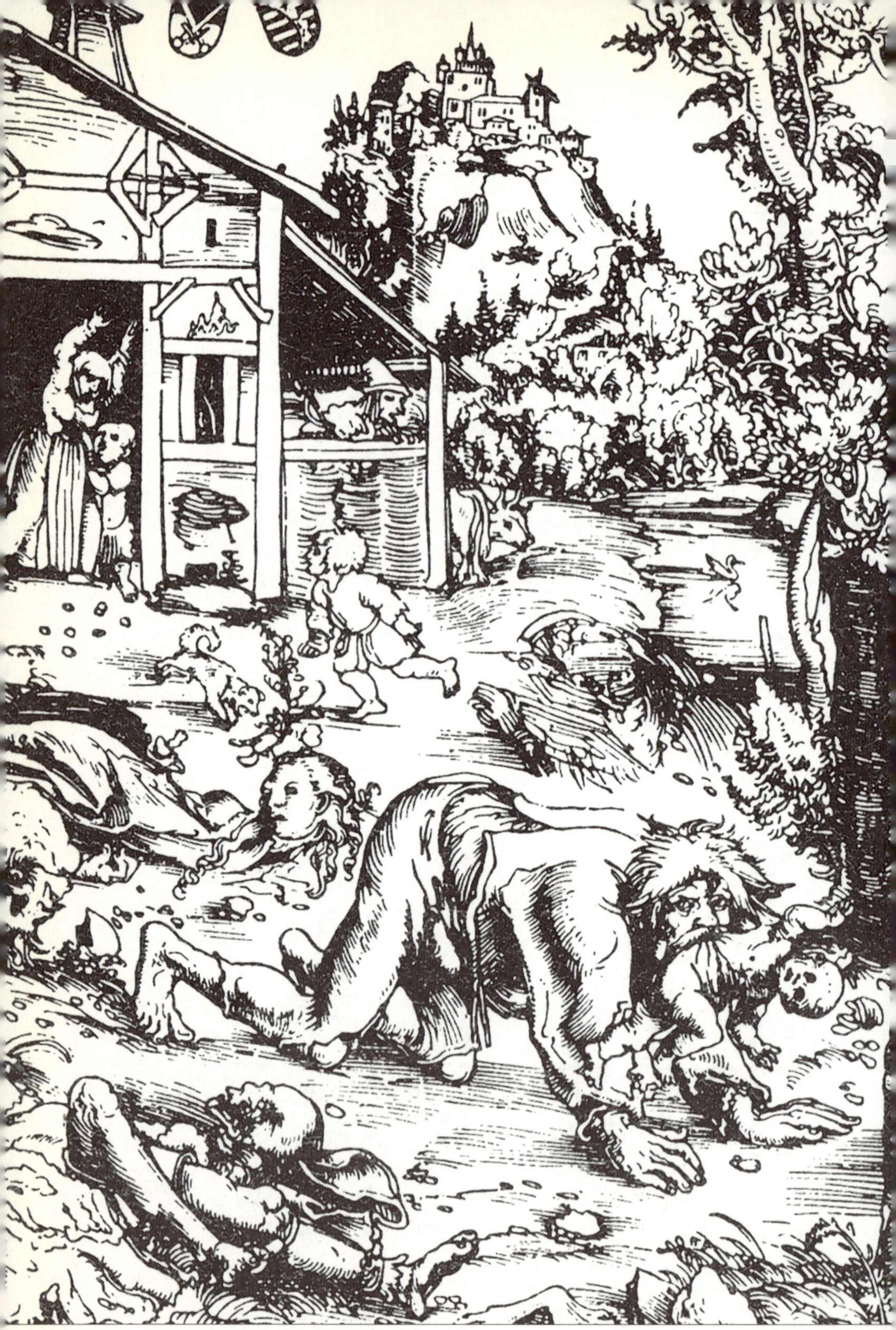

Above: *Witches are executed by burning in Germany, c. 1555. In the background another person is beheaded with a sword. (Original source unknown)*

Opposite: *A gory image of a werewolf on the rampage. From Olaus Magnus,* Historia de Gentibus Septentrionalibus, *originally published in Rome, 1555. This picture is thought to come from a later edition.*

The second problem is equally difficult to explain – women brought many of the prosecutions, and many women appeared as witnesses against those accused.[23]

The truth is that everyone – men and women – expected that in most instances witches would be women, and usually elderly ones at that. There was a stereotypical view of the witch: an elderly woman, often living alone (or, in Great Britain, with animals for company), poor, and eking out an existence on the margins of society. Accusations were most often made against those who fitted that stereotype; but, and it is an important but, not always. In some places – Normandy, Finland and Iceland for example – prosecutions against males were in the majority, and everywhere there were at least some men indicted.

European Casualties

Almost as contentious is the number of executions for witchcraft in Europe during the period of the witch trials. Estimates range from a total about 50,000 of both sexes to 9 million women (plus a few men). The higher figure has no basis in fact. It seems to have been pulled out of the air by Matilda Gage in the last decade of the nineteenth century:

> It is computed from historical records that nine millions of persons were put to death for witchcraft after 1484, or during a period of three hundred years, and this estimate does not include the vast number who were sacrificed in the preceding centuries upon the same accusation.[24]

'Nine million' was repeated by others, including Gerald Gardner, one-time owner of the Witchcraft Museum on the Isle of Man, and an important figure in the development of modern Wicca. Sadly the figure was also taken up by some members of the feminist movement of the 1970s, including the influential Andrea Dworkin.[25] It has now entered the folklore of witchcraft, and can be found in numerous books and web sites.

In recent years a great deal of work has been done on contemporary records. As the study progresses, the estimated totals of both trials and executions have been revised downward, because the reality tends to be lower than previous expectations. Brian Levack has estimated that for the whole of Europe there were in the region of 110,000 prosecutions, with perhaps 60,000 executions.[26] Current estimates run at about 50,000 executions. The figures may well go even lower. Though this figure is much lower than many earlier estimates, it still represents an enormous total, especially when it is remembered that witch-hunts tended to be localised both in time and geography. In Ban de la Roche in eastern France, between 1607 and 1630 some eighty-three people – about 7 per cent of the population – were executed for witchcraft. In some places the figure was even higher.[27]

3
WITCHES IN ENGLAND 1500-1736

Many of the traditions of English witchcraft are rooted in Europe, but there are significant differences, making the English tradition unique.

In the Middle Ages, the suppression of witches, wizards and sorcerers in England was a rather patchy affair, with few prosecutions and even fewer convictions. In 1441 Eleanor Cobham, Duchess of Gloucester, was condemned for 'compassing the death of the King,' Henry VI, by means of a wax image. She also tried to establish how high she would rise, a touchy question to raise in court, as it might imply the fall of the King. Her 'accomplices' were two priests, Roger Bolingbroke and Thomas Southwell, and Marjery Jourdemayne, the famous Witch of Eye. Jourdemayne had been in trouble before; in 1430, she had been imprisoned for two years for sorcery. Eleanor was ordered to do penance on three separate occasions, barefoot and bare-headed. She carried a two-pound candle, to be laid at the altar of St Paul's, St Mary Cree, Leadenhall, and St Michael's in Cornhill. Southwell died in prison, Jourdemayne was burned and Bolingbroke drawn, hung and quartered; their crime was treason[1], but such cases are unusual.

Ordinary folk appeared before Church Courts, charged with offences that often amounted to little more than superstitious practices, but the power of the Church to punish them was limited: penance, abjuration and excommunication, and occasional imprisonment, was about as far as they could go without passing the case to the secular authorities.

Continental Europe was ruled by Roman Law, and the tradition of heresy was strong; and although the *Malleus Maleficarum* ran to numerous editions, it was not translated into English until well after the witchcraft persecutions had ended. Thus the English witches did not often meet at Sabbats, nor was there a diabolic confederacy intent on overthrowing Christianity. Few Elizabethan witches signed a pact with the Devil.

The English 'black' witch was a malicious sorcerer, usually working alone, who blighted the lives of her neighbours. Like her continental counterpart, she caused illness and death in man and beast. She raised storms, damaging crops and threatening the lives of sailors at sea. She used sorcery to steal her neighbours' produce, and interfered with the day-to-day running of the farm. Her principle associates were her familiars; diabolical imps that carried out her commands. In return she fed them with blood, which they suckled from a supernumerary teat.[2] English witches rarely flew, though there are folktales of them having done so (for example Mother Haggy of St Albans, mentioned in Part Two). As on the continent, the majority of English witches were women.

At the end of the sixteenth century, the average Englishman believed implicitly in magic and witchcraft. There was no doubt in his mind that spirits and demons existed. His neighbours believed, as did his masters. And the law of the land confirmed his belief – the practices of magic and sorcery were amongst the most serious of offences.

Witchcraft and the Law in England

In the same way that the creed of witchcraft was passed from writer to writer, legal handbooks passed on advice as to how to deal with the witches themselves in the courts. Richard Bernard's *Guide to Grand Jurymen*, and Michael Dalton's *Countrey Justice* are typical examples. Both books gave similar advice on witchcraft cases – indeed, Dalton openly acknowledged that 'I thought good here to insert certain observations, partly out of the Book of Discovery of the Witches that were arraigned at Lancaster, Anno 1612 before Sir James Altham, and Sir Ed. Bromley, Judges of Assize there[3], and partly out of Mr Bernards Guide to Grand-jury-men.'[4]

The rules of evidence though were stacked against the defendant. According to George Gifford[5], 'Many jurors never weigh the force of the evidence which is brought, but as if they had their oth, for conjectures or likelihoodes, they are oftentimes very forward to finde guilty, being sicke of the same disease that the accusers be.' A reputation for witchcraft was indeed sometimes seen as acceptable evidence to be used against a suspect; Jane Wenham of Walkern had 'the common fame' of a witch, and Johane and Anne Harrison of Royston were also believed to be witches long before their indictment.

All classes of citizens were allowed to give evidence, including the very old and the very young. A single witness was in some cases enough to obtain a guilty verdict. Deathbed accusations were acceptable. A confession was absolute proof of guilt. Nonetheless in England, an accusation was a long way from a conviction.

As the seventeenth century progressed, the courts became steadily more demanding in the quality of evidence presented before them. Some judges were sceptical, one remarking that, as far as he was concerned, it was not a criminal offence to fly through the air… Others had fewer doubts. Sir Matthew Hale told a jury in 1665 that

> there were such things as witches he made no doubt at all; for, first, the scriptures had affirmed so much. Secondly the wisdom of all nations had provided laws against such persons, which is an argument of their confidence of such a crime. And such hath been the judgement of this kingdome, as appears by that act of parliament which hath provided punishments proportionate to the quality of the offence.[6]

To a certain extent a suspect's chances of acquittal depended upon the opinion of the judge: a hostile justice was likely to influence the outcome of the trial to a considerable degree.

The first statute against witchcraft appeared late in the reign of Henry VIII, in 1542.[7] In addition to criminalising the use of 'wichcraftes inchauntments and sorceries' for the destruction of 'persones and goods,' the act covered use of magic for treasure hunting:

> Where Dyvers and sundrie persones unlawfully have devised and practised Invocons and conjuracions of Sprites, p'tendyng by such meanes to understande and get Knowledge for their owne lucre in what treasure of golde and Silvere shulde or mought be founde or had in the earthe or other secrete places…

The first prosecution in Hertfordshire under any of the sixteenth-century Witchcraft Acts for which we have a record involved treasure hunting. In 1573 Thomas Heather 'late of Hoddesdon' was indicted for invoking evil spirits in the hope of finding treasure. He was convicted, but was probably pardoned on that occasion.[8] A man of the same name appeared before the Surrey Assizes two years later, charged with a similar offence. This time he was punished 'according to the statute.'

Treasure hunting was a popular pastime, indulged in by rich and poor alike. In a time when banks did not exist, it was believed that many wealthy people buried their treasures; and sometimes they failed to retrieve them. There were thought to be numerous treasures scattered throughout the country, and prehistoric burial mounds and such prominent sites were often the target of 'hill men.' After the Dissolution of the Monasteries, abbeys too became popular objects for the treasure hunters' attentions. It was difficult for the poor to become wealthy, and such a discovery was equivalent to winning the football pools or the lottery — there was little chance of success, but the hope was always there. But such activities were not confined to the needy by any means, and some wealthy people attempted to become wealthier.

Use of magic in the search for treasure was not uncommon, and tricksters who claimed to possess the means to tap the supernatural in order to detect underground hoards sometimes cheated the gullible.

The 1542 Act also forbade the use magic to recover lost or stolen goods, and to 'provoke any person to unlawfull love.'

Penalties were harsh. All offences were felonies, punishable by death. Contrary to popular belief, witches were not executed by burning in England, but by hanging. That was bad enough — it was death by strangulation rather than the more humane broken neck of later executions. Lands and goods were forfeited. Witchcraft was without benefit of clergy[9] or sanctuary.[10]

Reliable records of prosecutions do not begin before 1563, though there are occasional references to prosecutions. For example, Joanna Meriweather appeared before Archbishop Cranmer for using a wax candle to curse Elizabeth Colsey,[11] but it seems likely the Act was not heavily enforced. It was, in any case, repealed in 1547 by Henry's son, Edward VI. The repeal of Henry's Act did not mean there were no prosecutions, however; in 1560, eight men were tried at Westminster for conjuration and sorcery. Having confessed, they bound themselves never to use 'Invocation, or Conjuration of Spirits, Witchcraft, Enchantments or Sorceries' for any purpose again. The men were led through Westminster Hall, and on the order of Elizabeth I and her council they were set in the pillory before finally being released.[12]

Following Edward's untimely death in 1553, the Catholic Mary I acceded to the throne. In her five-year reign some 300 Protestants were burned for heresy, including William Hale at Barnet and George Tankerville, who died in front of St Albans Abbey Gatehouse. A third unnamed Protestant was burned at Bishop's Stortford.[13] The persecution caused many others to flee to the continent, where they saw at first hand the suppression of continental witchcraft. These returning exiles may have influenced events following Mary's death in 1558.

Elizabeth I succeeded Mary, and it was under her rule that the prosecution of witchcraft in East Anglia reached its peak (other parts of England, such as Middlesex and Chester, peaked somewhat later). There were more prosecutions, and more executions, under Elizabeth than in the rest of the period between 1558 and 1736 combined.

It was in 1558 too that Bishop Jewel of Salisbury preached a sermon before Elizabeth:

> It may please your Grace to understand that Witches and Sorcerers within these last few years are marvellously increased within your Grace's Realm.

Your Grace's subjects pine away, even unto Death, their Colour fadeth, their Flesh rotteth, their Speech is benumbed, their Senses are bereft. I pray God they never practise further then upon the subject.[14]

Whether the sermon influenced Elizabeth is unknown, but the following year enquiries were made through the Church as to 'whether you know any that do use charms, sorceries, inchantments, invocations, circles, witchcrafts, soothsaying, or any like crafts or imaginations invented by the Devil, and specially at the time of women's travel [labour]'.[15]

At the same time a Bill entitled 'An Act agaynst Conjuracions Inchantments and Witchecraftes'[16] was already in draft form and on its way through Parliament, having received its first reading in the Commons on 15 March. The Act came into full force on 1 June 1563. The provisions were less draconian than the Act of 1542:

OFFENCE	FIRST CONVICTION	SECOND CONVICTION
Using witchcraft to search for treasure or lost property	1 year's imprisonment, 4 appearances of 6 hrs in the pillory	Life imprisonment
Causing injury to persons or property by witchcraft	1 year's imprisonment, 4 appearances of 6 hrs in the pillory	Death
Causing death of persons by witchcraft	Death	
Conjuring evil spirits	Death	
Intent to cause death of persons by witchcraft	1 year's imprisonment, 4 appearances of 6 hrs in the pillory	Life imprisonment
Provoking a person to 'unlawful love'.	1 year's imprisonment, 4 appearances of 6 hrs in the pillory	Life imprisonment

The offender was also required publicly to confess her offence. The same penalties applied to 'Councelloures and Aydours [aiders].' Like the 1542 Act, the offence was without benefit of clergy or sanctuary. The rights of heirs and successors were protected, with the exception of those offences attracting life imprisonment. Though the punishment of a year's imprisonment might seem a reasonably light sentence, it could easily mean death for the offender.

¶ The Apprehension and confession of three notorious Witches. Arreigned and by Iustice condemned and executed at Chelmes-forde, in the Countye of Essex, the 5. day of Iulye, last past. 1589. ¶ With the manner of their diuelish practices and keeping of their spirits, whose fourmes are heerein truelye proportioned.

Three witches hang at Chelmsford in 1589. Joan Prentis on the right greets Satan in the form of a 'donnish coloured ferret, having fiery eyes.' The strange creatures on the left are the familiars of the other women accused of witchcraft with her.

Conditions in gaols were poor, and many died from 'gaol fever' (typhus), cruelty and neglect.

The sixteenth-century gaol was unlike modern prisons. Any type of building might be used. Hertford and Bishop's Stortford castles housed prisoners, and at St Albans the Abbey Gatehouse served the same purpose. Private premises were pressed into use. Responsibility for the prisoners rested with the turnkey, who made part or all of his living by exacting fees from the prisoners. They paid for everything – they even had to pay the gaoler to be released if they were acquitted. The turnkey's income from fees was supplemented by the sale of food and alcohol. For a wealthy prisoner life could be tolerable. For a poor one, it was unspeakable. Nor was the pillory the quaint village punishment of folklore. The missiles thrown by the crowd ranged from fruit to rocks and they were in some cases fatal. An unpopular prisoner was literally at risk of his life.[17]

The next significant piece of legislation relating to magic and witchcraft was a clause in an 'Acte against sedicious Wordes and Rumors uttered againste the Queenes moste excellent Majestie' of 1580.[18] There were concerns about diviners attempting to discover 'how longe her Highnes should lyve, and who should raigne after her Decease.' Attempts at prophecy of the Queen's death, or to establish the succession to the throne, became felonies punishable by death.

In 1581 Elizabeth declared a general pardon, but those convicted of offences connected with witchcraft were excluded.

Elizabeth died in 1603, and was succeeded by James I (James VI of Scotland). James did not at that time doubt the reality of witchcraft, believing himself to have been the target of a group of witches in North Berwick in 1590. Francis, the Earl of Bothwell, James's cousin, was accused of plotting the King's death. Amongst those charged were John Fian, a schoolmaster, and Agnes Sampson. The plot came to light following the torture[19] of a young woman named Gelie Duncan, who confessed and named her co-conspirators. According to Gelie and Agnes, the witches met in large numbers in the churchyard. Agnes further confessed to having made an image of the King in wax, which was given the King's name. Another attempt was made on his life by smearing the venom of a toad on an item of his clothing; it was thwarted by a loss of nerve on the part of the servant assigned to steal the garment to be used. The final attempt was by raising a storm as James returned to Scotland with his new bride, Anne of Denmark. The method used was to 'tie the chiefest part of a dead man and several joints of his body' to a cat, which was thrown into the sea to drown. James attended the examination of the prisoners, and what he heard convinced him of the truth of their confessions.[20]

This experience must have had some influence on James's book,

Dæmonologie, of 1597, though its main objective was to discredit the arguments of the sceptics Johan Weyer and Reginald Scot. Following his accession, James ordered the burning of all copies of Scot's *Discoverie of Witchcraft*, and a new edition of *Dæmonologie* was published in London in 1604.

In the same year an Act 'against Conjuration Witchcrafte and dealing with evill and wicked Spirits'[21] was passed. Its provisions were similar, if somewhat harsher, than the act of 1563:

OFFENCE	FIRST CONVICTION	SECOND CONVICTION
Using witchcraft to search for treasure or lost property	1 year's imprisonment, 4 appearances of 6 hrs in the pillory	Death
Causing injury to property or cattle by witchcraft	1 year's imprisonment, 4 appearances of 6 hrs in the pillory	Death
Causing death or injury to persons by witchcraft	Death	
Conjuring evil spirits	Death	
Removal of the dead, or any part of them for use in witchcraft, sorcery or enchantment	Death	
Intent to cause injury to persons or property by witchcraft	1 year's imprisonment, 4 appearances of 6 hrs in the pillory	Death
Intent to cause death of persons by witchcraft	1 year's imprisonment, 4 appearances of 6 hrs in the pillory	Death
Provoking a person to 'unlawful love'	1 year's imprisonment, 4 appearances of 6 hrs in the pillory	Death

The punishment for second offences was made more severe, and a new offence of using corpses or parts of them for witchcraft was introduced, perhaps as a result of the Berwick witches' reported methods; in Royston, Hertfordshire, the case of Johane and Anne Harrison in 1606, where human hair, and 'all the bones due to the anatomy of man and woman,' were found in the suspects' home, must have been one of the early prosecutions for this offence under this provision of the new Act.

The North Berwick witches, from the contemporary account, Newes from Scotland *of 1591. The Devil preaches to the witches from his pulpit, whilst a ship founders in the background, casting the crew into the sea.*

The rights of heirs and successors were protected. The same penalties applied to accomplices. Like the 1563 Act, the offences were without benefit of clergy or sanctuary.

In 1625 James ordered a general pardon, and in 1672 Charles II did the same. In both cases, offenders under the Witchcraft Act were specifically excluded. The 1604 Witchcraft Act was repealed in 1736. James's Act was to be 'of utterly void and of none effect.' That was not the end though. The Act went on:

> ...if any Person shall... pretend to exercise or use any kind of Witchcraft, Sorcery, Inchantment, or Conjuration, or undertake to tell Fortunes, or pretend, from his or her Skill or Knowledge in any occult or crafty Science, to discover where or in what Manner any Goods or Chattels, supposed to have been stolen or lost, may be found, every Person, so offending, being thereof lawfully convicted... shall, for every such offence, suffer Imprisonment by the Space of one whole Year... and once in every Quarter of the said Year, in some Market Town of the proper County, upon the Market Day, there stand openly on the Pillory by the Space of One Hour, and also shall (if the Court, by which

such Judgment shall be given shall think fit) be obliged to give Sureties for his or her good Behaviour, in such Sum, and for such Time, as the said Court shall judge proper, according to the Circumstances of the Offence, and in such case shall be further imprisoned until such Sureties be given.[22]

Thus by 1736 the perceived problem to the lawmakers was no longer witchcraft and magic, but fraudulent practices. This legislation remained in force until 1951, when it was replaced by the Fraudulent Mediums Act.

The Statistics of Witchcraft in England[23]

Prosecutions followed the legislation. Before long a trend became apparent that is difficult to explain. Essex consistently had more witch trials at assizes than the rest of the Home Circuit – Hertfordshire, Kent, Surrey and Sussex – put together.[24] Not only were there more prosecutions in Essex, but of those indicted, a higher percentage were executed:[25]

COUNTY	NUMBER OF PERSONS INDICTED	NUMBER OF INDICTMENTS	NUMBER OF EXECUTIONS	PERCENTAGE OF INDICTEES EXECUTED
Essex	299	473	82	27.4
Herts	52	81	9	17.3
Kent	91	132	16	17.6
Surrey	54	71	5	9.3
Sussex	17	33	1	5.9
Total/ Average	513	790	113	22.0

In addition, there are some mentions of witchcraft-related offences in quarter session records, and more in the records of Ecclesiastical Courts.[26] Neither of these courts had the power to hand down a sentence of death however. The quarter sessions could order imprisonment and/or whipping, and the Ecclesiastical Courts were limited to excommunication and penance. They tended therefore to deal with minor infringements and cunning folk.

It is possible that there were additional cases in some Borough or Liberty Courts; twenty-four have been found for Essex.[27] It is therefore possible some were tried at the Borough Courts of Hertford or the Liberty of St Albans.[28] Extrapolating the Essex figures across England, they might add an additional 400 cases.

We shall never know exactly how many people were executed for witchcraft in England. Making an allowance for the missing assize records, a total of about 145 executions for the Home Circuit during the most active period of suppression seems likely to be close to the truth. It may have been a few less, but my belief is that, if anything, it was a few more – I believe some individual indictments are lost. In Hertfordshire records exist of eight women and one man hanged.

C.L. Ewen found about 450 assize indictments for the rest of England, though the records for some circuits are very poor; for the Midland Circuit for example they are non-existent before the nineteenth century. Working from such records as do exist however, and assuming that Essex is an anomaly that was not repeated elsewhere, he estimated that the total number of executions for the whole of England for the period 1558-1736 was somewhat less than 1,000;[29] or an average of between five and six executions each year for the whole country. More recent estimates are lower still – perhaps as low as 300.[30] This is in stark contrast to earlier figures: one writer, Robert Steele, estimated 70,000 executions for England from 1604-1736 alone.[31]

How many cases were presented before the courts is also unknown. Indictments thrown out by the Grand Jury were usually discarded, and any record of the case detail lost.[32] There is therefore every reason to believe that there were more accusations of witchcraft than appear in the records.

Acquittals in witchcraft trials were common, though such a verdict was sometimes unpopular with the public.[33] It seems that some judges were intimidated by the mob; Roger North reported that

> It is seldom that a poor old wretch is brought to trial for witchcraft, but there is at the heels of her a popular rage that does little less than demand her to be put to death; and if a judge is so clear and open as to declare against that impious vulgar opinion, that the devil himself has power to torment and kill innocent children, or that good people's cheese, butter, pigs, and geese, and the like errors of the ignorant and foolish rabble; the countrymen (the triers) cry 'this judge hath no religion, for he doth not believe witches,' and so, to shew that they have some, hang the poor wretches.[34]

Sometimes a defendant prosecuted under several indictments was acquitted of the capital charges but convicted of those attracting imprisonment. Thus at the Hertford Summer Sessions of 1590, Mary Burgis was indicted on five counts: three of murder by witchcraft, one of bewitching a horse to death, and one of laming a man's arm. She was acquitted on the first three charges but convicted on the final two, which attracted a year's imprisonment and four appearances in the pillory. The conclusion might be reasonably drawn that juries were sometimes unwilling to condemn a person to death.

As the seventeenth century progressed, prosecutions declined until the 1640s, when there was a brief but significant flurry of activity initiated by the activities of one man: Matthew Hopkins, the self-styled 'Witchfinder General'; but before we look at Hopkins, we must consider the witch's familiar spirit.

The Witch's Familiar

Although there are cases of personal demons found in Continental Europe, they are far more common in England and Scotland than anywhere else. In these islands they seem to have been an essential aid to every witch. They were referred to as familiars or imps. Their origins are lost, but it is possible that they grew from tales of fairies, dwarves and suchlike; Robin Goodfellow and his companions in a demonised form.[35]

The familiar was usually given to the witch by the Devil, though in some cases it was passed from one witch to another: Margaret Ley, of Liverpool, confessed in 1677 to receiving hers from her mother some thirty years before.[36] A witch might possess more than one familiar – some had as many as three.

A witch feeds her familiars. This illustration is taken from a pamphlet describing events at Windsor in 1579. According to the text, the case involved familiars in the form of a toad, two cats, a rabbit that sometimes appeared as a cat, and a rat named Philip; though none of the accused had the combination of creatures shown in the picture.[37]

Familiars took many forms, but cats, dogs, toads or other small animals were the most common. The witch christened the familiar, giving it a name that was often bizarre: Jamara was a 'sandel spannell' (a brown spaniel); Holt was a white cat; Sack and Sugar was a black hare.[38] John Palmer of St Albans in Hertfordshire had a dog called George and an imp that appeared as a woman called Jezabell.[39] Occasionally the familiar took the form of no known creature, for example 'blacke and shaggy, and having pawes like a Beare, but in bulk not fully so big as a Coney [a rabbit],' which, according to his deposition in 1646, appeared to John Winnick of Thrapston in Huntingdonshire.[40]

Dorothy Ellis of Stretham, Cambridgeshire, confessed in 1647 that

> about thirtie yeares since shee being much troubled in her minde there appeared unto hir the Devell in the likness of a great catt and speak unto this ext [examinant] and demanded of hir hir blood wch she gave hime after which the spirit in the liknes of a catt suck upon the body of this ext and the first thing that this ext commanded her spirit to doe was to goe and be witch 4 of the cattell of Tho. Hitch all whch cattell presently died and further this ext confesseth that she sent hir catt spirit to bewitch and take away the life of Marie the daughter of Tho. Salter of Stretham which spirit forthwith kild the child of the said Marie and also this ext confesseth she commanded hir spirit to lame the mother of the child old Marie Salter which was done accordingly and that she commanded hir spirit to goe and be witch and lame John Gotobed because he cald this ext old witch and flung stones att this ext all wch command was performed by hir spirit and the said Gotobed lamed.[41]

This case is typical; the familiar carried out the witch's evil wishes, ranging from the relatively innocuous act of stopping the butter turning in the churn, through injury to man and beast, and to murder. In return, the witch fed it with blood, either from a supernumerary nipple or by pricking her finger.

Matthew Hopkins, Witchfinder General

Hopkins was the son of a puritan minister from Whenham in Suffolk. He settled in Manningtree in north-east Essex, where he practised for a time as a lawyer. According to his own account,[42] in 1644 he heard about a number of witches practising nearby, and took it upon himself to have them arrested. He later claimed that some of them had sent the Devil in the shape of a bear to kill him. Following the Summer Assizes at Chelmsford, nineteen women[43] were hanged.

Hopkins moved from town to town with his associates, John Stearne and Mary Phillips. He visited Essex, Suffolk, Norfolk, Cambridgeshire,

Huntingdonshire, Northamptonshire and Bedfordshire though for some reason he seems never to have visited Hertfordshire. Phillips organised the strip-searching of female suspects to check for witch marks and extra nipples. The witch-hunters charged a fee of twenty shillings to visit each town, and the same for each witch they discovered, though the rate must have been negotiable: seven women from Aldborough were hanged for a mere £6. At Stowmarket the Hopkins entourage made £23. During their first tour 124 suspects were identified, of whom sixty-eight were hanged. Others died in gaol. However, the witch-finders did not have it all their own way. On 4 September 1645 the Parliamentary periodical, *The Moderate Intelligencer*, commented on Hopkins' witch-hunting:

> whence is it that the Devill should choose to be conversant with silly women that know not their right hands from their left, is the great wonder... They will meddle with none but poor old women, as appears by what we received this day from Bury...

The Reverend John Gaule, vicar of Great Stoughton, then in Huntingdonshire, (now in Cambridgeshire), complained about the witch-finders' behaviour.[44] Gaule was incensed by Hopkins' arrogance in a letter in which he announced that he would give the town 'a visit suddenly... to search for evil-disposed persons called witches.' He had heard that Gaule was 'farre against us through ignorance,' and wanted to know if the Stroughton would 'give us good welcome and entertainment.' Under the circumstances it seems unlikely.[45]

But the tide was turning against him, and Hopkins wisely retired. He wrote *The Discoverie of Witches* in 1647 in an attempt to defend his actions, but he lived only one year more before dying of tuberculosis. Stearne carried on alone for a while, but he too was forced to retire and write a justification for his actions.[46]

Witch-finding did not disappear with Hopkins and Stearne. Scottish witch-finders continued to operate, sometimes crossing the border into northern England, but the heart had gone from the business. In some cases, their practices were so blatantly fraudulent that they were lucky to escape with their lives.

Hopkins' campaign would have been less likely to succeed had the normal mechanisms for justice been in place. But during the period 1644-1646 the assize courts were suspended, and local justices filled the gap; unfortunately some of them believed not only that witches existed, but that Hopkins was the man to root them out.

Was Hopkins sincere? It is possible that he was, but if so, he either suffered from delusions or he was prepared to invent evidence to support his belief. In *The Discoverie of Witches* he records one of the witch's familiars, named

The frontispiece of Hopkins' Discoverie of Witches *of 1647. This is one of the best-known contemporary witchcraft images. The creatures depicted are the familiars of witches Hopkins encountered.*

'Swimming' a witch in a mill pond. A detail from a pamphlet entitled Witches Apprehended, Examined and Executed, for notable villanies by them committed both by Land and Water. With a strange and most true triall how to know whether a woman be a Witch or not. *London, 1613. The sow and cart form part of the tale told in the pamphlet. The events took place a short distance north of Bedford.*

Vinegar Tom, which had 'an head like an Oxe, a longe taile, and broad eyes.' As Hopkins looked on, this creature 'immediately transformed himself into the shape of a little child of foure yeares old without a head, gave half a dozen turns about the house, and vanished at the doore.'

The Detection of Witches

According to popular belief, almost anyone might be a witch, though there were some that were more likely than others. John Gaule described the stereotype of a witch in England:

> In every place and parish, every old woman with a wrinkled face, a furr'd brow, a hairy lip, a gobber tooth, a squint eye, a squeaking voice, a scolding tongue, having a rugged coate on her back, a skull-cap on her head, a spindle in her hand, a dog or cat by her side, is not only suspected but pronounced for a witch'.[47]

It was one thing to suspect a witch, but how to prove it? There were a number of tests that were accepted by the courts at one time or another, and others that were accepted on an unofficial basis by the population as a whole. 'Swimming' was a relic from trial by ordeal. Sometimes the victim was stripped before the proceedings began. The right thumb was tied to their left toe, and vice versa. The suspected witch had a rope tied around her waist, and was cast into a pond. If she sank, she was innocent, and was pulled out and released. If she floated, however, she was thought to be guilty.[48] A floating suspect was usually ducked several times in order to give her every chance to sink. It is untrue that the suspect had to drown to prove her innocence, though there were occasions when the ordeal resulted in death by drowning or subsequent hypothermia.

According to James I, witches floated because

> it appears that God hath appointed for a supernatural signe of the monstrous impietie of witches, that the water shall refuse to receive them in her bosom that have shaken off them the sacred water of baptism, and wilfully refused the benefit thereof.[49]

Swimming of suspected witches persisted long after the crime of witchcraft was removed from the statute books, and Hertfordshire has the dubious honour in 1751 of being home to one of the more notorious occurrences of this test. John and Ruth Osborne were swum near Tring. Ruth died, and one of the ringleaders, Thomas Colley, was hanged (the case is examined in Part II).

The discovery of unusual marks on the suspect's body required a strip-search, and sometimes the shaving of the entire body. The search was thorough:

> Item, if she have any privie marke under hir arme pokes, under hir haire, under her lip, or in hir buttocke, or in hir privities: it is a presumption sufficient for the judge to proceed and give sentence of death upon hir.[50]

Witches' 'teats' are sometimes confused with witches' 'marks', but the two were quite different. The marks were caused by the touch of the Devil at the time the witch dedicated herself to evil. They were

> …sometimes a blue spot or red spot, like a flea biting; sometimes the flesh sunk in and hollow (all which for a time may be covered, yea taken away, but will come again, to their old form). And these Devil's marks be insensible, and being pricked will not bleed, and be often in their secretest parts, and therefore require diligent and careful search'.[51]

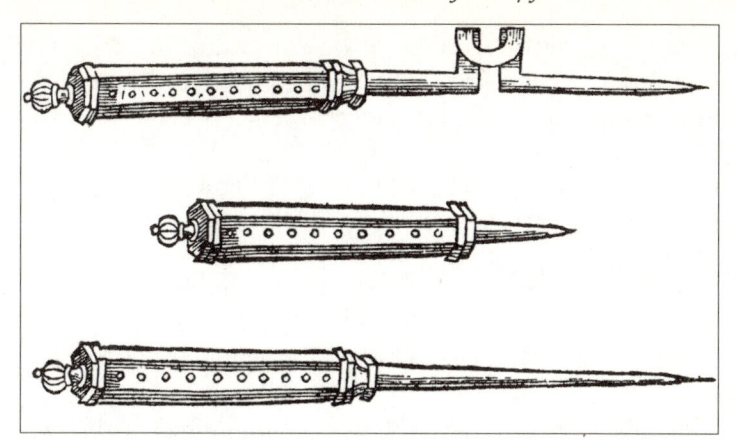

This illustration has appeared in a number of books as prickers' tools. They are not. They appear in Reginald Scot's The Discoverie of Witchcraft *of 1584 with the caption 'To thrust a bodkin into your head, and through your toong, &c.' They are in fact conjurors' props.*

Such marks and 'teats' are not uncommon, particularly amongst the elderly. As John Webster observed in 1677, 'Now if all these [warts etc.] were witch-marks, then few would go free.'[52]

The method used for their detection was to run a pin into the suspect's flesh. This was the job of the 'pricker.' It has been suggested that unscrupulous prickers used pins whose points retracted into their handles, but this is speculative.[53]

Witch-hunters used other methods to test suspects, including 'watching' and 'walking'. Watching involved shifts of 'watchers', who took turns in keeping the suspect awake. Sometimes food was withheld as well. The procedure could be lengthy – normally twenty-four hours, but in Suffolk there were cases of six or even eight days' sleep deprivation. According to the Reverend Gaule, the suspect was sometimes placed upon a chair or a stool, and if necessary, tied to it. A small hole was made in the door of the otherwise sealed room, in order to allow the witch's familiars to enter:

> As the imps come in less discernable shape, they that watch are taught to be ever and anon sweeping the room, and if they see any spiders and flies to kill them. And if they cannot kill them, then they may be sure they are her imps.[54]

The pain, hunger and disorientation, coupled with intensive questioning, often resulted in a confession, sometimes implicating others. That the confession might afterward be retracted helped the victim not at all; nor that he or she confessed to things that even to the credulous must have seemed unlikely. 'Walking' was a similar technique to watching, the chief difference being that the suspect was kept on her feet and 'walked' up and down the room.

Witches were said not to be able to cry. A variation of the same belief held that they could cry, but only three tears, and those from their left eye (or the right eye, depending upon the author). 'They cannot even shed tears, though women in general are like the crocodile, ready to weep upon every light occasion'.[55] Similar beliefs are found in the *Malleus Maleficarum*.[56] Arguably, then, any suspect weeping openly in court must be innocent.

Reciting the Lord's Prayer correctly was also thought to be impossible for a witch, and though the test was not a legal one, it was used in evidence in the trial of Jane Wenham of Walkern in Hertfordshire in 1712. It is worthy of note that Jane shed tears during her ordeal; this was conveniently ignored by her persecutors (see Part II).

Weighing against the Bible was an alternative extra legal test for witchcraft. If the suspect outweighed the church Bible she was innocent. Clearly for her to be declared guilty, the Bible would have to be extremely heavy, or the suspect very small.[57]

On 12 July 1737 an anonymous writer from Oakley[58] reported to the press an example in which several tests were used on the same woman:

>...the people here are so prejudiced against witches, that you would think yourself in Lapland, was you to hear their ridiculous stories. There is not a village in the neighbourhood but that has two or three.[59]

The suspect was about sixty years old, and had long been thought to be a witch. She was first swum, but floated. Her cap was checked for pins, because the crowd believed that she could not sink if there were any about her person, but still she floated. Some members of the crowd urged that she should be drowned, but the writer of the report argued with the crowd that everyone floats; he suggested weighing the woman against the church Bible. As the bible weighed only 12 pounds (5.5 kilos), she outweighed it and was released, though not without some grumbling.

The *Morning Post* for 28 January 1780 reported that a vicar had weighed two women in Bexhill in order to placate a suspicious crowd.[60]

Perhaps the most bizarre test involved the belief that if a witch touched the corpse of a person he or she had bewitched to death, the corpse would start to bleed. An old belief predating the witch-hunts, the bleeding test was also used for the detection of other crimes than witchcraft. According to James I,

>...in a secret murther, if the dead carkasse be at any time thereafter handled

by the murtherer, it will gush out of blood, as if the blood were crying to Heaven for revenge of the murtherer.[61]

The witch's victim could fire the suspect's thatch, or burn any animal thought to be bewitched by her. She would, it was thought, be forced to confess if she were guilty.

A search of the suspect's home might reveal some incriminating evidence, as happened to Johane Harrison and her daughter Anne of Royston (see Part II). A cunning man or woman might be consulted, and might appear in court as a witness, as seems to be the case of Elizabeth Lane, or Laine, of Walsworth in North Hertfordshire. Also worth trying were some of the countermeasures that involved the witch personally. If successful, they would prove the suspect's guilt, and break the bewitchment.

Defences, Countermeasures and Cures

Numerous defences were believed effective against bewitchment, ranging from herbs to charms, and from talismans to physical countermeasures. There were variations; for example some believed that merely to draw blood from a witch was enough to negate her spell, whilst others held that the blood must come from above the mouth or nose – 'scoring above the breath.' For some, charms were detestable: John Wycliffe, the fourteenth-century religious reformer, declared that 'charmis on no maner are letful [charms are in no way lawful],' and that 'it is supersticious to hang wordis at the neck.'[62] Though the Church considered Wycliffe a heretic, in this respect his attitude was in tune with the establishment.

The words worn as charms varied, but amongst the most popular was the first verse of the Gospel of St John, which in the James I version of the Bible runs 'In the beginning was the Word, and the Word was with God, and the Word was God.' Thus, the wearer might argue, wearing these words about his neck was equivalent to carrying God upon his person as a defence; and surely nothing could be more powerful than that. A Lincolnshire cure for ague also invoked the name of God:

> Father, Son and Holy Ghost,
> Nail the Devil to a post,
> Thrice I strike with holy crook,
> One for God, one for Wod and one for Lok

In this case the charm calls upon pagan as well as Christian gods: Wod is the Saxon Woden, and Lok is the Norse Loki.[63]

The word 'Abracadabra' was another firm favourite. It was usually laid out in a pattern:

```
A B R A C A D A B R A
 A B R A C A D A B R
  A B R A C A D A B
   A B R A C A D A
    A B R A C A D
     A B R A C A
      A B R A C
       A B R A
        A B R
         A B
          A
```

The word can be read from top left to top right, or from the bottom to the top right, and each letter forms part of a diagonal line. According to John Aubrey it was a cure for fever: 'with this spell, one of Wells, hath cured above a hundred of the ague.'[64]

There were other alternatives to calling for divine intervention. Reginald Scot collected numerous examples, amongst them these intended for use with bewitched animals:

A charme to find hir that bewitched your kine
Put a paire of breeches upon the cowes head, and beate hir out of the pasture with a good cudgell upon a fridaie, and she will runne right to the witches doore, and strike thereat with hir hornes.
Another, for all that have bewitched anie kind of cattell
When anie of your cattell are killed with witchcraft, hast you to the place where the carcase lieth, and traile the bowels of the beast unto your house, and drawe them not in at the doore, but under the threshhold of the house into the kitchen; and there make a fier, and set over the same a grediron, and thereupon laie the inwards or bowels; and as they wax hot, so shall the witches entrailes be molested with extreame heate and paine. But then must you make fast your doores, least the witch come and fetch awaie a cole of your fier: for then ceaseth hir torments...
A speciall charme to preserve all cattell from witchcraft
At Easter you must take certeine drops, that lie uppermost of the holi paschal [Easter] candle, and make a little waxe candle thereof: and upon some sundai morning rath, light it, and hold it, so as it maie drop upon and between the hornes and eares of the beast, saieng: In nomine patris, & fili, et duplex s s: and burne the beast a little betweene the hornes on the eares with the same

wax: and that which is left thereof, sticke it in crossewise about the stable or stall, or upon the threshold, or over the doore, where the cattell use to go in and out, and for all that yeare your cattell shall never be bewitched... [65]

As for humans, under the heading 'A knacke to know whether you be bewitched, or no, &c.' Scot says

> It is also expedient to learne how to know whether a sicke man be bewitched or no: this is the practice thereof. You must hold molten lead over the sicke bodie, and powre [pour] it into a porrenger [a small dish, often with a handle, for soup] full of water; and then, if there appeare upon the lead, anie image, you may the knowe the partie is bewitched.[66]

Written charms, especially older examples, rarely survive in any but recorded form. Witch bottles on the other hand have been found in reasonable numbers. These were intended to force the witch to break bewitchments by subjecting her to such agony that she would have no choice but to comply. Some are bellarmine jars, named after Cardinal Roberto Bellarmine (1542-1621), though early examples predate their namesake (see plate 3). The jars have bearded faces on them, and presumably they were selected as witch bottles for anthropomorphic reasons. Early bellarmines usually have a smiling face, whilst later examples are much less cheerful. Other types of vessel were used as well, and some have been found dating from the twentieth century. Catherine Parsons, in the proceedings of the Cambridgeshire Anthropological Society, described an example in 1915, at the village of Horseheath, not far from the Hertfordshire border. At that time a white witch known as Mother Redcap was practicing in the village.[67] The two may or may not be connected. The locations of bottles vary, but are quite commonly found close to thresholds, windows and fireplaces (see plate 4). The contents of the bottles also varies, but often include pins or nails (sometimes bent), human hair, nail parings, and cloth hearts with pins in them. The universal ingredient is the urine of the bewitched person.

This method of treating witchcraft had the approval of at least some of the medical profession:

> Another way is to stop the urine of the patient, close up in a bottle, and put into it three nails, pins or needles, with a little white salt, keeping the urine always warm: if you let it remain long in the bottle, it will endanger the witch's life: for I have found by experience that they will be grievously tormented making their water with great difficulty, if any at all, and the more if the Moon be in Scorpio in Square or Opposition to his Significator, when its done... The reason... is because there is part of the

vital spirit of the Witch in it, for such is the subtlety of the Devil, that he
will not suffer the Witch to infuse any poysonous matter into the body of
man or beast, without some of the Witches blood mingled with it...[68]

Sometimes the bottle was heated in order to cause suffering to the witch.
Should that fail, the intense pain of passing the bent pins when urinating
was likely to force her to visit the victim of the curse and implore him to
release her from her agonies.

Witches were thought to leave items in their victim's home as a means
of bewitchment. John Gaule referred to the belief that the bewitched
should

[search] for the witches signe or token left behinde her in the house under
the threshold, in the bedstraw; and be sure to light upon it, burning every
odd ragge, bone, or feather that is to be found.[69]

The burning of the charm was intended to rebound upon the witch. A
similar effect might be expected if the bewitched produce or animal were
destroyed by fire.

An allied but little-understood phenomenon is that of the ritual hoard.
They are quite common, and examples have been found dating from
between the thirteenth and the early twentieth century. The majority
however date from the nineteenth century, though whether this indicates
that the practice was more common in that period than hitherto is not
certain. It is possible that more of them survive for some other reason.[70]

Typically the collections include items of minimal value, but of a
personal nature: shoes, fragments of fabric or leather clothing, pipes,
ceramics, and iron items such as nails, knives and horseshoes. Sometimes
animal carcasses are included, sometimes they are found on their own.

The condition of the articles may well be significant. They are often in
a very poor state, at the end of their working life, as it were. It may be
that it is this very wear and tear that makes them suitable candidates for
inclusion in a ritual hoard. What is more personal than an item that has
been used by a person for years on end?

Shoes are the most common items,[71] from men, women and children,
in a roughly 2:3:5 split respectively.[72] Why are there more children's shoes?
It may be as simple as the fact that there were many children in large
families, or it may be that they were thought to be more at risk, coupled
with a strong interest in preventing child death. Infant mortality was high,
and if parents believed in witchcraft and magic it is quite possible that they
connected the large number of child deaths with such influences. The
shoes are rarely found in pairs – one was apparently enough to serve the
purpose. The age distribution by percentage is

Earlier than 1599	4.6
1600-1699	18.9
1700-1799	25.2
1800-1899	46.7
1900 onward	4.6

The reason for these hoards is a matter for speculation. The personal nature of many of the items may indicate that they are intended as 'lightning conductors' for evil energies caused by curses or evil spirits. The evil is diverted towards the hoard as it enters the house, allowing the intended victim to escape harm.[73] Locations of hoards near a threshold or chimney tends to confirm this interpretation, but they are not always found there – one of the Hertfordshire examples (the Long House, Walsworth, described in Part II) was found between a lathe and plaster ceiling and the floorboards of the room above. Other locations for these hoards have included behind walls, under floorboards, staircases and bricked-up ovens.

It is possible that in few cases the hoard might be akin to graffiti – intended to make a mark, to impose a person's identity upon a place or thing. If so, then any hoards with such a motive were probably deposited in secret by an individual, and as a personal act of superstition. It is significant however, that certain items are found more frequently than others. So many shoes have come to light that they must represent a widespread belief. Other examples involving cats and rodents are probably vestigial foundation or building sacrifices.

Joseph Blagrave had several methods of countering bewitchment, including the following:

> One way is by watching the suspected party when they go into their house; and then presently to take some of her thatch from over the door, or a tile, if the house be tiled: if it be thatch, you must wet and sprinkle it over with the patient's water, and likewise with white salt, then let it burn or smoke through a trivet or the frame of a skillet; you must bury the ashes that way which the suspected witch liveth. 'Tis best done either at the change, full, or quarters of the moon; or otherwise, when the witches significator is in square or opposition to the moon. But if the witches house be tiled, then take a tile from over the door, heat him red hot, put salt into the patient's water, and dash it upon the red hot tile, until it be consumed, and let it smoak through a trivet or frame of a skillet as aforesaid.[74]

The sufferer could ask a doctor whether he or she was bewitched. William Drage of Hitchin in north Hertfordshire could provide the answer:

> If the sick vomits gallons of blood, or the like goes by urine, and so continues day by day, and void 1,200 worms at a time, or several hundreds, and so continues, judge it fascination. Those that vomit, or void by stool, with greater or less torments, knives, scissars, bryars, whole eggs, dogs' tails, crooked nails, pins, needles, sometimes threaded, and sometimes with hair, bundles of hair, pieces of wax, pieces of silk, live eels, large pieces of flesh, bones and stones, and pieces of wood, hooks, and pieces of saltpetre; conclude they are bewitched; and that such have been vomited, or voided by stool, and that from witchcraft.[75]

Drage was well read on these matters — his list is drawn from a number of sources, both European and domestic. Amongst the 'preservatives against witchcraft' recommended by Drage were rosemary, mistletoe, ivy, coral, rue and lapis amiantes (asbestos in solid stone-form). The *Malleus Maleficarum* agrees that doctors could detect bewitchment,[76] but they could not cure the patient.

John Aubrey, the antiquary, reported that:

> ...it is a thing very common to nail horse-shoes on the thresholds of doors: which is to hinder the power of witches that enter into the house. Most houses of the west end of London have the horse-shoe on the threshold. It should be a horse-shoe that one finds.[77]

Iron had long been believed to have special powers, and the horseshoe charm may be no more than a remnant of that belief (see plate 5).

Various types of stone were also thought effective: Aubrey says that stones with natural holes in them were thought by some to protect man and beast from witchcraft and the 'night mare.' Hertfordshire puddingstone — a type of conglomerate — was also thought to be beneficial.[78] However, not everyone was convinced of the efficacy of these measures. John Cotta did not believe that some of the tests for witchcraft were reasonable:

> Neither can I believe (I speake with reverence unto graver judgements) that the forced coming of men and women to the burning of bewitched cattell, or to the burning of the dung or urine of such as are bewitched, or floating of bodies above the water, or the like, are any trial of a witch.[79]

But amongst the most popular options open to one who feared himself bewitched was, as in most of Europe, to go to a white witch, who would, they believed, be able to help.

The White Witch in England

The white witch, also known as a 'blessing witch', or wise or cunning man or woman, was everywhere. Most settlements of any size had at least one. There were estimated by some to be as many cunning men and women as there were clergy.[80] Unlike the black witch, cunning folk were more often men than women, but not exclusively so.

The term 'cunning folk' is difficult to define, because some offered a wider range of services than others. This chapter includes all kinds of white magician.[81]

The services offered were similar to the Continental version. They detected black witches, protected against them, found lost or stolen goods, told fortunes. They prepared charms to keep away evil spirits; and charms too to bring good luck. Love charms and philtres were available to gain the affections of members of the opposite sex.[82] They cured impotence, and gave mothers sedatives to help their children sleep. They could protect persons and property against storms. They cured disease in man and beast by charms and herbs, and advised the smallholder and farmer on how to get the best yield from his animals and fields. Some specialised: they might be wart charmers, or bone setters, or deal exclusively in horses. Others were 'strokers', who cured illnesses, as their name implies, by stroking the afflicted area with a charm.[83]

At a time when a woman's labour was often fatal, charms to ease the birth were also available. The following example dates from 1475 and has been translated from Latin, Hebrew and Greek.

> For woman in labour, tie this script to her thigh: In the name of the Father + and of the Son + and of the Holy Ghost + Amen. By the miraculous power of the Lord may the holy cross and passion of Christ be my medicines. + May the five wounds of the Lord be my medicine. + Saint Mary bore Christ. + Saint Anne bore Mary. + Saint Elizabeth bore John. + Saint Cecelia bore Remigium. + The sower Arepo holds steady the wheels. + Christ overcomes. + Christ reigns. + Christ to Lazarus to come forth. + Christ rules. + Christ calls you. + The world rejoices in you. + The law desires you. + Lord God of Battles free your handmaiden N. + The right hand of the Lord has performed a miracle. a. g. l. a.[84] + Alpha + and Omega.[85] + Anne bore Mary, + Elizabeth the one who went before, and Mary our Lord Jesus Christ without pain and grief. + O baby whether alive or dead come forth + Christ calls you to the light. + Holy. + Holy. + Holy. + Christ overcame. + Christ rules. + Christ reigns. + Holy. + Holy. + Holy. + Lord God. + Christ who is, who was, + and is to come. + Amen. bhurnon + blictaono[86] + Christ the Nazerene + King of the Jews son of God + have mercy on me + Amen.[87]

A demon is exorcised from a possessed man. From a fifteenth-century woodcut.

This is a typical charm insofar as it appeals for aid from Christian deities by means of sympathetic magic. The Roman magic square text 'Sator Arepo Tenet Opera Rotas,' which we have met before, presumably appears as words of power; it is not in a square, and there is no obvious link between 'the sower Arepo holds steady the wheels' and childbirth.

The combination of Christianity and magic was not new, and was practised by the Church itself. The power of the relics of the saints was accepted Catholic dogma. They could drive away demons, break spells and bewitchments, and cure illness. Particular saints were associated with particular complaints.[88] Many churches had relics; in fact their miraculous nature was such that in some cases duplicates existed. The wood of the Holy Cross held in Jerusalem was deemed so holy that every year pieces of it could be removed without reducing its size.

Pilgrimages to the church holding the relics of an appropriate saint were common, and brought in welcome funds to many religious establishments.

The Catholic Church had other cures for the possessed. A true faith was a protection, as was an Agnus Dei[89] worn about the neck (see plates 6 and 7). Confession, baptism, attendance at the Eucharist and prayer might help. The sign of the Blessed Cross was powerful. Holy water and oil were sold to pilgrims in small lead containers called ampullae (see plate 8).[90]

Either the Blessed Virgin Mary or a guardian angel might come to the aid of the deserving case. The sound of church bells was disliked by demons. As a last resort there was always exorcism.

Most ordinary folk tolerated, even venerated the 'cunning folk', in some cases preferring them to doctors. According to John Aubrey, Thomas Hobbes, the famed political philosopher and author of *Leviathan*, '...was wont to say that he had rather have the advice or take physic from an experienced old woman, that had been at many sick people's bedsides, than from the learned but unexperienced physician'.[91] Some folk cures had a basis of science behind them; for example the discovery in 1775 by William Withering of digitalis, which is still in use today, was based on a folk remedy learned from a gypsy healer, who treated one of Withering's Shropshire patients. Her potion contained a number of ingredients, but the active constituent – digitalis – came from foxgloves. An interesting cure for bellyache from the early twentieth century involved the use of a hot-cross bun, baked on Good Friday and kept in the chimney. This example includes a clear religious element, but its efficacy may have relied upon the growth of penicillin mould on the bun.[92]

Apart from the powers of herbs, there was the very real power of suggestion. The use of panaceas in medicine has long been known to be effective.

Physicians of the sixteenth and seventeenth centuries left much to be desired, and some of their methods were little more than superstition. A doctor was also trained in astrology, for the stars and planets were firmly believed to affect illnesses:

> And the stars do very much qualifie and alter the seeds in our humours... I have observed the mutations in divers' diseases to be from the Moon, and other planets, especially the planet that was Lord of the First and Sixth House... When the Plague did rage in this town of Hitchin, most fell sick or died at the change of the Moon, or the full Moon... when the Moon was at her full state, was the sickness in many in its crisis or exaltation...[93]

Not everyone was sympathetic to cunning folk. Some thought them frauds, intent on taking advantage of their clients' gullibility. Reginald

Scot considered that every aspect of witchcraft was a 'cozening art,' practised at the expense of the foolish. Richard Bernard agreed:

> These witches, to keep their credit, often deliver the medicines with an If: If it doe no good, come againe. When they returne and find that the Devill hath not removed the disease, the Wizards blame them, that they came not in time, or they applied not the means aright, or that they wanted faith to believe, or at least they acknowledged their power not great inough, and therefore they advise them to goe to a more cunning man or woman.[94]

Others were every bit as hostile, if not more so, but for a different reason; they believed the cunning folk to be a menace:

> By witches we understand not only those which kill and torment: but all Diviners, Charmers, Jugglers, all Wizards, commonly called wise men and wise women; yea, whosoever do anything (knowing what they do) which cannot be effected by nature or art; and in the same number we reckon all good Witches, which do no hurt but good, which do not smile and destroy, but save and deliver.... By the laws of England, the thief is executed for stealing, and we think it just and profitable: but it were a thousand times better for the land if all Witches, but specially the blessing Witch might suffer death. For the thief by his stealing, and the hurtful Enchanter by charming, bring hindrance and hurt to the bodies and goods of men; but these are the right hand of the Devil, by which he taketh and destroyeth the souls of men. Men do commonly hate and spit at the dandi-fying Sorcerer, as un-worthy to live among them; whereas the other is so dear unto them that they hold themselves and their country blessed that have them among them, they fly unto him in necessity, they depend upon him as their god, and by this means, thousands be carried away to their final confusion. Death therefore is the just and deserved portion of the good Witch.[95]

In many cases the white witch was known to his or her client, in others only by reputation or recommendation. Quite frequently a practitioner from another area was to be preferred,[96] perhaps out of embarrassment for a particularly personal affliction, or a consultation on a matter of the heart. The Hertfordshire cunning folk Thomas Harding and Elizabeth Lane both had customers who travelled some miles to consult them.

Apart from adroit questioning, the cunning man had other tricks up his sleeve. A client would be told that he had left the matter very late, providing an excuse should the prescribed remedy fail. Or he might be put off for a few hours, or longer, to allow enquiries to be made. Perhaps the cunning man knew the names of local people who already had reputations as witches or thieves; all he needed then to do is to confirm the client's suspicions. The customer might be invited to look into a mirror, being told that the person that was the subject of the consultation would be visible in it. Anyone with the temerity to say that they could see no one would be told that the fault was theirs: they lacked faith.

Some cunning men demanded a fee, whilst others refused payment. The fee might be left up to the client to decide, thus adroitly avoiding any suggestion of fraud. Many cunning men worked part-time, with another trade upon which they relied for the bulk of their income. Of the twenty-three cunning men whose other occupations have been identified in Essex,[97] there was a preponderance of educated people; more than half were doctors, or connected with medicine in some other way, and others were clerics or schoolmasters. There is no reason to believe that the pattern varied in other parts of the country. Though the cunning folk themselves seem to have been of the professional classes or lower, their customers were sometimes gentry, or even higher status.

Magic and Alchemy

Like cunning folk, magicians had an ambiguous status in sixteenth- and seventeenth-century England. Though their activities were often technically illegal, they were thought of for the most part as benign, or at least neutral. Magicians were at the top of the 'occult tree', and rarely prosecuted; they were too often consulted by those in power.

Perhaps the best-known magician and alchemist in England was John Dee. He was born in 1527, and educated at Chelmsford. He was a doctor, mathematician, astrologer and magician rolled into one. Dee moved in exalted circles: he was no stranger to the court of Edward VI. When Edward died and was succeeded by Mary I, her sister, Elizabeth, invited Dee to cast the horoscopes of the new queen and of Elizabeth herself. The results led to Dee's imprisonment. At around this time he became involved in magic.

When Mary died, Dee was asked to select an auspicious day for the Coronation of Elizabeth I. Shortly afterwards, a wax image of Elizabeth was found lying in Lincoln's Inn Fields, pierced by a pin. Dee was summoned before the Queen, but he assured her that she had nothing to fear. Much of Dee's work was spent in the company of Edward Kelly, whom Dee employed as a scryer.[98] Kelly seems to have had Dee's complete confidence for several years. Kelly claimed to have discovered the means to change base metals into gold, and Dee records in his diary that

A late-seventeenth century illustration of Edward Kelly raising a corpse in a churchyard, From the New and Complete Illustration of the Occult Sciences: or the Art of Foretelling Future Events and Contingencies, by the Aspects, Positions, and Influences, of the Heavenly Bodies. Founded on Natural Philosophy, Scripture, Reason, and the Mathematics, Book IV, *1790, by Ebenezer Sibly.*

E.K. made projection with his powder in the proportion of one minim [about 35 grams] …and produced nearly an ounce of best gold; which gold we afterwards distributed from the crucible, and gave one to Edward.[99]

The two men travelled to Prague to the court of the Emperor Rudolph.[100] Rudolph instructed them to set up an alchemical laboratory, but clashed with Pope Sixtus V, who was suspicious of anyone who claimed to speak to angels as Dee and Kelly did.

In 1588 Dee returned to England, leaving Kelly behind, where his failure to produce gold in significant quantities eventually led to his imprisonment, and he was killed in an escape attempt in 1593.

On Dee's return to England he found himself in dire financial difficulties. His friends provided some help, but nonetheless he died in poverty in 1608. Whatever else he may have been, John Dee was certainly an extremely clever man, as his writings reveal. Some of Dee's magical paraphernalia are held by the British Museum.

Alchemists have been portrayed as early scientists, but there is an important difference. The scientist carries out experiments to extend knowledge, while the alchemist attempts to rediscover the knowledge believed once to have been possessed by the ancients (normally defined as the Greeks, Romans and Hebrews). Alchemists rarely summoned spirits or demons to aid them in their work. They believed that they worked by natural laws.

The history of alchemy goes back 2,000 years or more. By AD 100 it began to spread through the Greek-speaking world, through the Middle East to Arab cultures, eventually reaching Western Europe in the thirteenth and fourteenth centuries. Alchemists claimed that base substances could be transformed by the addition of a seeding substance, sometimes referred to as the philosopher's stone. The trick was to find the seed.

Sincere alchemists genuinely believed in the possibility of transmutation of matter. Others were frauds, who fooled the wealthy into parting with considerable sums of money for their 'secret'. A typical scam worked like this: the 'alchemist' would let slip to his target the information that he had succeeded in transmutation of metals. Reluctantly, he would then agree to demonstrate the process, but only because he is temporarily short of funds. The alchemist would heat mercury in a crucible; stir it, add a little of his seeding material and allow it to cool. The victim was then invited to test the result. It was gold! – perhaps not pure, but certainly valuable. The victim would pay the alchemist for a supply of his seeding material, and that, of course, is the last he would see of him. How was it done? The alchemist's wand with which he stirred the mercury was hollow, and stopped with wax. The wax melted, and the gold hidden within it fell into the crucible. Most of the mercury vaporised under the heat, and therefore what was left on cooling was gold. Of course the cost charged to the victim for the seeding material far exceeded the value of the gold used in the demonstration.

A late example of a Hertfordshire alchemist was John Kellerman, from Lilley. In 1828 Sir Richard Phillips paid Kellerman a visit, and recorded the event in his Personal Tour through the United Kingdom. Kellerman claimed to have succeeded in making gold, but declined to show Phillips any examples, or to demonstrate the process. He lived barricaded in his home, and seems to have been a true eccentric, deluded in the belief that his investigations had been successful. The 'courts of Europe' were, he said, conspiring against him. He had been shot at, and attempts had been made to poison him. He had therefore destroyed all his notes.[101]

Almanacs, Fortune Tellers and Gypsies

On the popular side of the industry were almanacs, fortune tellers and gypsies. All three concerned themselves with selling the future to their clients. Then, as now, there were many who believed in the power of the stars, though not everyone agreed with them:

A visit to an astrologer in 1620, from The Astrologaster, or Figure Caster, *by John Melton.*

Those observers of time are to be laught at that will not goe out of their house before they have had counsell of their almanacke, And will rather have the house fall on their heads than stirre if they note some natural effect about the motion if the aire, which they suppose will varie the lucky blasts of the starres, that will not marry, nor traffique, or doe the like, but under some constellation. These, sure, are no Christians: because faithfull men ought not to doubt that the Divine Providence from any part of the world, or from any time whatsoever, is absent. Therefore we should not impute any secular businesse to the power of the starres, but to know that all things are disposed by the arbitrement of the King of Kings. The Christian faith is violated when, so like a pagan and apostate, any man doth observe those days which are called Ægyptiacia, or the calends of Januarie, or any moneth, or day, or time, or yeere, eyther to travell, marry, or to doe any thing in.[102]

Fortune tellers and purveyors of almanacs thrived. Early almanacs were not much more than calendars, and as late as the end of the seventeenth century wooden examples were in use in England. They were notched for each day of the year and engraved with symbols denoting significant days; for example, May Day might be signified by a green leaf, or St Katherine's day on 25 November by a wheel. Written almanacs had certainly appeared by the early sixteenth century, as the title of an example from 1532 collected by the folklorist J.O. Halliwell demonstrates:

> Pronostycacyon of Mayster John Thybault, medycyner and astronomer of the Emperyall Majestie, of the year of our Lorde God MCCCCCXXXIJ., comprehending the iiij. partes of this yere, and of the influence of mone [moon], of peas [peace] and warre, and of the sykenesses of this yere, with the constellacions of them that be under the vij planettes, and the revolucions of kynges and princes, and of the eclipses and comets.[103]

Moore's Almanac was first issued in 1697, and became the well-known Old Moore's Almanac of today. For many years the astrological predictions were prepared by Henry Andrews of Royston (1744-1820). Andrews was a mathematician and astronomer of no mean ability.[104] The modern edition has kept up with the times, including predictions of lottery numbers, racing tips, football pools forecasts and an astrological assessment of several celebrities.[105] Tide tables, phases of the moon, and recommended planting days for crops (the phase of the moon is most important) are also included. Mingled with all this are numerous advertisements for books on such subjects as salt rites and egg rituals. Whatever you believe, it's worth £1.75 of anyone's money.[106]

Almanacs gave general predictions for their readers. The personal touch was provided by a host of fortune-tellers and diviners. Some worked from home; others travelled. Some catered for the poor, whilst others numbered the rich and famous amongst their clients. One such was Simon Foreman of Lambeth, who at his peak had about 1,000 clients each year. Foreman was a Wiltshire man, born in 1552. With minimal education he convinced both himself and his clients of his powers. He was constantly in trouble with the authorities for practicing medicine without a licence, and was imprisoned on several occasions. Foreman was an inveterate philanderer, and recorded many of his conquests in his diaries. He is reputed to have predicted his own death.[107]

Amongst the travelling faction were the gypsies, often known as 'Egyptians'. They sometimes claimed that they did indeed come from Egypt, though their origin was actually further to the east. When the first gypsies arrived in Britain is uncertain, but by 1531 legislation was in place as a result of anxieties about their behaviour:

> An outlandish people, calling themselves Egyptians, using no craft nor feat of merchandise, who have come into this realm, and gone from shire to shire, and place to place, in great company; and used great subtlety and crafty means to deceive the people bearing them in hand that they, by palmistry, could tell men's and women's fortunes; and so have deceived the people for their money and also have committed many heinous felonies and robberies.[108]

Five years later, further action was apparently thought necessary:

> Whereas certain outlandish people, who do not profess any crafte or trade whereby to maintain themselves, but go about in great numbers from place to place, using insidious, underhand means to impose on his Majesty's subjects, making them believe that they understand the art of foretelling to men and women their good and evil fortune, by looking in their hands, whereby they frequently defraud people of their money; likewise are guilty of thefts and highway robberies; it is hereby ordered that the said vagrants, commonly called Egyptians, in case they remain one month in the kingdom, shall be proceeded against as thieves and rascals; and on the importation of any such Egyptian, he [the importer] shall forfeit £40 for every trespass.[109]

Nonetheless the gypsies stayed. In 1612, *The Art of Juggling, or Legerdemain*,[110] by S.R. (Samuel Rid), said that

> These kind of people about an hundred years agoe... began to gather... at the first heere about the Southerne parts... Certaine Egiptians, banished their cuntry, (belike not for their good conditions), arrived heere in England,

who being excellent in quaint tricks and devises, not known heere at that time among us, were esteemed and had in great admiration, for what with strangeness of their attire and garments, together with their sleights and legerdemaines, they were spoke of farre and neere, insomuch that many of our English loyterers joyned with them, and in time learned their crafte and cosening... These people continuing about the country in this fashion, practicing their cosening art of fast and loose legerdemaine, purchased themselves great credit among the cuntry people, and got much by palmistry and telling of fortunes, insomuch they pitifully cosened the poor contry girles, both of money, silver spones, and the best of their apparell, or any good thing they could make, onely to hear their fortunes...[111]

Deserved or not, gypsies had a reputation for dishonesty second to none:

Note, that these manner of persons are besides all of them for the most part theeves, cut purses, cozeners, or the like, and therefore the Just. of P. shall doe well to be carefull, not only in the examining of them, but also to cause them to be wel searched for counterfeit Passes, stoln goods, and the like.[112]

The quarter sessions records for Hertford in 1656 are said to contain a note that severe measures should be taken against 'all idle persons, using any subtle crafts... in feigning themselves to have knowledge in Physiognomy, Palmistry, or other like crafty sciences, pretending that they can tell Destinies, Fortunes, or such other phantastical imaginations.'[113] In 1703 a group of gypsies were prosecuted in Hertfordshire,[114] and according to a survey of 1810, there were thought to be about sixty families in the county; by then the majority of fortune telling was done by the womenfolk, the men either adopting no trade, or working as horse dealers, farriers, smiths, tinkers, braziers, grinders of cutlery, basket makers, chair bottomers or musicians.[115]

Groups of travellers — some genuine gypsies, others of different origins — still ply their trade today. They sell heather or small trinkets, claiming them to be lucky. An example from North Hertfordshire has just come to my notice: a middle-aged woman knocked at the door, saying, 'would you like to buy from a gypsy?' She offered a stone 'lucky animal' for sale for £2. There was a choice of two, and the householder opted for a lion because that was the only one that was recognisable (see plate 9). The caller told her that she should have been a nurse or a schoolteacher; she would be going on a journey with someone else; she should not worry, and look to the future, not the past. She would be healthy, and good luck lay in store for her. When the householder asked her to repeat her prognostications, she was told that would not be possible — it was part of the 'gypsy code.'

Astrology was only one of many methods used to predict the future. Amongst the more exotic were the following:[116]

Alectomancy	cockerels or chickens
Antinopomancy	the entrails of men, women, and children
Axinomancy	saws
Carromancy	melting of wax
Cephalonomancy	the braying of an ass's head
Cromnysmantia	onions
Gastromancy	the sounds of or signs upon the belly
Icthyomancy	fish
Logarithmancy	logarithms
Omphalomancy	the navel
Pedomancy	the feet
Spatalomancy	skins, bones, excrement
Sycomancy	figs
Typomancy	the coagulation of cheese

Other methods used included birthmarks, scars, dominoes, and, of course, tea leaves or coffee grounds. It would seem that almost anything would do – all one had to do was add the letters 'mancy.' In some cases there was some concurrence in interpretation; for example, to dream of a black horse was a negative omen: 'To dreame to ride on a blacke horse, signifieth losse & sorrow to ensue...'[117] 'To dream of white horses denotes a marriage, yours, if you are riding upon it. A black horse denotes death'.[118] 'To see horses signifies intelligence, black horses, death; white horses, marriage...'[119]

For those that are interested, there are today numerous books available on the subject of fortune telling. Why is the subject so popular? Why do people believe in the power of tea leaves to predict their future?

It is the desire to believe that is the significant factor, whether through fear of the future, or the difficulty in accepting the loss of a loved one; even the fear of making a decision without reassurance can be of sufficient influence that common sense is discarded.

Fakes and Fraudsters

As it is today, a great deal of occult activity in the past was fraudulent, both in Britain and in the Continental Europe. Unscrupulous confidence men played on the hopes and fears of what today would be considered a remarkably gullible clientele. But before we condemn them for their foolishness, consider how many times the Eiffel Tower has been sold for scrap by conmen (at least twice). Buckingham Palace, Nelson's Column and Big Ben have all found buyers.[120]

The field of the occult is such that excuses for failure are easy to fabricate. Most people believed in the existence of the supernatural, and the reality of spirits and demons. It was the conman's ideal environment. All sorts of activities were open to deception. Alchemy and fortune telling we have already met, but these were far from being the only opportunity for the unscrupulous. There were fake cures (both supernatural and natural); sham symptoms of bewitchment, and extraction of goods and money under the threat of a curse.[121] Even familiar spirits were up for sale: Adam Squier, Master of Balliol College at Oxford, apparently defrauded a group of Somerset men by selling them a familiar spirit, which he said would guarantee them good luck at dice.[122]

But perhaps the most frightening of all was the malicious allegation of witchcraft. During the height of the prosecutions the level of proof demanded by the courts was low. Testimony was accepted from children in a number of cases with disastrous results for the accused.

In 1616 John Smythe, a boy of thirteen who suffered from fits, was the main prosecution witness against a group of women at Leicester Assizes, presided over by Sir Humphrey Winch and Sir Randolph Crewe.[123] Nine of the defendants were hanged, but Smythe's fits continued. A further six suspects were arrested, one of whom died in prison before the trial. Fortunately for the remainder, James I visited Leicester in August of that year, and interested himself in the affair. He questioned Smythe, and concluded that his evidence was a fabrication. The boy was sent to the Archbishop of Canterbury for a second opinion, who agreed with James. The remaining five women were released. Smythe admitted that his motive had been attention seeking. James made clear his disapproval of the judges' conduct in the case.[124]

In 1634 there was another case involving a juvenile witness in Leicestershire. Edmund Robinson, aged ten years, from Pendle Forest, made a series of wild accusations about some of his neighbours. He claimed to have seen Frances Dicconson and an unknown child change from hares into human form. The unknown boy then became a white horse, and Dicconson and Robinson rode upon him to a meeting of witches. In a barn were six ropes, and when the witches pulled on them, food and drink fell down them into basins.

Twenty arrests were made, and at the trial at the Lent Assizes at Lancaster seventeen of them were convicted. One of the accused even confessed. The trial judge was not convinced, and the case was reported to Charles I. After re-examination of the witnesses and the accused it became clear that the prosecution was malicious, but by then some of the prisoners had died in gaol. The motive in this instance may well have been revenge; Robinson's father had argued with the Dicconsons over the sale of a cow.[125]

If these cases exhibit great callousness, at least the witnesses were children, and might be said not fully to understand the implications of their actions. Not so the Scottish pricker who admitted that he had been responsible for the deaths of 220 women, at a fee of 20 shillings each. He was eventually hanged in Scotland for his crimes.[126]

Less lethal were the small-time conmen and women who relieved the unwary of their money by simulating the symptoms of bewitchment. The Hitchin physician, William Drage, reported this precarious and unpleasant way of making a living:

> There are those that go up and down, that swallow pebbles, coals, pieces of iron, bones &c. and these may by use so facilitate their stomach, that they may vomit them when they will, and so be either admired, or pittied and relieved.[127]

There was probably more cash to be made in the construction of fake mandrake roots. A member of the potato family, the mandrake had been considered to have magical properties for centuries, in part because the root often grew in a shape reminiscent of a human form. The plant was used as a painkiller and narcotic, and as an ingredient for love potions. When it was uprooted it was said to shriek, the sound of which was supposedly fatal. For that reason dogs were trained for the task.[128]

As a native of the Mediterranean, the mandrake is not easily grown in Britain, though a demand existed; and where there is a demand, a supply frequently follows, though not always the real thing:

> Those counterfeit kind of mandrake, which couzeners and cony-catchers carry about, and sell to many instead of true mandrakes. You must get a great root of brionie, or wild nep, and with a sharp instrument engrave in it a man or a woman, giving either of them their genitories: then make holes with a puncheon into those places where the hairs are wont to grow, and put into those holes millet, or some other such thing which may shoot out his roots like the hairs of one's head. And when you have digged a little pit for it in the ground, you must let it lie there, until such time as it shall be covered with a bark, and the roots also be shot forth.[129]

To go to so much trouble indicates that mandrake roots fetched a high price. The forgery must have been quite realistic. How long it was before the customer realised that they had been duped depended upon the use to which they put their 'mandrake.' If taken internally, bryony is a purgative. The real mandrake can be highly poisonous however, containing alkaloids including atropine, scopolamine and hyoscyamine, and it must be used with extreme caution.[130]

Even exorcism was open to fraud. The Anglican Church did not much approve of the practice, especially after the activities of John Darrell came to light. Darrell's motive was probably not money, but glory. He was a Protestant preacher who seems to have taken his ideas from William Weston, a Jesuit priest who carried out several exorcisms in England. Weston was imprisoned in 1586, and banished in 1603.

Darrell began his career in the same year that Weston was imprisoned, with the exorcism of seventeen-year-old Katherine Wright. It ended in disaster when, with Darrell's support, Katherine accused Margaret Roper of bewitching her. The magistrate dismissed the charge and threatened Darrell with imprisonment should he persist.

About ten years later Darrell became involved in the case of Thomas Darling, a lad of fourteen who had claimed that during fits he saw visions of green angels and cats. His convulsions could be triggered by the first chapter of the Gospel of St John. The boy had claimed that he had met, and argued with, an old woman in a wood; from his description, the likely suspects were Elizabeth Wright or her daughter, Alse Gooderidge. Alse admitted meeting the boy in the wood, but denied that she had bewitched him. Nonetheless, after being searched for witch marks, she was committed to Derby prison. For some reason she confessed; she was tried and condemned, but died in prison before she could be hanged.

Tom Darling's fits continued, and his family called in Darrell. According to the exorcist, his efforts met with success, and his reputation was much enhanced. His next case, that of seven people living in Cleworth, became a *cause célèbre*. Members of Nicholas Starchie's household had been suffering from fits since 1594. Starchie had already consulted a conjurer, Edmund Hartlay, with some temporary success,[131] and had even contacted Dr John Dee. Once more Darrell was successful. After three days, six of the afflicted were cured; the last of them took one day more.

Only a few months later, Darrell seemed at first to have exorcised a demon from an apprentice, William Somers. The lad claimed that he had been bewitched by no less than thirteen women. They were all arrested, though only two committed for trial. But for some reason suspicions were aroused; Somers was taken to the house of correction[132] and closely questioned, and he finally admitted that his possession had been an imposture. Further, he said that he had been acting under instructions from Darrell. At an enquiry however he withdrew his confession.

Shortly afterwards, one of the accused women appeared at the assizes. The judge questioned Somers again, urging him to tell the truth; he capitulated, and admitted lying.

Darrell and George More, his associate, were summoned by the Bishop of London. Somers confirmed once again that he had lied. Thomas Darling also appeared, and said that he too had acted under Darrell's instructions. Though they denied any complicity, both Darrell and More went to prison for a year, and were stripped of their ministry. Shortly afterwards, the Church of England forbade any minister from undertaking an exorcism without authorisation from a bishop.[133]

No discussion of fraud and witchcraft would be complete without reference to Reginald Scot's Discoverie of Witchcraft. Scot was a Kent magistrate, and it is said that he became concerned about witchcraft following the trial of thirteen alleged witches from St Osyth, near Clacton-on-Sea in Essex, in 1582 (also known as St Oses). They were accused of the murder of twenty-four people between them. In addition, they were charged with causing injury to people, cattle and livestock. Most were acquitted or reprieved, but two were hanged: Ursley Kempe and Elizabeth Bennet. Amongst those who testified against Kempe was her eight-year-old son. She confessed to a number of offences, including the murder of her neighbour's baby. She had, she said, sent one of her familiars, Tyffin (a white lamb) to tip the child from its cot, breaking its neck. Kempe implicated Bennet, who confessed to sending Suckin, a familiar in the form of a black dog, to murder William Byett. Her motive was said to have been revenge, after he had called her 'old trot, old whore' when refusing to give her the milk she asked for.[134]

Others might wonder whether there was any truth in tales of witches, but Scot did not; he was sure they were fictitious.

> The fables of Witchcraft have taken so fast hold in the heart of man, that fewe or none can (nowadays) with patience indure the correction of God. For if any adversitie, greefe, sicknesse, losse of children, corne, cattell, or libertie happen unto them; by and by they exclaime upon witches.[135]

The powers attributed to witches were impossible, Scot assured his readers, and the authors of the *Malleus Maleficarum* and Jean Bodin came in for special criticism. There were no genuine references to witchcraft in the scriptures, said Scot; all the examples quoted by the witchmongers were mistranslations.

A good proportion of Scot's book is taken up with the secrets of the conjurers' arts. He lists numerous tricks that would not be out of place in the repertoire of a modern stage magician:

> To burn a thred, and to make it whole againe with the ashes thereof.
> To cut a lace asunder in the middest, and to make it whole againe.
> To make a little ball swell in your hand till it be verie great.

There are coin tricks and card tricks ('how to tell what card anie man thinketh, how to conveie the same into a kernell of a nut or cheristone, &c.: and the same againe into ones pocket: how to make one drawe the same or anie card you list...') Some of the tricks are somewhat cruel – 'Brandon's pigeon' involves poisoning the bird – but it was a cruel time. Bull and bear baiting were popular; 'mumble a sparrow' was a game involving trying to bite the head off the bird; and 'cat in a barrel' resulted in a most unpleasant end for the cat.[136]

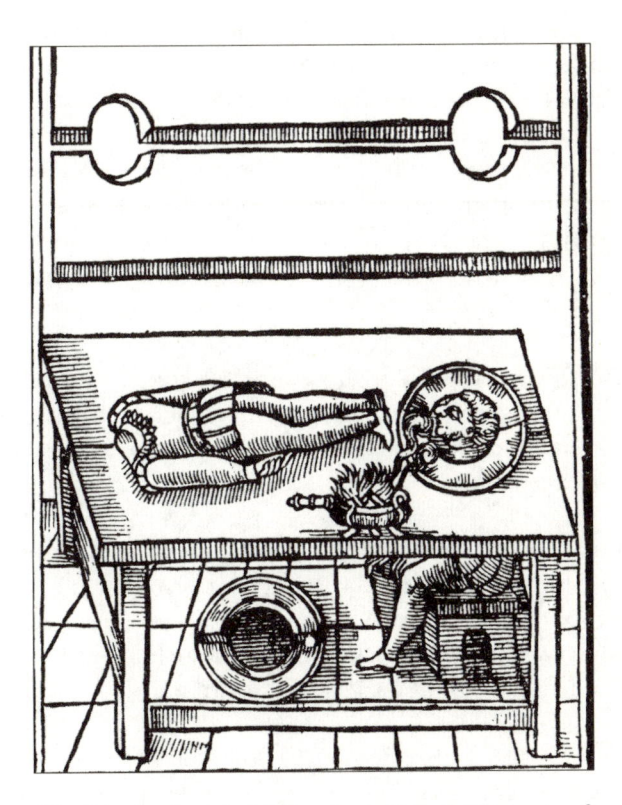

The 'John the Baptist' trick, from Reginald Scot's Discoverie of Witchcraft, *1584. An example of the 'cozening art.' As far as the audience is aware, the victim is decapitated. Two accomplices are involved; the first lies on the table, the top of which is in two pieces as shown at the top of the diagram. His head hangs down through one of the holes. The other sits beneath the table with his head through the other hole, which is surrounded by the two-piece plate (shown beneath the table). A table cloth, omitted here for clarity, hides from the audience what they are not intended to see.*

Scot goes on to explain tricks that sound highly dangerous, including how to

> eate a knife, and to fetch it out of anie other place;
> thrust a bodkin into your head without hurt;
> cut halfe your nose asunder, and to heale it againe presentlie without anie salve;
> thrust a dagger or bodkin into your guts verie stranglie, and to recover immediatlie.

Performers throughout the land used all these tricks, and many more, in order to make a living, but they had a secondary effect: they confirmed in the mind of the ordinary man the reality of magic. Like modern magicians, the 'jugglers,' as Scot called them, kept their secrets to themselves – there was no advantage to them in disclosing their methods (unless they found themselves in court charged with witchcraft).

Scot also lists the hierarchy of Hell,[137] with the names of the seventy-two principal devils, their powers, and the legions of demons subservient to them. But

> He that can be persuaded that these things are true, or wrought indeed according to the assertions of couseners, or according to the supposition of witchmongers and papists, may soone be brought to beleeve that the moone is made of greene cheese.

Fraud and trickery continued beyond the era of witchcraft suppression, and as we have seen the 1736 Act recognised its existence. Fraudulent conjuration (or any other 'crafty or occult science') remained an offence long after the real thing was struck from the statute books. Occasionally the courts acted. In 1867 *The Daily Telegraph* reported that

> At Leamington yesterday, a woman named Hannah Maria Moore was charged with fortune-telling. The defendant resided at a lonely cottage in the outskirts of Leamington, and has long been celebrated for her knowledge of the occult arts, and her skill in divining the future. If report be true, the rich were as credulous as the poor, and even carriages might be seen waiting after nightfall in the vicinity of her dwelling. At last, so notorious did the scandal become, that the police took steps to obtain a conviction. Accordingly, on Monday night, the wives of two of the constables paid her a visit. If her powers of divination are to be judged by what she revealed to them, they certainly were not great, for she not only failed to discover the true object of their visit, but showed great consideration for them, and, out of compassion for their indigence, only charged threepence for all her glowing promises of

A series of illustrations from Saducismus Triumphatus, *Joseph Glanvill's defence of the belief in witchcraft and the supernatural.*

sweethearts, weddings and a long line of descendants. It would appear, however, from a letter found in her possession when apprehended, that she occasionally engaged to exercise her arts so as to send sweethearts to young women, as in the communication alluded to her correspondent upbraided her for not having fulfilled her promises, and exhorted her to redouble her efforts. The bench committed her to gaol for a month with hard labour.[138]

The last person convicted under the 1736 act was Helen Duncan, known as 'Hellish Nell.'[139] She was arrested on 19 January 1944, for pretending to conjure the dead at séances in a room above a chemist's shop in Plymouth. Some of her supporters testified on her behalf, claiming that she could indeed raise the dead. If anything, their testimony damaged her case, and she went to prison for nine months. There have since been claims made that the real reason she was prosecuted was the fear that she might be giving away military or naval secrets, or lowering morale in wartime.[140]

The Decline of Witchcraft Prosecutions in England

The pattern of rise and decline of prosecutions in England was similar to most of Europe. There was an unusual second peak in prosecutions during the period of the Civil War and the Commonwealth, but such surges were not unique. No single cause was responsible for the steady decline in prosecutions; several influences combined to make acceptance of magic and witchcraft less popular with those who wielded power.

Many clerics were reluctant to concede to the Devil the degree of power that belief in the supernatural implicitly demanded. Perhaps just as significant was the manner in which the supernatural was portrayed in literature and the theatre. In medieval mystery plays, the Devil frequently had an important and sombre role. Christopher Marlowe's *Doctor Faustus* is a tragedy in which the title character sells his soul to Satan. The witches of Macbeth are menacing, evil creatures.

But John Webster's [141] *The White Devil* shows that fraudulent magicians did not fool everyone. In reply to Brachiano's query as to how he will murder Camillo, the conjurer replies:

> You have won me by your bounty to a deed
> I do not often practise. Some there are
> Which do sophistic tricks aspire that name,
> Which I would gladly lose, of nigromancer [necromancer];
> As some that used to juggle upon cards,
> Seeming to conjecture, when indeed they cheat;

Others that raise up their confederate spirits
'Bout windmills, and endanger their own necks
For making a squib; and some there are
Will keep a curtal [an animal whose tail has been docked]
    to show juggling tricks,
And give out 'tis a spirit; besides these,
Such a whole realm of almanac-makers, figure flingers,
Fellows, indeed, that only live by stealth,
Since they do merely lie about stolen goods, –
They'd make men think the devil were fast and loose,
With speaking fustian [pretentious] Latin.'

As the seventeenth century wore on, the pendulum swung away from the supernatural as a serious subject for literature; Ben Jonson's comedy *The Devil is an Ass* of 1616 was an early example of the Devil being treated in a disrespectful manner.[142]

Increasingly, books on witchcraft called the power of witches into question and expressed doubt about the witchcraft trials themselves. When Scot wrote in 1584, he was in the minority as a sceptic. His contemporary, George Gifford, published his *Discourse of the subtill Practices of Devills by Witches and Sorcerers* in 1587; he too was sceptical. In his *Dialogue Concerning Witches and Witchcraftes* (1593) though, he recognised the violence of feeling of others, and one of his characters says 'If I had but one faggot in the world, I would carry it a mile upon my shoulders to burn a witch.'[143]

The majority scorned the sceptics' views. William Perkins in 1608 we have already met; likewise Michael Dalton and Richard Bernard a few years later. All three were firm believers.

As the century wore on, the sceptics became either more common or more courageous. Some still believed in Satan and his power upon the earth, but doubted the guilt of those brought before the courts. Others, like Thomas Hobbes, dismissed the power of witches entirely, but still thought them evil:

> As for witches, I think not that their witchcraft is any real power; but yet they have been justly punished, for the false belief that they have that they can do such mischief... [144]

John Gaule, in 1646,[145] and John Webster, in 1677,[146] were both deeply concerned by the difficulty in obtaining reliable evidence, and convictions obtained without it. The believers did not disappear overnight however. William Drage of Hitchin was writing in the 1660s when he described the symptoms of possession and bewitchment.[147]

Joseph Glanvill's *Saducismus Triumphatus*, a defence of belief in witchcraft, in which he claimed that to deny it was tantamount to atheism, appeared in 1681.[148]

But the last serious witchmonger's book in England was Richard Baxter's *Certainty of the World of Spirits* in 1691. Baxter was a fervent Puritan who accepted as true some dubious material, especially if the source was known as a pious person, and his book is a collection of witchcraft and ghost stories from around the British Isles.

The final serious refutation was Francis Hutchinson's essay in 1718.[149] Hutchinson was the vicar of St James's Church in Bury St Edmunds. He investigated a number of cases of supposed witchcraft, visiting some of those concerned personally; he corresponded with others. He noted the swimming of John Lowes in 1645, when several 'honest' people were put into the water at the same time as the accused; they all floated. Lowes confessed after being 'walked' for a protracted period. Witch-hunters came in for condemnation for their brutality to elderly suspects. Hutchinson visited Jane Wenham of Walkern in Hertfordshire, the last woman sentenced to death for witchcraft in England, and found her to be an inoffensive woman; he had no doubt as to her innocence. Following publication of Hutchinson's book, few amongst the learned classes openly professed a belief in the power of witches, but it was another eighteen years before the 1604 Witchcraft Act was repealed.

In the closing years of the seventeenth century many of the judiciary, following the lead of Gaule, Webster and others, became increasingly uneasy about the quality of evidence being presented to them. They were increasingly unwilling to accept guilty verdicts for witchcraft. Prosecutions became rare, and acquittals, never unusual, became even more common. A leading light in this respect was Sir John Holt. Born in 1642, he led a wild youth, but achieved respectability as Lord Chief Justice of the Court of the King's Bench in 1689. According to a tale that may be apocryphal, in his youth he paid an alehouse bill by writing a charm to cure the landlady's daughter of the ague. Many years later she appeared before him charged with curing fevers with the same charm he had given her. Her daughter had recovered, and convinced of the power of Holt's scribble, she had used it to cure friends and neighbours ever since.[150] Holt tried a number of witchcraft cases, and secured acquittals for the accused. In his last case, at Guildford Assizes, not only was Sarah Morduck discharged, but her accuser was committed for trial as a 'Cheat and Imposter,' found guilty, and sentenced to a year in prison, with three appearances in the pillory.[151]

The last execution for witchcraft in England was that of Alice Molland in Exeter, in 1684. Neither she nor Jane Wenham of Walkern, Hertfordshire, were the last prosecutions, however; that dubious honour goes to Jane Clarke, who, with her son and daughter, was tried at the

Leicester Assizes in 1717. Though the people of Great Wigston were convinced of the family's guilt, and twenty-five of them were prepared to testify to that effect, the Grand Jury returned a bill of ignoramus.

But amongst the working men and women of the country, a fear of the evil that witches might do persisted well into the twentieth century. Assaults in an attempt to 'score above the breath' continued to occur. In Monmouth in 1827 four men set upon Mary Nicholas, aged ninety, whom they accused of being a witch. They scratched her face with a briar to break the spell. Such occurrences were not rare. Swimming of witches continued too, even though in 1712 Lord Chief Justice Sir Thomas Parker declared that if 'the party lose her life by it, all that are the cause of it are guilty of wilful murther.'[152] Occasionally a swimming was indeed fatal. In 1751 Ruth Osborne lost her life near Tring, Hertfordshire, whilst being ducked by a mob. In 1863 an elderly fortune teller was so barbarously treated during a ducking at Sible Hedingham in Essex that he never recovered, and died a month afterwards in the workhouse. Emma Smith and Samuel Stammers were charged with assault, and received remarkably lenient sentences of six months in prison.

Eventually the witch became the subject of storybooks and fairytales, used either to amuse or to send a shiver down the spines of small children. Though the witch was nearly always evil, ugly and female, she was not invulnerable, and often came to a sticky end. New myths have appeared – in parts of Germany the witch is now benign, and as a herald of spring, she sweeps the snow from the mountains. A little ironic, bearing in mind that Germany saw some of the worst excesses of the witch-hunts in the whole of Europe. Even today however there are many people who accept the truth of superstitions that a few moments' thought would show to be ridiculous. Whilst the witch has all but vanished, a new pantheon of beliefs has sprung up. Crop circles, alien abduction, spiritualism and the like all have their adherents. The number of people that turn first to their 'stars' in the newspaper each morning is astonishing. Perhaps we are not as rational as we like to think.

Today there is an industry catering for those who choose to believe, but few would accept the existence of the classical witch of the fifteenth, sixteenth and seventeenth centuries, with all that goes with her: the pact with the Devil; the flight to the sabbats, where blasphemies, child sacrifice and orgies took place; the ability to raise storms, blight crops, even to kill men and animals, either by a curse or even no more than a glance. The witch is no longer a figure of fear, and toy witches are available as corn dollies and mementos.

4
THE REALITY OF WITCHCRAFT

There can be no doubt that until comparatively recently there was widespread belief in magic and the supernatural. Some people still believe in it. People have been, and are still, prepared to believe in fortune tellers, mediums and astrologers. Cunning folk – white witches – existed throughout Europe, but as they were rarely prosecuted they ran little risk of punishment. Indeed, their activities gave them a higher status than they might otherwise have aspired to. A few were itinerant, but many more practised in the village or town in which they lived.

Some were sincere, believing in their powers, and relying upon herbs and folk medicine to effect cures on their clients. Others were less scrupulous, and can only be described as charlatans and frauds. They exploited the fears, desires and anxieties of local people for their own profit. In some cases, they combined both folk healing and fraud, depending upon the demands made upon them.

Fortunes were told in much the same way as they are today, using elaborate magical props at one end of the spectrum and tea leaves at the other. Common factors are skill in assessing the client, and deliberate vagueness in prediction. But what about the black witches, those darker sisters of the cunning folk?

There is no evidence of the pan-European witch-cult, intent on the overthrow of society and the Christian Church that the elite of society had feared. There was no widespread organisation of devil-worshipping sorcerers, murdering children and boiling their bodies down to fat to make a flying ointment. Nor did groups of witches meet at midnight at secret rendezvous to celebrate the black mass at a sabbat.

But most people believed in the power of magic, and mankind has shown great capacity for evil throughout history. It would be inconceivable if no one attempted to cast magic spells or charms for material gain, or to revenge themselves against their neighbours. We can be sure that individuals made wax images in the belief that they could harm their enemies. The only thing to stop them was fear of damnation, which is small deterrent for those whose faith in the Church was weak.

Of course such activities were necessarily carried out in secret, and the evidence is sparse. Nonetheless, it does exist. We have seen Roman examples; a similar lead curse from the seventeenth century was found at Wilton Place, near Dymock in Gloucestershire, and like the Roman curses it is written backwards. There are a number of astrological symbols, followed by the curse, which is directed at Sarah Ellis: 'make this person to Banish away from this place and countery amen to my desire amen'.[1] Another lead curse, dating from the sixteenth century and found at Lincoln's Inn in 1899, ill-wished Ralph Scrope, one of the Governors of the Inn.[2] In January 1960 an example of a paper curse was found in a cellar during renovation work at the Hereford Rural District Council offices. Dating from the nineteenth century, it read:

> Mary Ann Ward
> I act this spell upon you with my holl heart
> wishing you never rest nor eat nor sleep the
> resten part of your life I hope your flesh
> will waste away and I hope you will never
> spend another penny I ought to have
> Wishing this from my whole heart

It was tucked in the skirt of a small female figure, which had a plait of hair inserted in it. It wore a cap or bonnet, and was made from a patterned material (dark blue, with red spots), with a head of pink cotton.[3] Bearing in mind the perishable nature of the medium in many curses, and the secretive nature of their preparation and concealment, it seems likely that elaborate curses were in fact laid quite frequently.

The ordinary Englishman's concept of the black witch came closer to reality than her Continental counterpart. She was a malevolent person, acting alone and in secret, preparing a curse in order to harm an enemy. How many of those convicted of being witches were in fact guilty of attempting malevolent witchcraft is impossible to say with any certainty, but most of those that denied the charges laid against them were probably innocent. Confessions made under duress are similarly unreliable.

A small number of English witches were said to have confessed without pressure being exerted upon them. Perhaps they really had attempted to cast a spell; perhaps they were simply attention seekers. It is possible, in view of the advanced age of many suspects, that some were merely senile, and scarcely knew what they were saying.

The Causes of the Witch-Hunts

Some writers have looked for a single explanation for the witch-hunts, and as a result they have failed to make a convincing case. The truth is that there was no single explanation. There were a number of them, and one or more explanations may be appropriate to each individual accusation.

A witch-hunt must have the right conditions to flourish. A belief in witchcraft must exist; there must be someone prepared to lay the accusation; a legal mechanism must exist for their prosecution; and there must be a willingness on the part of the judicial authority to take action. Fear was often the key. The accuser was frightened of what the witch could do to him; the elite feared a witch cult, in league with the Devil and his cohorts. Witches were believed to be numbered in tens, perhaps hundreds of thousands; maybe even more. Demons were counted in millions. For those in power, this was a formidable threat.

People from all walks of life believed in the stereotype witch as a result of a steady change in ideas between the tenth to fourteenth centuries. A number of factors combined to create her; the concept of a threat from within society, and the suppression of it, arose from fear of invaders and the persecution of such groups as the Cathars, Knights Templar, Jews and lepers. The Church came to view any form of magical activity as heresy, thus placing it under the jurisdiction of the Inquisition. In some areas, the breakdown of centralised control resulted in local persecutions, as in parts of England during the Civil War.

The philosophy of proof by resorting to authorities of the past, coupled with developments in printing, resulted in a rash of books such as the *Malleus Maleficarum*, and the works of Bodin, Remy, Guazzo, De Lancre and their ilk, all of which helped spread the fear and persecution far and wide. The legality of torture through most of Europe led to confessions made either as a result of torture or the threat of its use. Questioning included demands for acomplices' names, which, not surprisingly, were often forthcoming. Each arrest led to more arrests, and a full-scale witch-hunt resulted.

Some cases might have been due to poisoning, accounting for both accusations and confessions. Various plants and fungi have been credited with producing hallucinations in both witches and their victims. Ergot is frequently quoted as a prime suspect, and in a few cases it may have been the culprit. But the effects of ergot have been known since the Middle Ages; the fungus was used by midwives to stimulate contractions.[4] It seems likely therefore that ergot poisoning might be recognised as such, and the symptoms attributed to natural rather than supernatural causes. And ergot poisoning does not fit all cases by any means. Many victims 'languished until they died,' in some cases many months later. Some of those deaths may have been murder by some other form of poison, but most were more likely natural deaths.

In most of Europe, the goods of convicted witches were subject to confiscation, and this too has been suggested as a motive for the witch-hunts. There were however few wealthy people amongst the accused. The organisation of an expensive trial and execution in order to seize the goods of a poor man was unlikely to yield a profit. It is possible however that in isolated cases, where the proceeds made it worthwhile, some accusations were made with this motive; and perhaps some were made with a political motive, such as that made by Henry V against his stepmother, Joan of Navarre, in 1419.[5] The light sentence passed on the alleged conspirators tends to support this view.[6]

That the Catholic Church used witch-hunts as a means to attack Protestants is sometimes proposed as an explanation. However, though Catholics did prosecute Protestants, they also prosecuted large numbers of their own faith; and Protestants too prosecuted people of both faiths. The picture seems to be of Christianity against supposed witches rather than a sectarian purge.

It has been claimed that the Reformation was the cause of the witch-hunts. As the persecutions began before the Reformation, this is clearly not true, though the Reformation may have had some impact on the scale of the purges. With the loss of the Catholic Church to perform rituals for the protection or cure of the bewitched, it is likely that ordinary people turned instead to white witches, or to the secular courts.

Doctor Margaret Murray, a respected Egyptologist, proposed in her book *The Witch Cult in Western Europe* that witches had really existed. They were, she argued, the remnants of a pre-Christian pagan faith that had survived to the Middle Ages, worshiping a horned god. The witchcraft suppressions were the result of the Church's attack on a rival, and thriving, religion. Doctor Murray collected evidence from far and wide in support of her theory, and for some time it became extremely popular; but that popularity rested in part upon its romantic appeal. The appeal works still, and I should be delighted if I could say that I believe it to be true.[7] Unfortunately Murray was highly selective with her evidence, accepting that which fitted her hypothesis and rejecting that which did not. Whilst there is evidence of the survival of pagan practices, such as the dance of the Deermen in Abbots Bromley,[8] Staffordshire (see plate 10), this should not be confused with the survival of a pagan religion. It is possible that some of the witches' sabbats reported to the authorities were indeed pagan survivals, but this is mere speculation.

There is a second serious problem with the pagan religion theory. There are some, admittedly sparse, records of magicians and sorcerers in the period between the Christian conversion and the persecution of supposed witches; but there is no mention of an organised witch cult. Supporters of the theory might say that there is no proof that the cult did not exist: but that is not proof that it did.

At about the same time as Doctor Murray was working on her theories, Montague Summers published a number of books on the subject of witchcraft.[9] He also produced introductions and notes for a number of translations of classic witchcraft texts.[10] Summers was a Catholic priest, and his explanation for the witch-hunts was perhaps the most unusual of all: he was convinced of the reality of the satanic version of the witch cult. Summers' writings are strongly biased in this direction, and in favour of the Catholic Church, to the extent that he refers to one of the authors of the *Malleus Maleficarum* as 'the erudite Sprenger.' 'Only the trained theologian can adequately treat the subject [of witchcraft],' he says.[11]

What were the causes of individual accusations? A compelling suggestion is that many of them were the result of social pressures. In a changing world where village society, with its tradition of caring for the poor, the elderly and the infirm, was in decline, feelings of guilt arose in those who refused charity to their neighbours. An accusation of witchcraft against the old woman who came begging, and who was rebuffed, meant that the feeling of guilt could be dismissed. The wrongdoer was the witch, and the person that had snubbed her became the victim. The hypothesis is supported by the large number of cases that meet the scenario, in which an elderly woman is refused charity, and who is subsequently heard mumbling under her breath; after a while the person who refused the charity suffers some misfortune.

In Protestant countries, the loss of the Catholic Church's support for those who believed themselves bewitched, either by appeal to saints, relics or exorcism may have resulted in some prosecutions.

Reginald Scot believed that many accusations were the result of people choosing to assign the blame for their own failures, moral or material. It was far more comfortable to blame someone else than to admit one's own shortcomings.

There seems too to be some correlation between periods of social stress and witchcraft accusations. The connection may be real, or illusory. During such times central authority was often diminished, and local justice administered; the check on witch-hunts provided by the higher courts in normal circumstances was lost.

Not to be dismissed is the malicious accusation, made through hatred or envy, or even for as slight a motive as attention seeking. The acceptance of the testimony of children in several cases resulted in death for the defendants. During the peak of the witch-hunts there seems to have been little punishment for such accusations, even though they might result in death for the accused.

And of course some accusations were sincere. Prosecutions were laid by people who believed in witchcraft, and were convinced that they, their family or their possessions had been bewitched. Under such circumstances their motives in bringing the prosecutions were a combination of self-defence and a real belief that their actions would result in justice.

Summary

There were many white witches, the cunning folk; they might be found in most settlements of any size throughout Europe, but their stock in trade was very much the same throughout. It was frequently to these witches that the ordinary people, and often their social superiors, turned in time of need. Some were sincere, but many were charlatans, taking advantage of the superstitious beliefs of their neighbours. Others combined folk healing with the less reputable roles of the trade.

There were also some, but fewer, black witches. They were not the witches of the stereotype however. In most cases they were individuals dabbling in magic, sometimes in the hope of revenge, sometimes using magic in the hope of financial gain. There was no satanic cult of witches dedicated to the overthrow of Christianity, as described by the *Malleus Maleficarum* and other contemporary books on the subject. The concept of the stereotypical witch and the diabolic conspiracy arose from several sources: the persecution of religious groups such as the Cathars and Templars, with allegations of Devil worship and sexual orgies and deviance; the acceptance of torture as a legitimate means of interrogation, and its use in obtaining denunciations; the Wild Hunt, with its midnight meetings, and combination with the flying women of the *Canon Episcopi*; social tension amongst the group most likely to make accusations – the lower classes; the willingness of the Church to prosecute heretics, and to see them executed; and acceptance of the view of women as inferior to men, and easily seduced by the Devil. By the early fifteenth century, the stage was set. All that was required was the accusations and the will of authority to act.

Though there were relatively few victims of the purges in all, they were often localised, both in geography and in time; the result to a small community could therefore be devastating.

The majority of victims, between 70-80 per cent, were women, though a significant number were men. The male-female mix varied in different areas.

The cause of the witch-hunts was not down to a single factor. Different hunts might have a different origin, or combination of origins.

The witch-hunts spread slowly, not reaching some parts of Europe for a hundred years or more. But the spread was not even; in some cases neighbouring communities had very different experiences. On the whole larger towns were less likely to be hit than smaller, rural districts.

In England the pattern followed similar lines to Continental Europe, but differed in detail. The concept of the diabolic cult arrived late, and had less impact on the witch trials — by the time it became widely accepted, the trials were already in decline.[12]

The belief in this country was that witches worked alone, carrying out evil acts against their neighbours; they might cause bad weather, injure or kill man or beast, and cause misfortune and ill luck. The British witch was believed to have a familiar imp, an idea that occurred much less frequently on the Continent. The number of prosecutions was relatively low, in part because torture in its more extreme forms was forbidden in Common Law.

PART TWO
HERTFORDSHIRE IN DETAIL

NOTE ON THE SOURCES

The cases that follow are drawn from a number of sources. Indictments and Assize Court records come from the HMSO publications for Elizabeth I and James I, and from Cecil Ewen's trawl of the assize rolls published in *Witch Hunting and Witch Trials*, which, despite being more than seventy years old, is still the best place to start in searches for witchcraft cases in the Home Circuit.[1] quarter sessions items come from W. Le Hardy's Quarter Session Rolls (Hertfordshire County Session Rolls, 1581-1698), published by Hertfordshire County Council in the early twentieth century.

Unfortunately, in most instances the assize records preserve only the indictment, though it is sometimes supported by lists of prisoners in gaols or discharged recognisances.[2] The sort of information contained in these documents is restricted:

> the person accused, their trade and where they come from
> if a married woman,
> the name of the victim
> and (usually) the trade of her husband
> the nature of the offence
> the date of the offence
> sometimes the names of witnesses
> (usually) the plea, the verdict and the sentence.

Take for example the case of Sara Assar in 1601: she was from Little Munden, and a spinster. On 28 February 1601, she bewitched Mary (or Mercy) Ireland of Little Munden, who languished until 20 March following, when she died at Little Munden. The witnesses were Robert Ireland, Susan Ireland and Ellen Gibson. The Grand Jury found a case to answer (a true bill). Sara pleaded not guilty, and was acquitted.

Occasionally depositions and other documents are preserved, but they are quite rare, and are more often found in cases that came before the quarter sessions than the assizes.

Events are sometimes described in pamphlets or books, but here the reliability of the information has to be viewed with caution. Who wrote the account? Was the author a believer in witchcraft and magic or not? Why was it written? Is there any supporting evidence of the case? Does the account ring true? Some are more believable than others. Even those that report cases that can be verified may well have been written by someone with an axe to grind. But even pamphlets that are clearly biased one way or another tell us something about the person that wrote them, and the society in which he lived.

Further information on particular cases might be available from local documents such as parish registers, many of which are available at Hertfordshire Archives and Local Studies, County Hall, Hertford. To carry out searches on all the people mentioned in this collection would be a daunting task indeed, and I leave it to those with an interest in particular cases. I would be delighted to hear of the results of any such research however. A list of all the cases for which there is a mention in the assize and quarter sessions records can be found in Appendix A.

Finally, it is worth pointing out that spelling in the sixteenth and seventeenth centuries was a pretty hit-and-miss affair. Phonetics ruled, and the same person might well have his or her name spelt in a variety of ways in the same document.

1 The oak plaque on the wall of the parish church of Great Giddings, Cambridgeshire. The words have been corrupted – 'AREPO' now reads 'ARIPO', and 'TENET' has become 'TENIT', so the magic square no longer works. The significance of the 'E R' is unknown – the death of Elizabeth I predates the plaque by more than ten years. (Author's collection)

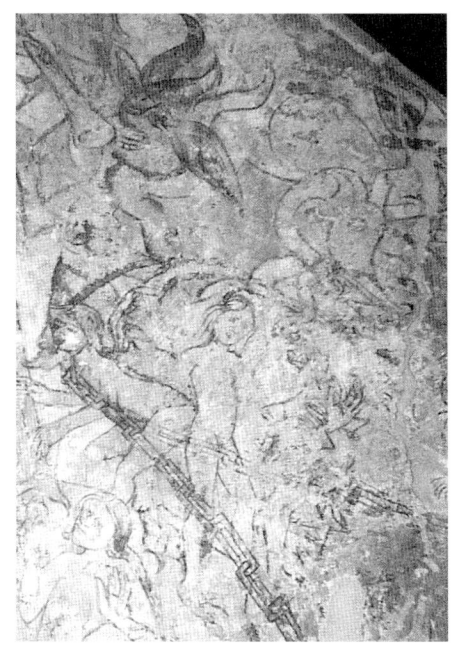

2 A detail of the 'Doom' painting at Great Shelford, Cambridgeshire. Demons herd sinners towards the jaws of Hell. The chains are clearly visible. On the opposite side of the painting (not shown) the righteous ascend into the Kingdom of Heaven. (Author's collection)

3 A seventeenth-century bellarmine witch bottle from Felmersham, Bedfordshire. It tested positive for urine. (Robert Fletcher)

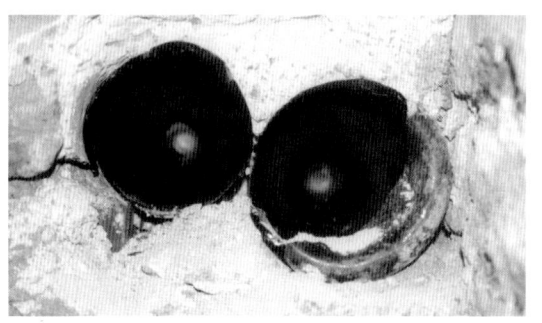

4 Two late eighteenth-century bottles walled up to the left of a hearth in a large house in western Essex. Finds like these should never be cleaned before examination and testing. In this case the contents leaked away before it could be collected, but it is likely to have been urine. (Brian Hoggard)

5 This horseshoe has been in position since at least the 1930s, and perhaps longer than that. In Hertfordshire the horseshoe has to be this way up 'to keep the luck in', but in some parts of England the shoe should be the other way up. (Author's collection)

6 The Agnus Dei, or Lamb of God, appears in many forms, not just as a charm. Here it is as a ceiling boss at Burford, Oxfordshire. (Author's collection)

7 The Agnus Dei on a medieval green glaze pottery fragment, found in St Albans. (Author, courtesy Museum of St Albans)

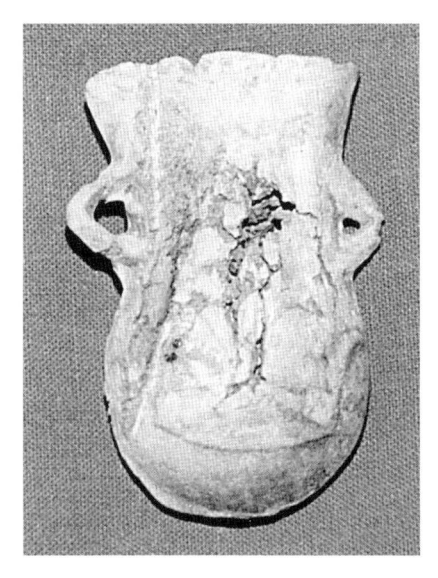

8 *A medieval lead ampulla. This one was buried in a field in Gloucestershire. It is likely that its contents were spread on the field to bless it. It is about 50mm in height, and has been flattened by pressure of the ground above. (Author, courtesy Janet Newman)*

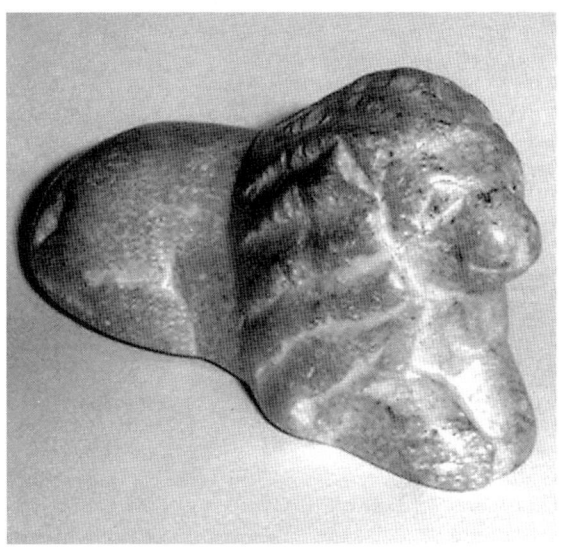

9 *A 'lucky lion', bought in September 2003 for £2 from a caller claiming to be a genuine gypsy. It is about 6cm in length, and made of a pinkish stone. (Author's collection)*

10 *The Deermen of Abbots Bromley, in Staffordshire, in the 1930s. Such pagan survivals have been taken as evidence of the survival of a pre-Christian religion, worshipping a horned god.*

11 *According to local tradition, this cottage in Church Lane, Walkern, was once the home of Jane Wenham. It is possible, but seems unlikely; Wenham was extremely poor, and this house seems a little too fine for her. (Author's collection)*

12 *Ruth Osborne's body was taken to the Half Moon public house, Wilstone, after her swimming. Part of the original building at least has survived since then. Corpses likely to be subject to an inquest were often taken to pubs until the Licensing Act of 1902, which stipulated that inquests were not to be held in licensed premises unless there was nowhere else to hold them. (Author's collection)*

13 Above: *The ritual hoard found at the Long House, Walsworth, Hertfordshire. The shoe dates the hoard to the last twenty years of the nineteenth century. (Author, courtesy Bryn and Julie Lerwill)*

14 Left: *A close-up of the shoe from the Walsworth hoard. The heavy wear and tear is typical of the condition of items in ritual hoards. (Author, courtesy Bryn and Julie Lerwill)*

15 A ceramic bottle from a hoard found at Weston, Hertfordshire, dating from the end of the seventeenth century. Unfortunately it was not tested for urine before cleaning. (Author, courtesy North Hertfordshire Museum Service)

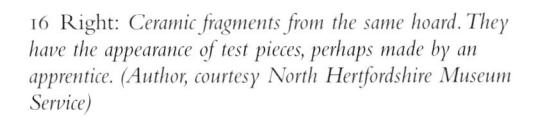

16 Right: Ceramic fragments from the same hoard. They have the appearance of test pieces, perhaps made by an apprentice. (Author, courtesy North Hertfordshire Museum Service)

17 Below: An iron snaffle bit, with leather fragments, and two flint pebbles, all from the Weston hoard. Neither of the pebbles have holes in them, suggesting that they are included for their unusual shape. (Author, courtesy North Hertfordshire Museum Service)

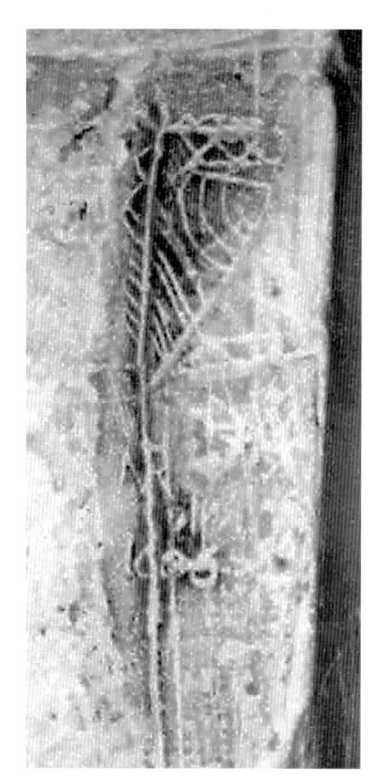

18 Above left: *A hobbyhorse from the church porch at Wallington. The reasoning behind this graffito is unknown, as is its date, though it seems to cut through another graffito of 1606. (Author's collection)*

19 Above right: *A similar example of a hobbyhorse, taken from just across the Bedfordshire border at Shillington. (Author's collection)*

20 Below left: *A daisywheel in the belfry of All Saints church in Willian, near Letchworth. (Author's collection)*

21 Below right: *Daisywheels in the porch of the church of St Mary the Virgin, between Willian and Letchworth. (Author's collection)*

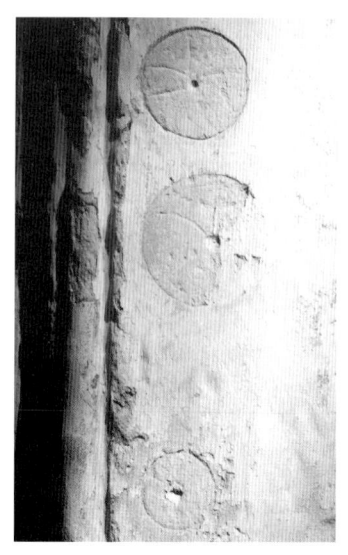

22 Right: *An unusual daisywheel found at St Mary Magdelene Church, Great Offley. As in this case, an oblique view sometimes shows feint graffiti to advantage. The engraving is symmetrical. The dots are intriguing; they also appear at Willian and many other churches. There is research being carried out into them at the moment, but as yet their significance, if any, remains unexplained. (Author's collection)*

23 Far right: *A horned mask graffito from St Mary's Church in Gravely. The damage is recent and due to the use of Rawlplugs. (Author's collection)*

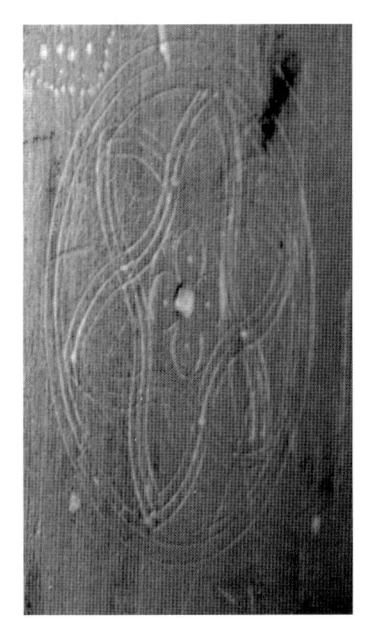

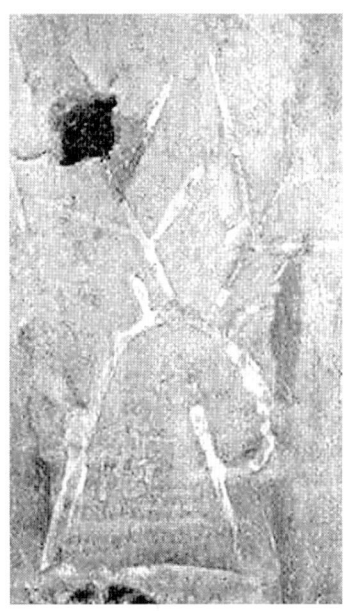

24 Above: *The dagaz, a rune associated with light and good fortune. This form certainly dates from the Saxon period, but is probably much older. It sometimes appears rotated by 90 degrees. This example is on the door latch at Wallington church. (Author's collection)*

25 Right: *The 'witch' in St Helens Church, Wheathampstead. The graffito has been enhanced for clarity. (Author's collection)*

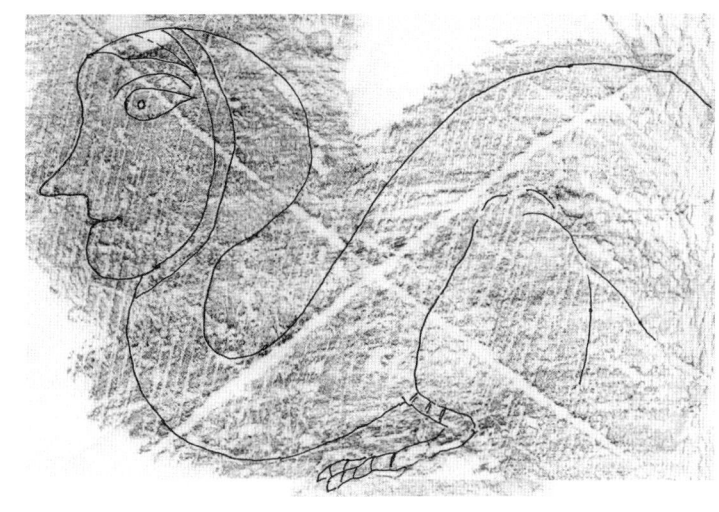

26 *The seventeenth-century view of the witch. Apart from her familiars, she is just like any other elderly person. From* The Wonderful Discoverie of the witchcrafts of Margaret and Phillip Flower, *1619.*

27 *By the eighteenth century things had changed; this woodcut comes from* The Famous History of the Lancashire Witches. *The leading witch rides a broomstick and wears a pointed hat – the modern stereotype had begun to evolve.*

5
Maleficium

Maleficium was the evil art practised by black witches – the killing or injuring of men or beasts, storm raising, damaging crops or produce and so on. The majority of prosecutions in English secular courts were for this type of activity; after all, most prosecutions were brought by common men or women, and it was this form of witchcraft most feared by ordinary people.

Mary Burgis (or Burgess), 1590

In 1590 Mary Burgis of Bengeo was accused of a number of acts of witchcraft dating back several years. In this respect her case is typical. Accused witches frequently had a reputation for the offence, and when eventually a prosecution was brought, all the earlier suspicions were rekindled. In Mary's case, the earliest accusation was four years in the past. She had, according to the indictment presented to the Hertfordshire Assizes in the summer of 1590, bewitched a horse, brown in colour, belonging to George Grave of Bengeo. Horses were expensive animals – this one was valued at five pounds. There exists no record that anything was done at the time. Far more serious charges were laid against her however. It was alleged that she had killed three people, and attacked George Grave for a second time. With the exception of Grave, her victims were apparently children.

On 6 October 1589, Susan Hill, daughter of John Hill of Bengeo, was struck down with illness. She lived until 25 November, when she died. On 7 October 1589, Elizabeth Noble, daughter of Thomas Noble of Hertford, was taken ill. She did not recover, dying on the 20 November. The Noble household can scarcely have recovered from their loss when a son, William, was struck down on 20 December.[1] He languished for just two days before succumbing to the ailment that afflicted him.

The final allegation was that on 4 April 1590, at Stapleford, Mary struck at George Grave once more, crippling his right arm for a significant period. The deaths of the three children prompted action, and Mary was arrested. On 31 July 1590 she appeared before the assizes. The judges for the Summer Sessions that year were Sir Robert Clarke, Baron of the Exchequer, and Serjeant John Puckering, later Lord Keeper of the Great Seal. The hearing was held at St Albans.

The Grand Jury decided that there was a case to answer on all five indictments, and Mary Burgess's full trial commenced.

Whether the Petty Jury was unwilling to bring in a 'guilty' verdict on a capital charge, or whether they judged the case on the evidence alone we shall never know, though I suspect the former – there were other cases with a similar result. In any event, Mary was acquitted on the three charges of murder, but convicted of killing the horse and crippling George Grave.

The punishment was clearly stated in the Act of 1563 – a year in gaol, with four appearances, each lasting six hours, in the pillory. Though this may seem a far better option than the alternative – death by hanging – it was still pretty bad. On occasion prisoners in the pillory were killed by the missiles thrown, especially if they were unpopular; and the death rate in gaols by disease, especially typhus, was a significant concern for both inmates and turnkeys. The last we hear of Mary Burgis is a short entry in the Gaol Delivery Roll for 1590/1, where she is listed as an inmate in the prison. We can only hope that she completed her sentence safely and was released.

Alice and Christian Stokes; Johane and Anne Harrison, 1606

Royston was the location for our next case, which is a particularly interesting one; it presents problems for the historian that are difficult to resolve.

According to assize records of the Summer Sessions of 1606 at Hertford there were only four sentences of death passed for the whole county of Hertfordshire. The first two were George Dell of Hatfield, and his mother, Annis, for the brutal, but conventional, murder of a young lad, Anthony James. The second pair was Alice and Christian Stokes of Royston, for murder by witchcraft. Shortly afterwards a pamphlet was published in London entitled:

> The most cruell and bloody murther committed by an Inkeepers wife, called Annis Dell, and her sonne George Dell, foure yeeres since. On the

bodie of a childe, called Anthony James in Bishops Hatfield in the countie of Hartford, and now most miraculously reuealed by the sister of the said Anthony, who at the time of the murther had her tongue cut out, and foure yeeres remayned dumme and speechlesse, and now perfectly speaketh, reuealing the murther, hauing no tongue to be seen. With the seuerall witch-crafts, and most damnable practices of one Iohane Harrison and her daughter vpon seuerall persons, men and women at Royston, who were all executed at Hartford the 4 of August last past. 1606. London: Printed for William Firebrand and Iohn Wright, and are to be sold at Christs Church dore, 1606.

Here is the difficulty: The assize records and the pamphlet agree on the names of George and Annis (or Agnes) Dell. But why does the pamphlet say that the two witches from Royston were Johane and Anne Harrison? Are they in fact Alice and Christian Stokes?

The indictment detail we have is as follows:

ACCUSED	OFFENCE	VICTIM	VERDICT
Alice Stokes	Murder by witchcraft	Richard Bland	Guilty
Alice Stokes	Causing injury by witchcraft	John Rumbold	Pardoned
Christian Stokes	Murder by witchcraft	Roger Gybbons	Guilty
Christian Stokes	Murder by witchcraft	John Peirse	Guilty
Christian Stokes	Causing injury by witchcraft	Jane Wakefield	Pardoned

Unfortunately the pamphlet does not give the names of the victims, so we cannot match those details. Nor do the offences described in the pamphlet match the indictments listed above. That in itself however does not prove that this is the same case – it is possible that some of the indictments have been lost.

Let's have a look at the contents of the pamphlet. The first part deals with the murder of Anthony James by the Dells, and though it is outside the scope of this book I will give a brief outline of the events.

The James family – father, mother, son and daughter – were the victims of robbers, and the parents murdered. The children, Anthony and Elizabeth, were lodged at a Hatfield inn run by Annis Dell and her son George. A short time later Anthony was murdered and his body dumped in a pond. His identity was established when a local tailor recognised his jacket. Elizabeth's tongue was cut out, and she was given to a beggar, who agreed to take her 'for a peece of money.' In fact he abandoned her. After four years begging, she found herself once more in Hatfield, where she recognised the Dell's inn. She was fostered with a local family, and eventually recovered enough speech to recount her story. The Dells were arrested, tried and hanged.[2]

The account of the Harrisons as told in the pamphlet is as follows: the two women already had reputations for witchcraft before the events described took place. After their arrest, their home was searched, and some incriminating evidence was found in a chest. The searchers found 'all the bones due to the anatomy of man and woman', human hair, and a parchment hidden in a compass about the size of a groat [a four-penny piece]. The parchment opened up to the size of two spans (46cm). In the middle was a life-size representation of a heart. From the heart ran divided branches, variously coloured, to the edge of the parchment. At the end of each dangled something like a key. 'At the end of them in some places figured and others proportioned a mouth, in briefe the whole joynts and artries of a man.'

According to the pamphlet, Johane realised that the game was up, and confessed that 'by the help of that parchment, man and woman's bones and man and woman's haire,' and the help of her familiars, 'which she reported to have two attending on her, one for men another for cattell, in any joynt synnew or place of the body by only pricking the point of a needle in that place of the parchment where in his or her body she would have them tortured, which torture of hers once begun in them their paine should continue so restless that a present death had been more happier than so lingering a calamity and those whome she intended to kill had the same in effect, if she gave a prick in the middle of ye parchment where she had placed the heart.

The pamphlet describes the two women's crimes. Johane had argued with a neighbour, 'a good country Yeoman,' and he had called her an 'Old Hagge.' In view of her reputation, a dangerous move; for she replied, 'I will say little to thee, but thou shalt feele more of me hereafter.' Only half an hour later the man was stricken with pain, so intense that it was compared to the 'Scotch Boote,' the strappado[3] or the French evil [syphilis]. He fell into alternate fits of hot and cold. Before long he found that he could not get up, let alone walk. No medicine helped, nor eased the pain. He became convinced that he was bewitched, and that the only solution was to scratch Johane Harrison and draw her blood in order to break the spell. At his neighbour's suggestion he invited her to visit him, but unsurprisingly she declined. Eventually a meeting between the two was organised, and the witch was 'well Scratcht.' Within three of four days the yeoman recovered.

Johane Harrison laid a complaint for assault with the local justices, and was awarded five shillings in damages, plus costs. As soon as the fines were paid, the yeoman relapsed, and shortly thereafter died. A second unnamed man was killed in a similar manner.

Both these events had blown over when a young woman who was washing clothes inadvertently threw rinsing water over Anne Harrison. She was furious: 'Do you throw your water upon me gossip, before it be long I'll be revenged for it.' The young woman thought little more of the occurrence; she went into the next room, leaving her baby in its cot alone. In her absence the cot was thrown over and 'shattered all to piece', and the infant killed. 'Thus we see', says the pamphlet, 'the Devil hath such power on these his damnable servants that neither men nor infants are to be pitied by them.'

A short time later Anne bewitched the daughter of a wealthy Royston townsman. Her brother rode to Cambridge to consult a friend of his, a 'scoller', (presumably a cunning man), who told the young man that his sister was bewitched, and offered his assistance. By the time the brother had returned to Royston the girl had recovered. Anne, in revenge for his interference, 'caused such a plague upon all his cattell that they all perisht and consumed.'

These supposed bewitchments, and the reaction of the people of Royston to them, have a ring of authenticity. The description of the parchment, and the manner in which it was used, is an unusual form of image magic, but plausible. So too is the claim that Johane herself resorted to law in order to restore her reputation. The failure to prosecute in what was a difficult crime upon which to gather evidence is also credible. This final episode however bears the hallmarks of an addition, and is presented as a humorous and slightly vulgar tale. Here it is as it appeared in the pamphlet:

How the Witch served a Fellow in an Alehouse.
There was an honest fellow and as bon a companion dwelling in Royston, one that loved the pot with the long necke almost as well as his prayers, for (quoth he) as I know one is medicinable for the soule, I am sure the other physick for ye bodie.

It was this Fuddle-caps chance (with 3 or 4 as good Maltwormes [drinkers] as himselfe, and as sure where the best lap [drink] was to be found together as four Knaves in a payre [pack] of cards) to be drinking, where this witch came in and stood gloting upon them.

Now this Good fellow not enduring to looke upon a bad face but his owne especially when he is Cup-shot [drunk], called alowde to her: 'Doe you heare witch, looke tother wai as I cannot abide a nose of that fashion or else turne your face ye wrong side outward, it may looke like raw flesh for flyes to blow maggots in.' Still as the witch was ready to reply, hee would crosse her with one scurvy jest, and between every jest drink to her yet sweare: 'God damn him, she should starve ere she should have a drop on't since the pot was sweet and he'd keep it so, for should but her lips once looke into the lid on't her breath's so strong and would so stick in the cup, that all the water that runs by Ware would not wash it out again.' At last the witch got so much time to call to him 'Doth thou heare good friend,' (quoth she). 'What sayth thou, ill face,' (quoth he). 'Marry I say' (quoth she), 'that thou throwst in thy drink apace, but shall not find it so easy coming out,' (answered the fellow) 'I throwd it in above and it shall come out beneath and then thou shalt have some of it if thou wilt because I am in hope it will poyson thee.' Then with this greeting away goes the Witch in a chafe and the fellow sits down to follow his drink but as the end of all drunkards is, to ming [urinate] or to sleep.

So out goes this felloe and drawing his Gentleman Usher [penis] against a pale-side [bucket], finds me a top of his nose a red lump as big as a cherry and in his belly felt such a rumbling as if the Tower of Babell had falne about his eares. Oh! the sight thereof draw his hart to an ague and his tongue to an alarm and out he cries: 'The Witch, the witch, I am undone, I am undone, O God, women of Royston helpe; helpe, the Witch, I am a man spoyld, help, I am undone.' At that word 'help, the Witch,' in comes one of his fellows running in hast and asked him what they should help. 'The Witch Oh,' (quoth he) 'to the gallows, for I am undone by her.' Well, yet out he runs, where for that night she would not be found but the next morning meeting her in a lane his pain rather increased than lessened and there casts his ten commandments upon her, he almost scratcht out her eyes, nay left her not till he brought her to ye towne where for this and the rest she was apprehended and she and her daughter with George Dell and his mother worthily suffered death the 4th of August.

I think that the Harrisons were indeed Alice and Christian Stokes, although I do not know why the pamphleteer changed their names. It seems unlikely that the only two persons convicted of witchcraft at the Summer Assizes that year came from the same small town as the pair named in the pamphlet. Regarding the events reported in the pamphlet, they reflect the beliefs of the time, though the items found during the house search are unusual – perhaps sufficiently unusual to be evidence of accuracy in the description of them. The bewitchment of the man in the alehouse however smacks of an apocryphal story; I suspect that it was gleaned by the author from an entirely different source.

George and Sarah Adownes, 1613

Although it was not until 1613 that members of the Adownes[4] family appeared before the assizes charged with murder by witchcraft, the family had been in court before, and on both sides of the dock.

At the Lent Assizes of 1602, Elizabeth Davy of Caddington was accused of the murder of Thomas Adowne. Elizabeth was recorded as a spinster, but we know no more about her or her victim. It was alleged that Elizabeth had, on 1 June 1601, at Caddington, put ratsbane[5] in 'a mess of pottage' eaten by Thomas. He died on 3 June. Found guilty, Elizabeth was sentenced to hang.

Two years later George Cordal, a 'gentleman' from Flamstead entered into a recognisance before Sir John Luke to give evidence against George and Sarah Downes, also of Flamstead, on suspicion of witchcraft. At the same time Hugh Harrison from Studham, Bedfordshire, and Thomas Andrewes from Flamstead guaranteed their appearance in court.

There is no further record of this particular charge, so either the evidence was weak or the offence a minor one; in any case, George and Sarah were freed. Matter came to a head in 1613. On 15 March, once more before Sir John Luke, several people laid information against the couple. Their accusers were Henry Osmond of Markyate in Caddington, a carpenter; John Walker of Markyate in Flamstead, a labourer; and Robert Adownes (alias Clothier) of Studham, Bedfordshire, also a labourer, and presumably a family member[6], all gave recognisances to appear as witness against them. George was wealthy enough to enter into recognisances for the appearance of both himself and Sarah.

Very shortly thereafter they appeared before the assizes at Hertford. The judges Serjeant Henry Montague and Serjeant John Davis presided. The accused were alleged to have bewitched Hugh Adownes of Caddington on 6 March; he lingered for a week, and then died. In addition to the witnesses already mentioned, Helen Androwe, Henry Botele junior, Philip Godfrey, John Sutton, and Thomas Lea also gave evidence.

The Grand Jury found a true bill against both of the accused, but the Petty Jury acquitted Sarah. George however was convicted, and sentenced to hang. The last we hear of him is in a Gaol Delivery Roll, with the comment 'hanged by the neck until etc.'

But we have not done with the Adownes family. In 1614 Solomon Carpenter, a husbandman[7] from Harpenden gave evidence against John Adownes (alias Clothier). William Adownes of Harpenden, shoemaker, and George Anderson of Wheathampstead, miller, gave recognisances for his appearance. There is no record of the charge, nor of the trial and its outcome. The recognisances were discharged though, so it seems likely that John Adownes was more fortunate than George, and was acquitted.

Alice Nashe and Margaret Hullett, 1618

This case is included because it demonstrates how accusations could divide a village. Barkway is quite a small place, though it was once important locally for its market; and for more than twenty of its inhabitants to be directly involved on one side or the other in accusations of witchcraft must have caused uproar and enmity. Most people in the village probably took one side or the other. There were two accused, and two alleged victims: Alice Nashe, a widow, on 12 January 1618, was accused of bewitching Margaret Bishopp. Margaret languished until 5 February, when she died. Margaret Hullett, wife of Richard Hullett, on 7 September 1616, was accused of bewitching Henry Braie, who languished until 12 September following, when he died.

In the months of June and July Sir Robert Chester, JP, took recognisances from the interested parties, either to appear as witnesses, or for the appearance of the accused. In the case of Alice Nashe, William Bishoppe (perhaps the husband of the victim), Susan and Thomas Fitch, John Kinge, Henry Michaell, and Elizabeth Dowse appeared as witnesses. Thomas Moyses and Richard Hullett (husband of the other accused) entered into recognisances for Alice's appearance in court.

Against Margaret Hullett, John Osland, Richard Dewe and Agnes Bray agreed to give evidence. Edward Walleys entered into a recognisance on behalf of his wife Agnes to do the same. Richard Hullett and Richard Downeham entered recognisances for Margaret's appearances.

There are a couple of common threads in the two cases. Susan Fitch appeared as a hostile witness in both instances, and Richard Hullett, husband to one of the defendants, entered into recognisances for the appearances of both of them. The case was heard by Sir Robert Houghton and Serjeant Ranulph Crewe at Hertford on 24 July. In both cases the Grand Jury found a true bill, but both women were acquitted.

The result must have caused fury amongst the accusers. Not only had Margaret and Alice walked free, but the jury had chosen to disbelieve the evidence that the witnesses had presented. The prosecutions were over, but it is reasonable to suppose that their echoes continued for considerably longer.

John Palmer, 1649

The main source of information concerning John Palmer is a contemporary pamphlet:

> The Divels Delusions or A faithfull relation of John Palmer and Elizabeth Knot two notorious Witched lately condemned at the Sessions of Oyer and Terminer in St Albans, 1649.

The pamphlet is in the form of a letter, a not uncommon means of presentation for the time. It is written under the pen name of 'Misodaimon', which means 'hater of demons.' At the time of its publication doubt in the existence of witches was gaining ground, and it may be that the motive for publication was to convince doubters of the reality of the witchcraft rather than to make money. There is no doubt about which side of the fence Misodaimon comes down on – he is a firm believer, and convinced of the power of the Devil. The essential elements of the text of the tract are given below.

A letter sent from St Albans to a friend in the country concerning the Tryall, condemning and execution of John Palmer and Elizabeth Knott, two notorious witches:
Sir,
According to your earnest desire, I have taken the best care I could to satisfie you, concerning the Witches lately tryed, condemned and executed at St Albans: It had been very difficult to convince me of that which I find true, concerning the wiles of that old serpent the Divel, for the supporting of his subtile trade hee drives for the enlarging of his territories; by strengthening of himself upon the weaknesse of his subjects, relapsed men and women.

I shall the more clearly give you to understand what you desire concerning these two, by name John Palmer and Elizabeth Knott, of Norton, within the Liberty of St Albans...

Palmer confessed [Marsh of Dunstable] to be head of the whole Colledge of Witches, that hee knows in the world: This Palmer hath been a witch these sixty years (by his own confession), long enough to know and give in the totall summe of all the conjuring conclave, and the Society of Witches in England. This Marsh hath so long gratified the country people with his conjurations, that time and ignorance stiles him a good witch or a White Witch; I suppose you easily grant that the Divel is never blacker, and more to be abhorr'd than when hee transforms himself into an Angell of Light. Sir, I easily believe that if Marsh was brought to his tryall, hee might confesse as much of his brother Lilly[8] as Palmer hath of him...

By the plain confession of Palmer, it may certainly be guessed that the Divel took advantage of him at this breach, and brought him into bonds upon this ground; in as much as hee was (as hee said) of a fretfull and revengefull nature, and not being able of himself to avenge himself of his adversaries, hee adjoyned himself to the Divel, and wrought much evil in the eyes of the Lord: upon his compact with the Divel, hee received a flesh brand, or mark, upon his side, which gave suck to two familiars, the one in the form of a dog, which he called George, and the other in the likeness of a woman, called Jezebell, when the Divel first made this mark he drew his blood and caused him to write his mark upon the ground with his own hand therewith; his trading in this horrid and abominable practice of Witchcraft was (as hee confessed) betwixt the space of fifty and sixty years, the hurt which from time to time hee had done was very much; and this I account his prime pranck that he notoriously seduced Elizabeth Knott his kinswoman, to consort with him in his villany, who hath assented to him more especially in the death of one Goodwife Pearls of Norton, whom Palmer said he would do nothing to occasion her death unlesse this Elizabeth Knott would assent: whereupon they presently agreed to frame the picture of the woman (Pearls) in clay, which was forthwith hid upon the fire, and duly raked up in the embers; while it was consuming and mouldering away the woman lay in miserable torments; when it was quite consumed the woman immediately died; and this hee confessed to be done by him, and his kinswoman out of revenge which hee ought her, for hanging a lock upon his doore, for the not paying of his rent. At another time, to satisfie his revengefull humour, hee kill'd an horse of Mr. Cleaver's by sending his familiar; and this Elizabeth Knott bewitcht a cow of John Laman's, by sending an evil spirit into her, which was in the likeness of a Catt, but had no hand in the death of anything, save the death of Goodwife Pearls. The familiar which she entertained came to her about three weeks before the said cow was bewitched at twelve of the clock in the night, and the familiar promised her that she should have her desire in anything she should desire, except money: and the reason why she bewitched the cow of William Laman was, because she demanded money which was due to her from the said Laman's wife, and it was denied her. We understand also from this Elizabeth Knott that when she was cast upon the water her familiar sucked upon her breast, but after she came out of the water she never saw it any more.

It would be tedious to reckon up the multifarious exploits of this old witch Palmer; for Knott, his kinswoman was but a novice, in comparison of him, and, as I conceive, had made no direct covenant with the Divel, as Palmer had.

A little before his execution he confessed to Sampson Clark, the Keeper of the Prison, that, falling out with a young man, hee transformed himself into a Toad, and, lying in the way where the young man came, he kick't it. Immediately Palmer complained of a sore shinne, where upon hee bewitched the young man for many years to his great woe and torment.

That you may further understand what society hee had on your side the country, with such as were in bond to the Divel, I shall signifie to you what hee confessed before his execution. In Hitchin he reckons two, Mary By-chance and widdow Palmer; in Norton, John Salmon, senior, Joseph Salmon, and Judeth his wife. John Laman, senior, and Mary his wife. John Lamen, Junior, Mary, the daughter of John Lamen, senior, John Lamen, the daughter of the aforesaid John Lamen, and the wife of one Mayer, in Weston. And at the place of execution he confessed two more, Sarah Smith and Anne Smith, servants, the one to Mr. Beamont, the other to Mr. Reynolds.

I am in haste but rest, yours

B. Misodaimon.

It has been suggested[9] that the reference to Marsh in Dunstable might well have been Francis Marsh, who died there in 1685. John Aubrey's *Miscellanies* provides some details about Marsh:

> Dr Richard Nepier, rector of Lynford, was a good astrologer, and so was Mr Marsh of Dunstable; but Mr Marsh did seriously confess to a friend of mine, that astrology was but the countenance; and that he did his business by the help of the blessed spirits; with whom only men of great piety, humility and charity, could be acquainted; and such a one he was. He was an hundred years old when my friend was with him; and yet did understand himself very well.
>
> At Ashbridge in Buckinghamshire, near Berkhamsted, was a monastery, (now in the possession of the Earl of Bridgewater) where are excellent good old paintings still to be seen. In this monastery was found an old manuscript entitled Johannes de Rupescissa, since printed, (or part of it) a chymical book, wherein are many receipts; among others, to free a house haunted with evil spirits, by fumes: Mr Marsh had it, and did cure houses so haunted by it.[10]

Marsh seems to have been a cunning man, or white witch. Misodaimon's attitude towards him reflects the elite attitude that cunning folk were more dangerous than black witches. The reference to a 'Colledge of Witches' is unusual, as most people in England believed that witches operated alone. The author seems to have been familiar with Continental beliefs. This is not unlikely – Reginald Scot more than sixty years before had known all about them.

The description of the witches' mark is unusual. In most cases the mark and the supernumerary nipple used to feed familiars are differentiated. In Palmer's case they are confused. Unusual too is a familiar in human form, Jezebel; small animals were more common. George the dog fits the normal pattern far better. The pact Palmer signed with the Devil is another example of Continental witch-lore, and connects nicely with the alleged 'Colledge of Witches.' According to the pamphlet, Palmer said he had been a witch for between fifty and sixty years, and so must have been quite elderly when he made his confession. The circumstances would have been interesting. Was he 'walked,' or 'watched?' Was he 'cast upon the water' (swum) as Elizabeth Knott was? How voluntary was the confession? Was Palmer in full possession of his faculties? As he claimed to have the power to turn himself into a toad, there must be some doubt about the truth of his statements.

Following his trial Palmer implicated others in his 'Colledge.' These unfortunate people may have been acquaintances, or they may have been people against whom he had a grudge. According to W.B. Gerish, John

Lamen died in 1688; Mary Lamen in 1706; Joseph Salmon in 1684; and Judith Salmon in 1692. Luke Beaumont and Richard Reynolds were men of some substance. A Joan Mayes died a pauper in Weston in 1649. Thus we know that some at least of the characters named existed, but there is no trace of one of the Hitchin women, 'widdow' Palmer. If she existed, she might have been a relative. Mary Bychance, or By-chance, however crops up elsewhere:

> Mary by chance, (so nick-named) 'tis here publickly known how she swam, and could not sink with all the means she could use; and some say, She had got Iron next to her to make her sink... a very honest Man told me, (he saw it) That about the year, 1637.[11]

It is interesting that of these people accused by Palmer of complicity most seem to have survived him by a good many years. Presumably either his denunciations were not taken very seriously, or no corroborative evidence could be found and they were acquitted.

John Palmer and Elizabeth Knott leave no trace in the Assize Rolls, nor do any of those accused by him. The only Hertfordshire indictments for witchcraft in 1649-50 name three defendants: William Litchfield and his wife Prudence, of Ardley, and Anne Man of Ashwell. No plea, verdict or sentence is recorded for any of them, though we know that Prudence at least was remanded in gaol. The charges against them involved the bewitchment of animals. But these cases were heard at Hertford, not St Albans. Bearing in mind however that the events described are said to have taken place during the Civil War, it is possible that records have been lost.

In summary then, we have a pamphlet that includes the names of people whose existence is verifiable from other sources; some of them were also associated with witchcraft; but we have no court records or other corroborative evidence that the events described ever took place, let alone resulted in an execution.

Alice Free, 1659

Had Alice Free been accused of witchcraft during the reign of Elizabeth, it is quite possible that she would have been convicted. As it was, by 1659 witchcraft prosecutions were on the wane, and guilty verdicts rarer still. In fact it is probably only because of this that we know about the events at all. The allegation was one of murder by witchcraft, and was heard by Hertfordshire Quarter Sessions,[12] and some of the documents were preserved – three depositions and a recognisance.

Sarah Smith, the widow of John Smith, gardener, of Little Hadham, deposed that she was with Frances Rustat, the late wife of Samuel, as she neared her end. According to Sarah, Frances was 'strangely handled with great pain, wracking and torment... the said Frances did often say... that if she died of that distemper that was then upon her, Goody Free[13] was the cause of her death.' She had never been well since she had bought a penny worth of eggs from Goody Free, especially after Goody sent her son for the money, which was to be part payment for his schooling. Frances had given the excuse that she had no small change.

Edward Samm of Little Hadham laid information that Samuel Rustat had said, weeping, after the death of his wife Frances (but before her burial), that 'the forementioned Alice Free had bewitched his wife to death; his wife said so.'

Martha Rockwell, of Little Hadham, deposed that Samuel had spoken to Alice Free after the death of Frances; he had said that 'while she lay by the walls, that he would take his oath that she had bewitched his wife to death.' Alice had to enter into a recognisance 'to appear and answer to such things objected against her for matter of witchcraft.'

The nature of the evidence is highly unsatisfactory, consisting of a deathbed claim of bewitchment,[14] a statement confirming that Samuel had said so, and finally a witness to Samuel's accusation of Goody Free. It is hard to believe that the Grand Jury found a true Bill, let alone that the case was referred to the Court of Assize with any success. There is no further record of the case, and it is reasonably safe to assume that it was dismissed.

Agnes Gardiner, 1658, and Susan England, 1674

As the seventeenth century wore on, conviction of an alleged witch became less and less likely. In fact we know of only three more cases that got past the Grand Jury: Agnes Gardiner, Susan England and Jane Wenham, the last of whom is described in a chapter of her own.

Agnes was the wife of a labourer, Christopher Gardiner, from the village of Bennington, just east of Stevenage. According to the indictment, on 3 July 1658, Agnes bewitched Marcy Spencer, who was wasted and consumed. A second indictment alleged that ten days later she 'fed, employed and entertained two evil spirits, one in the likeness of a black cat and the other in the likeness of a toad.' John Wallis, Henry Walker, Abraham Hurst, Thomas Norwood, John Chapman, Joseph Noone and John Kent appeared as witnesses.

On the charge of murder the Grand Jury acquitted her; but the allegation of entertaining spirits was apparently sufficiently compelling for them to return a true Bill. It made no difference in the long run – Agnes was acquitted. Susan England, a widow, was charged with the murder by witchcraft of Thomas Gold the younger. Thomas languished between 20 June 1673 and 5 April 1674, when he died at West Berkhamsted. The Gold family turned out in force as witnesses – Thomas senior, John, Anne and Edward all gave evidence, as did Mary Ward, Elizabeth Puddeford and Anne Bird. The indictment is endorsed with a not guilty verdict, and Susan was discharged.

6

Cunning Folk and Fortune Tellers

Cunning folk, as we have seen, had a number of strings to their bow. They countered bewitchment, cured their clients of natural disease, and acted as animal doctors. They provided amulets and charms against evil spirits and ill fortune. They found lost and stolen property. They told fortunes and provided love magic.

Rarely prosecuted, they do not often appear in court records. In Hertfordshire we have only two cases in the secular court records that we can firmly identify as real cunning folk, though there are other practitioners who carried out one or more of the services listed above. For the sake of convenience I have included them all in this chapter.

Thomas Harden, or Harding, 1590

Harding almost certainly provided the full range of services of a real 'cunning man'. He appeared before the courts not because he attempted to provide these services, but because he failed to come up with the goods, and his customers turned on him. The information comes from depositions taken for the quarter sessions.

> *Taken before Thomas Docwra, esquire.*
> *Matters against Thomas Hardeng of Ikelford.*
> Mary Pennyfather, of Hippollettes, hath a woman childe of the age of fower years which could nether go or speke, whom she caryed to Thomas Harden, because it is noysed in the country that he is a wyse man and can skyll of many thinges, who tolde her that her childe was a changelinge, but would in tyme help her. The next tyme she came unto him he bade her to take a nutt and to pick out the curnell and fiyll yt with quicksilver, and to

stoppe the hole with wax and to bynde a thread a cross over the nutt and to lay yt under a pylow wher the chylde should lye, and that shoulde help yt. Her chylde having thereby no helpe, she repaired to him againe and then he bad her to sette the childe in a chare upon her dungell [dunghill] by the space of an houer upon a sonny day, which she did and the childe had no helpe. She paid him six pence and promysed him more.

John Bigge, of Hippolettes, 'being very syke of a fever,' went to Harden for a cure. Harden wrote some words on a parchment scroll and told him to hang it around his neck, promising that it would heal him. The sick man, however, became sicker and died: but before he died he cut away the scroll, repenting that he had ever dealt with Harden.

Robert Dickenson of Codicote, having a 'wastecote porloyned from him' at one time and certain linen at another, went to Harden to find out where it was, and gave him 12d. Some time afterwards when Harden visited him, Dickenson asked him where his linen was; Harden said that the person who had his linen in her possession would come into his house the following Monday, with a feather through her nose. No one came, and when Dickenson asked for further help, he was promised that the person would come and confess her guilt; but nothing came of it.

Goodwyfe Strate of Kings Walden said that after 'having a good parcel of newe cloth stollen away,' she went to Harden for help, since she had heard he was good at telling where things could be found. On her first visit he promised to help her, but when nothing happened she went back to him and received further promises, for which she gave him money, bacon and pigeons to the value of 5s; but to no avail.

William Kinge of Gamlingay, Cambridgeshire, 'having lost two horses whiche were stollen from him' went to Harden for help, for which he paid him 12d and promised him 20s more. Harden told him to go to Hoddesdon market, where he would see his horses; they were not there. Oliver Burgen, 'being desirous to know who fired his mother's house at Weston,' went to Harden to find out, paying him 40s and promising £20. Harden asked for time and when pressed said he would 'consult with one Caull.'[1] After a time Oliver was told that if Harden came in sight of the offending person 'he had such marke of him, that he could descrye him.' None of the suspects were charged, and Oliver, believing himself cheated, asked for his 40s back. It was refused, and he brought a civil action to recover it.

A Mr Gothe, a schoolmaster of Highgate, was the agent of Oliver in this action, and it was to him that Harden afterwards confessed, claiming that he had lost the powers he had once had; and that he had a familiar spirit, which a nobleman had cheated him of, together with a great many books.[2]

There are marginal notes on the document that Harden confessed to the first two charges in full, and in part to the remainder.

This is the most complete picture we have of a Hertfordshire cunning man. Harden used charms on the sick, and purported to be able to find stolen goods, as well as identify the culprit. There is no evidence in the records that he was a herbalist, nor that he provided charms against witchcraft or told fortunes. It is probable that these were services he would provide if asked; all we know of him results from his failures. Unfortunately for him he managed to build up a significantly hostile clientele. His fate is unknown, but the quarter sessions could hand down only non-capital sentences; so unless his case was referred to the assize court – and there is no record of it if it was – Harden either received a whipping, a period of imprisonment or a spell in the pillory, or perhaps a combination of the three.

It is interesting that one of his clients travelled from as far away as Gamlingay to see him, a distance of some fifteen miles, whilst others travelled from Codicote and King's Walden.

Elizabeth Lane, 1597/8

In the case of Elizabeth Lane of Walsworth, near Hitchin, it was slanderous remarks that got her into trouble. It is not known why she chose to blame the Minister, John Knightly, of Guilden Morden in Cambridgeshire, for her clients' misfortunes. It would seem however that her remarks got back to him, and he decided to take action.

On 30 January 1598 he gave a recognisance before Thomas Docwra, JP, to appear and give evidence against Elizabeth, charging her with witchcraft. On the same day she gave a recognisance of £20 for her appearance; Richard Spede and Michael Wylkenson, or Wilkenson, both of Walsworth, gave recognisances of £10 each on her behalf, all substantial sums of money at the time. Knightly gathered information about Lane's clients:

John Smythe went to see her, because his wife was 'in desperation' and was told by her that she was bewitched by 'deep and profane learning' by Knightly. Robert Frost, troubled with a pain in his throat, visited her and was told that he was possessed by spirits and bewitched by John Knightley, but that she could help him; she received 16d and said he had promised to give her 6s 7d more. Joan Shatbolte admitted to the churchwardens that she had been to see Lane about her husband who was then ill, and was told that he was 'beworded and bewatled' by Mr Knightly, and she should cut off his hair and send her son with it to Lane. She should also turn his bed another way and throw his water on the fire. Shadbolt gave Lane 2s and a cheese. Her husband had since died.

Thomas Payne went to her on behalf of his wife and paid her money, but was not prepared to say what actually happened.

Walter Copis went to see her for a pain and said that she spoke evil words of the minister. Henry Wood went to see her about his horse that was stolen, for which she received money. John Kidd was sent to her by Anne, wife of Richard Lilley, with their daughter Grace.

Elizabeth Follye, servant to Richard Lilley was sent by her mistress to see her with Grace Lilley, but she would not repeat what Elizabeth Lane said. Anne, wife of Richard Lilley, went to speak to her about her daughter, but she too refused to go into any details of the meeting. Elizabeth Lane also went to her house to see her about things stolen from her buttery. Agnes Cooper went to her about a gown that had been stolen.

Robert Shatbolt the elder went to see her because his wife was ill, and was told she was bewitched.

Kidd, Follye and Anne Lilley's visits are probably concerned with a childhood ailment in Grace Lilley. The last reference we have of this affair is a clerk's note that Elizabeth Lane was to appear at the next assizes. Wilkenson and Spede gave recognisances of £40 each that she would appear at the assizes to answer the charges against her.[3]

Unfortunately there is no mention of her appearance at the assizes, though the records for that year and the subsequent few years still exist. It may well be that the Grand Jury threw the case out, and any indictments were therefore discarded. As Lane and her supporters provided recognisances for her appearance, there would be no record of her in Gaol Calendars.

But that is not the last we hear of Elizabeth Lane. Some years later, in 1613, an 'Elizabeth Laine' of Walsworth in Hitchin, described as a widow, and William Burr, husbandman, of Aspenden, entered recognisances to give evidence against Thomas and Agnes Hamond on a charge of witchcraft.[4] The hamlet of Walsworth was a pretty small place, not even meriting a church until the 1890s, so it seems likely that the two Elizabeths are one and the same person; this time though, she seems to be appearing on behalf of a prosecution, perhaps as an 'expert witness.'

Johanna Leper, 1446

Here is a tantalising glimpse of the sort of information to be found in the Church Court records. It involves a Hertfordshire woman who was accused of several offences from 1446 onward.[5] Ickleford was administered at that time by the Archdeaconry of Huntingdon, which in turn was part of the Diocese of Lincoln.

Bishop Alnwick's Court Book:

'Hunt[ingdon] 10

Johanna Leper of Ickleford in the parish of Pirton uses divination, necromancy and incantations and makes certain things to be put about the neck as is made clear by the presentment... and it is said that she has abjured other things.

23 Nov 1447: in the church of Lidyngton Derby the commissary decreed that the said Johanna who was in hiding should be summoned by edict.

19 Sept 1448: in the church of Bugden (Buckden)... appears and swears. She denied the charge from whence the other things fail.'

The last entry implies that there was little evidence against Johanna, and as she refused to confess the charges were dropped.

Joseph Heynes and James Domingo, 1676

The quarter sessions records document visits to Ware and Bishops Stortford of a group of fraudulent fortune tellers from London.

From information given against Joseph Haynes, James Domingo and Sarah, his pretended wife, by John Hockley, John Grindley, Peter Holdsworth, and Rivers Dickinson, all from Ware, it seems that the prisoners came (the woman being in man's clothing) into Ware pretending to tell fortunes both by publishing papers to that end and verbally, taking from Hockley and Grindley 6d apiece.[6] They also pretended to provide medicine that cured 'almost all deseases by an elixir as may appear by their bill; they saying that money came in very slowly at Ware by 6d and 3d apiece, but at Bishop's Stafford they got £20.'

Joseph Haynes on being examined, 'doth acknowledge that he went out of London with a designe to assist James Domingo and by naturall magicke and other artifices to tell fortunes, but denyeth that hee tooke any money, and pretends whatever hee did was without any designe but as a frollicke.' Haynes boasted that he 'had gotten five pounds and three maydenheads at Ware and a broken shinne,' which is scarcely compatible with his claim that he 'tooke no money.'

James Domingo, on being examined, 'owneth that hee was at Bishop's Stortford with Joseph Haynes and a woman in man's apparell,' who he pretended was his wife, and that he was also at Ware on the 1 August, 'and owns the printed paper now showed to him and did accordingly practise the said art of telling fortunes, but got not above 7s at Bishop's Stortford. Further saith that he hath noe house but that his dwelling and his wives are at Doctor Revells, in Salisburie Court, London.' Domingo said he made about 26s that day.

The record also contains a slip of paper thought to be one of the fortunes Domingo sold. Unfortunately it is damaged, and only partly legible:

> ...I should advise you not to proceed in law. You shall be married Candlemas Day to a pretty tall merry-speaking man with black haire, a mole on his chin, you do not know him yet – his name is Simon Peters, a farmer's son, he is worth £80 and heire to his father. The water has been an enemy to you and almost [spoiled]... fortune but ...

Tall dark strangers, it seems, are nothing new.

Thomas Ingroom and his group, 1703

The quarter sessions rolls contain a warrant dated 31 March to the keeper of the County Gaol in Hertford to receive Thomas Ingroom, his wife Margaret, Easter Joanes and Susan Wood, the heads of a group of some fifty travelling folk who told fortunes, 'calling themselves Egyptians.'

Hertford had just had a new gaol built; the old one in Back Street was in poor condition, and there had been a number of prisoners who successfully escaped from it. The new gaol opened in Fore Street in 1702, just in time for the Ingrooms and their companions. Unfortunately it was an unpleasant place, and overcrowding resulted in outbreaks of typhus and smallpox.

'Egyptians,' or Gypsies, apparently had a reputation for some skill in foretelling the future, as they continued to do for many years to come. 'Genuine Romany' still appears in some advertisements for fortune tellers today. We know no more of this itinerant group.

7

POSSESSION AND BEWITCHMENT

Possession and bewitchment were phenomena that were far more common in England in the seventeenth century than in the century before. Hertfordshire followed the national trend. Bewitchment was often referred to as obsession. The line between obsession and possession was a fine one – possession was the control of a person's body or mind by a spirit or demon, whereas obsession was control exercised from outside the body of the victim. In England the two expressions were often used interchangeably.

Incidents frequently involved adolescent children, most often girls. Group possession of young people in the same household was also a common feature, though only one of the Hertfordshire cases involves more than one person (the Baldwin children of Sarratt).

All of the possessed were however young people; five girls and three boys. Whether the phenomenon is a real one, or whether it is the result of childish pranks is difficult to say. The subject was, and still is, much confused by the religious implications; though religion cannot be completely ignored – it may, for example, be an important factor in cases in which the possessed person is from a devout background.

Certainly there is a strong religious element to the Hertfordshire cases of possession – every instance took place in a devout environment, where prayers were said for the bewitched or possessed. It may be that some of the afflicted were reacting against surroundings they found, consciously or otherwise, unbelievably stifling.

Mary Hall, 1664

This remarkable case is extracted from William Drage's *Discourse of Diseases proceeding from Witchcraft*.[1] Drage was a doctor, and lived in Hitchin.

He was a firm believer in the reality of witchcraft and the spirit world. The diabolic dialogue is so striking that I have included the whole story as it appeared in Drage's book. I have kept to his spelling and punctuation.

A Relation of Mary Hall of Gadsden, reputed to be possessed of two Devils, 1664.

Mary Hall, a Maid of Womans Stature, a Smiths Daughter of little *Gadsden* in the County of *Hartford*, began to sicken in the fall of the Leaf, 1663. It took her first in one foot with a trembling shaking and Convulsive motion, afterwards it possessed both; she would sit stamping very much; she had sometimes like Epileptick, sometimes like Convulsive fits, and strange ejaculations: she was sent to *Doctor Woodhouse of Barkinsted*,[2] a Man famous in curing bewitched persons, for so she was esteemed to be; he seeing the Water and her, judged the like, and prepared stinking Suffumigations, over which he held her head, and sometimes did strain to vomit, and her distemper for some weeks seemed abated, upon Doctor *Woodhouse* direction; Then reinvigorating, were heard in her strange noises, like mewing of Cats, barking of Dogs, roaring of Bears, &c. at last a Voice spoke in her, *Pus Cat, what a Cat? nothing but mue*; this was about the beginning of *August*, 1664. and after this evil Spirit spoke often, exercising the tricks and torments, convulsions, and elevations of the Maid, as before it spoke, with some Additions. The manner and matter of the Spirits speaking was on this wise:

If any said, *Get thee out of her, Satan*; the Spirit replyed, *We are two*; and as oft as any said, *Satan*, or *Devil*, it would reply, *We are two*; and would say, *We are only two little Imps*, Gfe Harods, *and* Youngs; *Sometimes we are in the shape of Serpents, sometimes of Flyes, sometimes of Rats or Mice; and Gdf Harod sent us to choak this Maid, Mary Hall; but we should have choaked Goodman Hall, but of him we had no Power, and so possessed his daughter; we came down the Chimny, riding on a stick, and went first to Mary's foot, whereupon her foot trembled first of all her distemper.* At other times upon diverse occasions, either voluntarily, or in answer to questions of those that came to see her, they said, *They would do more mischief if they could; yea, they would destroy all Mankind, and be revenged on their Adversaries, but God was above, they had not Power*, yet many times they would speak Blasphemously of God; and say, *God cannot cast us out, we are above God; we are four to one*, (meaning the two Witches that sent them, and they two, against God), *and do you think we cannot deal with him well enough*. When some came to pray, they would say, *You shall not cast us out, we will tire you all out*; and when they had done praying, the Spirits would say, *Did we not tell you, you should not cast us out? where is your God now?* When one of Saint *Albans* came to pray, the Spirits said, *Get you gone, for we cannot abide you*: to another they said, that spoke to them of God, *Get you gone, it is dark, it is late, you will be benighted.*

Sometimes to those that came to cast them out, they would say, *They would be gone to morrow; or that they had a short time, and therefore must be busy in showing a few pranks more, ere they went out*; at another time they would tell them, *They must choak her, and they would not out yet.*

Sometimes they would bid her, *Mary, choak yourself,* when she went to eat; and when she went nigh water, *Mary, dround your self*; and when she would not do it, and they wanted Power to make her, they would say, *Ah Fool, Fool, Fool, Fool, what will you not drownd yourself?* When she was nigh the fire, they would say, *Mary, put you head into the Fire*; or, *Mary, put your head into the Pot*; and sometimes of a suddain they would drop down her head, as if she should put it into the Scalding Pottage, but could not effect it.

Because many People came to her, her father, in *September,* sent her to several Friends Houses, five or six miles more or less distant; where Friends met to pray; and the Spirits would say, *Mary shall not ride,* and would lift her up, and make her shake, so that they were fain to hold her on the Horse; but formerly they suffered her to ride without interruption; since they began to speak, when she went to read in the Bible, they would say, *Mary, do not read*; or, *Mary, you shall not read, for Books are all against us*; her father would say, *She shall read in spight of all the Devils,* and so she did always without interruption; for when she read, she was not molested, but once they did convulse her Arms, and threw the Books far from her.

When some prayed by her, and said, *At the Name of God shall all Flesh Tremble; and at the Name of Jesus shall every knee bow,* they would make her to tremble, and her knees to bow, and when so done laugh and sing, *We know how to cheat you, and make you believe anything.*

Yet sometimes they would say, *We are Lyers, and God is true; and when God speakes the word, we must out*; and at other times they would howl, and lament, and condole their condition, and cry out, *We are undone, we are undone, we are miserable and tormented!* and immediately thereupon they would bark, or sing, or howl, or make a jearing, and set a tune, and make Maryes feet move thereto according.

And when any blamed them for mocking at God, who was able to make them miserable to all Eternity, they would answer, *They could be no worse than they were, and that if they were out of* Mary Hall *they must go again to service, to the Witches that sent them in; to them they must return, and their work they must do; and as much mischief as they can against all that are their enemies.*

Sometimes when questions were asked, they would make no answer; and sometimes, answer to each question; sometimes indirectly and sometimes directly; sometimes seriously, sometimes scoffingly; and sometimes would do nothing, but say and gainsay themselves: one spake to them in Latine, and they answered, *We cannot speak Latine*; and presently they said, *If we can, we will not*: the father thinks one speaks one thing and the other another.

They would often repeat what Doctor *Woodhouse* had done, and said, about their casting out, and remember all exactly, and laugh at him, saying, *Doctor* Woodhouse *would have cast us out, but he could not; he is a cunning fellow, but we are cunninger than he; let not him think a few slaps will expel Satan.*

Sometimes they would Blasphemously say, *God was a Bastard*, let him come if he dare; and when some good men had done praying, the Spirits would say, *Where is your God now?* and afore they began, they would tell them, *They should weary them out.*

When Goodwife *Harwood*, the Witch, that sent them (as they say) came, they said, *Oh Gfe* Harwood! *are you come! that is well; it is well you are come; we were sent by you Gfe* Harwood: she denyed it; then said the Spirits, *What! will you deny us now!* Gfe Harod, *you sent us to choak the Father, and having no Power of him, we were to go to his Daughter; and we have endeavoured to choak her, but cannot.* And when Gfe Harwood was going away, the Spirits cryed, saying, *We will go with you Gfe* Harod: *Oh let us go with you; will you leave us, Goodwife* Harwood? but Gfe *Young*, the other they accused, never came to vindicate herself.

Doctor *Woodhouse* got *Mary Halls* nailes that were cut off, and with somewhat he added, hung them up in the Chimny a reefing over-night; and by next morning Gfe *Harwood* came, which they thought to be caused by the aforesaid things.

When it we talked amongst the Household that Gfe *Harod* should be had before a Justice; upon the Spirits accusation, the Spirits would plead for her, and say, *Do not have Gfe* Harod *afore the Justice*: But after she had come, and denyed them, they would say, *Let Gfe* Harwood *be hanged, if she will, because she denyed us.*

The voice these Spirits uttered, differed; the father said, he thought one had a shrill voice, and the other a great; sometimes they would speak like a Child, and drawling; sometimes greatly, and sonarously; sometimes they would imitate the voices of those that were in the House.

Ere they speak, the Spectators beheld her Breast to rise, and by the gradual lifting up of her Breasts towards her Throat, somewhat seemed to ascend; then it came into her Throat, and distended that, so that her neck seemed at sometimes as if a roll was in it.

Sometimes her lips in speaking were not moved, but commonly they were, and her tongue alwayes; for the Spirits by the pains she felt, and by the swelling of those parts seen to the Spectators, came to the root of the Tongue, and moved it.

Sometimes they came thus to her Throat, to try if they could choak her, and her breath would be stopped for a while, and then be at a little more liberty; and presently they would distend and swell her Throat again, so that she was ready to swoond, and for a while laboured for breath: sometimes she had many of these fits, and sometimes was freed a good while; she slept well, and eat freely, and all the while she read, the Spirits troubled her not; so that eating, reading, and sleeping, were her immunity, or times of reprieve.

But when People prayed, they tore and tormented her; yet at sometimes they lay still, and if she sat, on a suddain they would make her leap up a good height; sometimes in length she would leap an Extraordinary way; sometimes as she lay on her bed, and was fain to be held, on a suddain (while others were praying, the Spirits lying still a good while) she would leap up and hit her head against the Beds Testor.

Sometimes she would beat herself, sometimes with one, sometimes both hands, chiefly on the Breast.

Sometimes her legs would go, fast and violently, kicking of the ground, and the Spirits would say, *Come, Mary, Dance*: and then they would make a tune, and make her feet to Dance it; sometimes they would say, *Mary, make a mouth*; and then they convulsed her mouth, so that her lips seemed gristles, and her Nose was sometimes drawn up; another time they should say, *We will put out your Eyes*; and then they would so draw together her Eye-lids, that scarce any extuberance of the Eye could be perceived.

Sometimes they would say, *Come*, Mary, *turn round*; and then they would whisk her round; sometimes they would say, *Turn half round*, and she would do accordingly.

Sometimes when the Spirits moved her Tongue, some of the House would catch hold of it, to stay it, and it was pulled from them.

They read out of Master Culpepers Books, that *Misleto of the Oak was good against Witchcraft*,[3] wherefore they got some Misleto, and applyed about her neck, and she trembled; and to what part soever they applied it, so as it touched her Flesh, she trembled; by which they perceived it had prevalency against Diabolical Incantation; but did the Maid no good, as to the Expulsion of the *Cacodæmons*.[4]

When Doctor *Woodhouse* ordered some things to be boiled for her, as soon as they began to boil, the Maid, or the Spirits in her, did tremble and shake, and so continued all the while those *Antidæmoniack*-Medicines boiled.

Though she was for the most part most tortured and molested when any prayed by her, yet she was willing thereto, because desirous to be rid of that enthralment; yet commonly we cannot tell how to entertain willingly a present misery, though it bring to us an after extraordinary happiness.

All this while she looked pretty well for colour, and kept her Flesh; she was a Civil fair-conditioned Maid, and her Friends inclined to the *Anabaptists Sect*, and most that came to pray by her were of their Teachers.

She would sometimes be forced against the walls, scrabbling with her hands as if she would run up; the Spirits would precipitate her in diverse manners, but that they wanted Power, as sometimes they said they could not hurt an hair of her head, and though they tortured her body, they could not damnifie her Soul; her mind was free and unhurt, when her fits were off, and when the Spirits were no way occasionally moved.

As soon as Doctor *Woodhouse* had given her a Spoonful of some Liquor, being scarce got down her Throat, she fell down in a swoond; so that it is apparent some things are Antipathetick to *Dæmons*.

I told them I doubted natural Remedies would do no good, otherwise I could have advised them to give her Powder of Coral, of *Piony*, of *Misleto*, of Herb True-Love, and of Saint *Johns-wort*, severally, now some of one, and anon some of another; and to have hung *Rosemary*, *Misleto*, *Ivy* and *Coral* in the house, and about her neck, or to have given her the Decoction of them at any time, specially in the fits, in such manner as she could best take them.

The Evil Spirits would rarely take notice of any, or speak to them if they stood civily in the Room, unless they first spake to, or concerning the Spirits; they would sometimes say, *We may easily be cast out, one word will cast us out*; the standers by would presently ask, *What word? Adjure*, said the Spirits: but they tryed that, & many others ineffectually.

I went over to have seen her, but she was not at home, and her Father and Uncle said, *they knew not whither she was carryed by some other friends she had, that used to pray with her*; Therefore I made it my business to examine strictly, her Father, Brother and Sister, at different times, and also her Uncle, who were most constantly with her and saw all her changes; and also in the Town I examined some that were present with her in her fits, and of some Neighbour Towns; who held alike in their confession.

Since, in *September*, *October*, and *November*, little talk hath been of her, but I hear she is so afflicted still: but the Spirits lie still for the most part, unless by questions, or praying, they are disturbed; sometimes they say, *they lift her up to a great height*, but say, *they cannot hurt one Hair of her head*.

Since, on *December* I. I was there, and saw the postures and carriage of the Maid: when I went first into the house the Maid was feeding, and looked well-bleed, seemingly she was very well: I asked the Spirits some questions, and they answered me, but very foolishly; they said, *They were sent by* Gfe Harod, *who gave them her Soul to come into Mary Hall*; I asked them if they were sent by a Councel of Superiour *Dæmons*? they answered thus: *We will not tell you, that we won't, that we won't, that we won't*. I asked them, if they did not fear God's punishing them to all Eternity, for these endeavours of wrong to mankind? they answered, *We do not fear God, we care not for God*. I asked if their Superior *Dæmons*, or Masters, sat in a Local Hell, to give out commission, to such as they, to go and do their service, or whether the chiefer Spirits also did possesse any, as they did? they said,

We won't tell you, that we won't. I asked them, how they liked the Bible? they made no answer. I asked to what purpose were their foolish, idle, unnecessary tricks, they tended not to advance the interest of their Master's Kingdom? they answered nothing. Both in her reading and feeding, both her fits of speaking, and convulsive fits molested her: alwayes when she spoke, her voice was intelligible, plain and modest; they spoke scarce to be understood: always afore they spoke, her Throat swelled, her Face grew red, her head shook, and was wreathed about, until they had done; when I caused her tongue to be held out of her mouth, their voice was more obscure; it is sometimes hoarser, sometimes shriller; sometimes small, sometimes great; sometimes her Throat swells more, sometimes lesse, and her Breast is elevated; she went to read, they told her, *she should not*, yet she did; she then had a shaking of one Leg; I laid my hand upon her knee, and then the motion ceased there, and writhed her body; in her going, one Leg was took, as it were, with a cramp; but sometimes she goeth very well; nothing happens always, and each sometimes; sometime one member, sometime another; sometime in one manner, and sometime in another; sometimes almost all the members, and sometimes scarce any.

While I was there, Goodwife *Hall* told me, that the night before the Spirits told her, *she should not sleep*, and would sometimes heave her up in bed, and tell her, *Mary, we will buy you a black Gown, Hoods*, and *Scarfs*, and *Ribbins, Hay! Ribbins, Ribbins, Ribbins, Ribbins.*

Not being satisfied with what I saw, I went over to *Barkinsted* to see Doctor *Woodhouse*, who was her Physitian, and he told me, *he really thought she was possessed*, and he told me two able Physitians (whose names I have now forgotten) were with her, and told him *she was Dæmonically possessed*, and that they being very lately in *France*, saw there a whole Covent of Nunns so handled as *Mary Hall* was, with their Abbatesse;[5] onely this Symptome was more in *Mary Hall*, then any of that Covent (who were to the number of thirty possessed with Devils) that ere when the Spirits spoke in *Mary Hall*, in their presence, her Throat, on each side, was extended to the bigness of a man's fist; Also Doctor *Woodhouse* said, *one of her keepers told him, that he and another man held her in her Chair, and she leaped up from them, and they thought she would have gone out of their reach, had they not pulled her down and held her; and another time two men held her, and she leaped out of her Chair, and until her fit was over, they could not force her down again*: her fits commonly are very short, especially when they are very often. When she came to be cured, with Doctor *Woodhouse*, she sat very still a while in his Physick room, and on a suddain she fell a stamping, and so continued half an hour, till she was all on a sweat, and made the house shake.

Doctor *Woodhouse*, gave her a Venificifuge, a Chymical preparation, given in the third part of a grain for one dose; *Opium* the strongest of all things, many times in a Grain, makes very little alteration in the body; but this rid her, in part for a while, of her fits; but then the Spirits had never spoke in her: he hath used that Venificifuge to other bewitched persons with good successe; and to a Child in his own Town, that the People brought information it was in convulsion fits, he sent convulsive Remedies; they did no good: then he questioned the *Querents* what fits they were, *They come,* said they, *every day, at six of the Clock*; he went there to see it, and found it to begin its fit, with pulling off its headcloaths; then it fell a pulling off its Hair, and then scratching the skin off its face; Mr *Sanders*, the *Astrologer & Chiromancer*, was there, who told Doctor Woodhouse, *It was bewitched*, & accordingly, with other Remedies, it was cured; but the chief thing he trusteth to, is a Sigil to hang about their Necks: He cured one in *Barkamsted* also, that two learned Physicians (many there be, that know Greek and Latin, though perhaps nothing else truly, and as they ought, which many a Boy of twelve or fourteen years old knows) said, *had Hysterick Fits*, said he, You will not believe that there be Witches, but you shall see that the Party is not handled as you imagine, for Hysterick Medicines will do her no good; but I will cure her with one thing, once given in the third part of a Grain; which was accomplished.

A Friend of his, used *Amara Dulcis*,[6] a *Mercury Placit*,[7] gathered when *Mercury* was strong, essentially and accidentally, and applyed about the parties Neck, when *Mercury* was well posited in House, and aspected friendly by the Fortunes, and most significant Planets.

And *Tragus* saith, *The People in* Germany *used to hang* Amara Dulcis, *or Wood-night-shade about their Cattels Necks, when they feared Witchcraft.*

The Spirits in Mary Hall told them, That if they would go to Redman, of Amersom,[8] (whom some say is a *Conjurer*, others say, He is an honest and able Physician, and doth abundance of good) he would cast them out. This *Redman*, by relation, is unlearned in the Languages,[9] but hath abundance of Practice, and is much talked of in remote parts; he was once sent to Prison for these things.

A Child being very sick, likely to die, *Redman* bids them, *Take the length of the Child with a Stick, and measure so much ground in the Churchyard, and there dig, and bury the Stick of the Childs length*, and the Child suddenly recovered.

Another troubled with an Ague, he bid *go into the Medow, and where two Cart ruts crossed one another, just there to dig an hole with his stick, and make water therein*; and the party thus doing was freed of his ague.

A third was wished *to boil an Egg in his Urine, and bury it in an Ant-hill, where were many Ants, or Pismires*; and he presently recovered of his distemper.

But the Judge could not for these things do any thing to him, and set him free; these do not deny but he may be a Witch (or Wizard as some will have men to be called) but do not prove he must be so; and I have in my Observations, collected from the Vulgar, diverse of their practices of this kinde, ridding their selves thereby of divers distempers, especially Agues, which we have shewn in our *Puretology*, or *Treatise of Agues*, writ in Latine, and in the chapter of *Transplantation.*

Redman, as I am informed, pretends to do these, and the like feats by *Astrology*; much indeed may be done lawfully by *Astrology*, but there be many that make that their pretence and defence, and probably use other Arts that may be unlawful, that go beyond *Astrology.*

Goodwife *Hall* told me, *that her Daughter was worse when the Spirits lay still, and did not actuate her parts, for then she was heavy, and Melancholy, and like a weight lay at her Stomack.*

The Maid is very young, and seems bashful, and modest; her Parents and Kinred are held by all very conscientious and honest People, and wealthy; so that they need use no such impostures to get money, nor would use such blasphemies and abuses of God to gain pity or admiration.

Indeed many a Jugler, or Tumbler, may by use come nigh to imitate these things, but what can such a silly, young, bashful well-disposed, and religiously-educated Maid do in these things?

Since one told me, that a Minister that was with *Mary Hall* told her, that when he came in presence, the Spirits said, *What do you want with that little Book in your Pocket?* he wondered, when as he knew none saw or heard of it; if this be true, it is *Præcognition*, and that is not Natural; it was a little Pious Book, that troubled them.

Following the relation of Mary Hall's story, Drage discusses the symptoms of possession, and whether it is real.

[They are possessed] that leap five or six yards; that speak Tongues they never learned; that foretel things to come; that are stronger then four or five men; that fly, or stand in the Air; or run up Walls without use of their Hands; or have their Face bent quite behind them, so long remaining, *Consideratis considetandis*, must be possessed of Spirits; but they that are not thus handled, may be possessed of Spirits.

Those that were in the Evangelists possessed, were not alike possessed.

Different kinds and degrees of a thing, shew it may, but do not prove that it must be another thing.

It is best judging what may be, by what hath been; but Histories mention divers that have been so possessed, therefore divers may be so possessed...
Some are thought to be bewitched, that are not; and some are thought not to be bewitched that are.

If *Mary Hall* is falsely possessed, it doth not prove another not to be truly possessed; or if *Mary Hall* be truly possessed, it doth not prove that there are no such counterfeits.

Neither have the Imps, or Inferiour Dæmons, the power and knowledge of the Superiour, to exercise; nor can the Superiour alwayes exercise the power and knowledge they have.

Neither are all Diseases natural, cureable by Natural Remedies; nor are all Diseases Supernatural, incureable by Natural Remedies.

There is nothing of the Will of God, that is not in his Power; and if his Will did restrain Witchcraft, it were in his power to do it: But his Will is two-fold.

1 Of Ordination.
2 Of Permission.

He ordains Good, and suffers Evil.

It is lawful to use all the means ordained of God to cure Witchcraft, but all the means that are used to cure Witchcraft, are not ordained of God; and cure only by his permission, who brings good out of all evil.

Neither have the Dæmons licence from God to hurt whom they please, nor have the Witches licence from their Dæmons to cure whom they will.

All that are bewitched, are handled after some extream or strange way or both; but all that are handled after some extream and strange way, are not bewitched.

All that cause Preternatural Sickness, through the power of the Devil, be Witches; but not all the Witches that be, for some cause Diabolical Sicknesses, and some cure them (called *White Witches*) and some both. Spirits frequently work without, but sometimes by, but then commonly above the power of Natural Causes, or means.

Those that deny any powers or influences, to be here in or upon Natural things, from any other then Natural and common Causes, deny anything to be supernatural; and consequently must conclude that God could make the order, progress, and nature of this World, and it contents, no otherwise then what it is; and to go on, act and alter by no other Causes, Methods, or Wayes, then what we see commonly to be.

Therefore whatsoever Supernatural and Spiritual may be proved to arise from the common force, and usual order of natural things, is thereby proved to be Natural; and whatsoever cannot be solved by the ordinary force, and usual course of any Natural Causes, is thereby proved Supernatural and Spiritual.

There was Printed last year, about two sheets of Paper, concerning two possessed or bewitched; the one was *James Barrow* of *Olaves Southwark*, whose condition was writ by his Father, to whom did divers in witness accord: He was almost two years possessed, of Five Evil Spirits, and was at last dispossessed by constant prayer, at which the

Devils roared, and were tormented, so that they went out of him, not in any visible shape, but as it were with Belches, and like Suffocation: He was sometimes dumb for long time, sometimes stark mad, sometimes beat himself, and endeavoured to make himself away; strange noises were heard in him, singing and cursing were sometimes present; He said, at first like a Rat came to him; the Imp of the Witch, or the Witch herself might so transform her self: And some imagine that *Nebuchadnezzar* was transformed into the shape of an Ox (see *Dan.* 4.33.36) and that, that saying, *He eat Grass like an Ox*, should be translated, *He eat Grass, being like an Ox, or in the likeness of an Ox*.

The other Relation, in that Paper, of *Hannah Crump* of *Warwick*, had nothing extraordinary, but the Symptoms of madness, yet might be bewitched: They went to one in *Winchester Park* in *Southwark*, to unbewitch her, he asked *Five pound; for* (said he) *I am not sure to cure her, and if I do, if I cannot be strong enough for the Witch, after I have taken the affliction from the Maid, I must bear it my self; but if I can be strong enough for the Witch, she must bear it, until she dispose of it to some other, for none of her Familiars will bear it*:[10] Doubtless Spirits are loth to go out of the possessed; and the Evangelists shews some reason, saying, *When the unclean Spirit goeth out of any man, he wandereth up and down, seeking rest, and findeth none*; and then he taketh counsel of a greater number of foul Spirits, and they possess the same party again, or others, more grievously.
VALE.

Non gens sed mens, non genus sed genius; virtus nobilitat, & Ratio homines a brutis & inter se discriminat, Symboli Emiliani & Claudij Jmperatorum.

Deo Gloria, Homini pax.[11]
FINIS

In the main body of Drage's book there are two further references to Mary Hall:

> ...sometimes they are, as we have received information of the Maid *Mary Hall*, now possessed, as the Spirits say, with two; and she said she saw two Flies come down the Chimney to her, before she was distempered; she lives at, or nigh *Gadsden*, nigh *Dunstable*...

> ...if many women may bewitch those they have not seen, but it is rarely seen; sometimes they intend (as the two Spirits in *Mary Hall* in *August* 1664 about *Gadsden* did expresse; they were sent to her father, but had not power, given of God), to bewitch one, and cannot, and so bewitch another of the family.

Unfortunately Drage does not reveal Mary Hall's eventual fate.

Jane Stretton, 1669

Jane Stretton was baptised on 24 June 1649,[12] which means that at the time of the events described she was no older than eighteen, and may have been younger. Her tribulations are recorded in a pamphlet entitled

The Hartfordshire Wonder, or, Strange News from Ware, Being and exact and true Relation of one Jane Stretton the Daughter of Thomas Stretton of Ware in the County of Herts, who hath been visited in a strange kind of manner by extraordinary and unusual fits, her abstaining from sustenance for the space of 9 Months, being haunted by Imps or Devils in the form of several Creatures here described, the Parties adjudged of all by whom she was thus tormented and the occasion thereof, with many other remarkable things taken from her own mouth and confirmed by credible witnesses. London, 1669.

The pamphlet tells the tale of Thomas Stretton, who had a bible that he particularly valued, but lost. He therefore went to a cunning man to track it down. Stretton was rude to the man, saying that he must be a witch or a devil. The cunning man sent his wife to Stretton's home, where she asked Jane for a drink. Apparently this was the opening the cunning man required to send an imp to possess the girl, and she suffered a number of fits.

A week later the cunning man's wife called again, this time asking for a pin, which Jane innocently gave her; her fits became even more violent. For six months she ate nothing, nor did she evacuate her bowels.

The story became known, and onlookers intruded upon Thomas's privacy, so he sent the girl to stay with John Wood, a neighbour. She was constantly watched, and

> there appeared the resemblance of Flax and Hair to fall down upon a white sheet that was laid over her bed, which they narrowly taking notice of, and perceiving her tongue to hang or loll out of her mouth, upon a nearer view found the perfect resemblance of Flax, Hair and Thread points to be on the same which, being by them removed, there presently proceeded from her mouth two flames in resemblance of fire, the one of red colour and other blew, and soon after in some short distance of time eleven pins, in several crooked forms and shapes, some bowed one way, some another. The report of these more strange accidents soon flew about not onely all over Ware but to the adjacent villages and more remote Towns, so that people came in multitudes to see her, some out of pitty, to help and comfort her, others out of curiosity, to be ascertained of the truth of these relations, and some who were diffident of any such thing as Witchcraft, who being fully satisfied in the truth of what is here set down, went home fully convinced of their errors.

Jane suffered excruciating back pain, and felt as though 'she were continually slashed with a Knife, or had her flesh cut and mangled, and the people about her, with setting her up in her bed to give her some food, found a naked Knife there, no body knowing how or which way it should come thither.' The onlookers could see 'the Devil, or his Imps, or what it was we cannot determine, but sometimes it was in the shape of a Toad and at others like a Frog, or a Mouse...'

The neighbours, when told of what had happened between the Strettons, the cunning man and his wife, concluded that the latter were responsible for Jane's illness. They decided that if necessary, violence should be used against them. In the meantime, some of the foam expelled from Jane's mouth during a fit had been put on the fire, where it burned. As a result, when the neighbours came upon the cunning man's wife, and told her of their intention on forcing her to appear before Jane, she said that 'if they had not come she could not have stayed any longer from her.'

For nine months the girl took no solid food, though she ate some 'liquid meats,' which the writer states were quite inadequate to sustain life. At the time the pamphlet was published, Jane was still on a similar diet:

> At present she takes nothing but surrups and such like liquid ingredients, being in such pain yet it is hoped by the blessing of God and the endeavours of those under whom she is in cure that at last she may be eased of her misery...

Some are of that belief that stories of witchcraft are but idle Chymeras, but we know that no part of Scripture was spoken in vain and one place thereof saith, Thou shalt not suffer a Witch to live, those who are so, I wish them grace to repent and get out of their damnable estate, and should admonish all persons whatever, not upon any loss or disaster to go to these Sooth sayers, Wizards, or Cunning Men, for as the Scripture saith in one place, Cursed be the image and the image maker, so I say there can be no blessing to those who are either Wizards or go to them for help and Councel.

The author is of no doubt then of the source of Jane's illness, but puts the blame in part upon her father, in the first place going to a cunning man, and secondly for being so foolish as to insult him. Jane's eventual fate is unknown.

The Baldwin Children, 1700-1704

This case is a classic example of bewitchment: young girls, succumbing in turn to similar symptoms. There has been a good deal of speculation as to whether these cases are the result of some form of hysteria, or no more than the antics of groups of children as a device to draw attention to themselves.

The pamphlet recording the events was written by Thomas Aldridge of Tring, but he died two years before its publication in 1717. It was entitled *A Short Rehearsal of the Sad Condition of three of the Children of John Baldwin of Sarret, in the County of Hertford, and also the Manner of their Deliverance.*

The case of the Baldwin children was another in which Doctor Woodhouse, who also treated Mary Hall, was involved. There are similarities between the two, though the account of the Baldwin case is not as detailed, nor as dramatically told. John and Rebecca Baldwin had at least four children, all girls, three of whom were 'possessed' between 1700 and 1704. The affected children were Anne, Rebecca and Mary.

Rebecca was the first afflicted. She was born in 1688, and early in 1700 she was 'taken with great pain in her sides.' This was soon followed with shaking of various limbs, sometimes for hours on end. She also suffered fainting fits, during which she frothed at the mouth.

> ...one day she made a strange humming noise, much like a bumble-bee; after that mew'd like a kitten and so louder and louder until like unto a cat; then fell a barking like unto a small dog, and that louder and louder, at last so eagerly that she could scarce fetch her breath, and continued so doing

until night. She also had other kind of fits, in which, if she was near the fire, she would be ready to sink down into it, and sometimes it would be said by her mouth 'I'll burn ye,' and then it was hard work to hold her, so as to keep her out of the fire; then she also striv'd to beat herself with her hands very much.

She reported seeing apparitions, both human and animal; something appearing like a boy 'caught her head, and beat it against the wall, making it ache sadly.' John and his wife called in a Dr Parker, but he seems to have been little help to Rebecca. During that first year she experienced periods of relief, but they were only temporary. Late in 1701, or in early 1702, the family called in Dr Woodhouse. After only three or four visits, the fits ceased for between three and six months.

During this period of relief for Rebecca her sister Mary, who was by now twelve (the same age at which Rebecca had been first afflicted), was struck down. Her symptoms were somewhat different; she whined, sang and laughed in a strange manner, and said that she saw men and women invisible to the rest of the family. She experienced periods of blindness too. A short time later Rebecca was taken ill once more, though the symptoms were more acute. Mary was even worse, however, and was so badly affected that she was sometimes unable to walk. On occasion she could only walk backwards, or with the aid of crutches. She lost the strength in her arms, and had to be fed. The figures she reported seeing were regular visitors, and she knew them by name. Rebecca claimed she saw them too. The two girls caused their parents great distress:

> Sometimes one of them would fall down in the house and lie as though she was in a swoon or dying and froth at the mouth, and sometimes the other; and sometimes before one of them fell down, it would be said by her mouth 'Now she shall fall down,' and then so she did and there lie like one in a swoon and froth at the mouth and her tongue turn about in her mouth very strangely for a considerable time; and then when she got up, it would be said by the other's mouth 'Now she shall fall down,' then she would do as the other did, and thus it would be several times in a day some days.

The girls had to be watched constantly for fear that they would take their own lives. On one occasion when Mary was left alone, she reported that 'an Appearance' told her to set fire to the house. The elder daughter, Elizabeth, who was free from the affliction, reported that Mary had threatened to kill her. She heard noises and saw lights, as did the father, John Baldwin, but no more than that. Doctor Woodhouse was consulted once more, and though there was occasional respite, the symptoms continued. In desperation their parents sent them to stay with a friend, William Brewer. Oddly, while they were away the symptoms disappeared; but should anyone suggest they go home, or should they be brought home, they were taken ill once more.

It was at this time that the power of prayer was suggested as a solution. The girls seemed willing, and Rebecca's suffering at once abated. Mary's symptoms continued for a while, but after several sessions of prayer, she too showed some signs of improvement. The Baldwins organised a religious meeting at their home for 19 May 1704,[13] and thereafter both girls were restored to health.

The family's troubles were not over, however. In April 1704, the eighteen-year-old Anne was taken ill, initially with what was thought to be the ague (fits of shivering or fever), but developed after some three months into the same symptoms suffered by her two sisters. She was struck with dumbness and convulsions, and when offered a Bible to read, she said 'I can't endure it, I will tear it,' though both her fits and silence disappeared once she began to read. The relief was only temporary however, and the Baldwins decided to organise another day of fasting and prayer. Anne seemed distressed at the plan, and expressed the hope that the visitors' horses might throw them, or that they might lose their way. On one occasion she said to her mother 'I'll rest that I may be strong to overcome them and then I will stay.' After a false start due to confusion amongst the participants, on 18 August, 1704, several friends met at the Baldwin home to pray for Anne's relief.

> In the former part of the opportunity (though the poor maid was willing and agreed to endeavour to keep the day with us) yet she in some little time began to be bad with fits and grew greatly discontented and could not bear hearing prayer; and after some time the influences the poor creature was under, grew so outrageous and strong in her, that she on a sudden sprung out of the chair she sat in and leaped about the room crying out 'I'll kill ye, I'll kill ye.' Then we got her into her chair again, and kept her in it by holding of her, and when the person (that was then engaged) gave over praying (for he did not leave off when she raged so) it was said by her mouth 'Now you have done, I will have done,' and then she ceased to be in such a rage and was very calm.
>
> After some discourse with her, they desired her to kneel down and to endeavour to join (in her desires) with them in their prayers, and she did kneel down with them, and two of them kneeled down, one on one side and the other on the other side, and each of them laid the hand next to her upon her, to help her to keep herself upon her knees, that she might not be raised up by that Power that acted against her will; and then one of them prayed again, and when they prayed she was strangely stirred and had

strange snatchings in her arms, and, as she said she was ready to be raised up, do what she could, yet the persons on each side helped her without much difficulty, though sometimes her knees were raised (as one of them said he thought) from the boards, but as they continued kneeling and praying and she and we with them, the Power that acted her grew weaker and weaker in her, and after some time there appeared to us nothing at all outwardly, she being neither lifted up, shook or snacked in her arms or head, etc., as before, but could continue kneeling with us in prayer as quietly as the rest. And when they ceased praying, they asked her, whether she felt anything of those workings within her still? And she told them 'No.' Yet they prayed again, she kneeling down with them. And they afterward asked her again if she felt any remainder of the workings in her? And she said 'No'; whereupon they spent some time in endeavouring to give thanks unto God for his great mercy and then gave over.

Thereafter the girls were free of affliction for some time. The pamphlet bears the names: 'John Baldwin, the father, Jeremiah Baldwin, the uncle
The mark of X Rebecca Baldwin, the mother of the children
Witness our hands Sept 7th, 1706'.

The narrative is followed by the statements of some of those involved, including both parents, Elizabeth and Rebecca. Thomas Aldridge recounts how Rebecca (the daughter) told him about some strange yeast designed for baking which found its way into three pans of milk by unnatural means. Some of her clothing was torn, and she had seen visions in her room and other parts of the house.

Joseph Munn says that John Baldwin told him that the Devil visited the household again on 9 January 1714, and Anne and Mary were afflicted. This visitation was short lived, being curtailed by the 103rd Psalm. Richard Carter tells of the prayer meetings, and the swooning of the girls, their dumbness and blindness, and their fits.

> In the time of prayer Mary Baldwin was taken very ill; and after prayer was over it was declared to me by her, and others who saw it, that towards the end of that day of prayer Mary was so ill that she thought she should vomit and went out of the room, (and her sister Rebecca went out with her) and Mary cast up (as she thought) a piece of flesh as big as a mouse, and she said then she see several of the appearances standing about it and her, and they said they could not meddle with her any more, and she said she thought the piece of flesh crawl'd away, and the appearances went away with it snivelling and crying.

On his way home Satan, in the form of Mary, waylaid him and threatened to throw him in the pond.

It may be significant that Rebecca and Mary were about the same age when they were afflicted. Anne was of course older. The family were devout Nonconformists, and prayer formed a large part of their daily ritual. Rebellion by the young girls against such a regime may explain the events recorded.

In the same pamphlet Aldridge mentions three other local cases of possession, but there is no great detail. They are as follows:

Isaac Tockfield of Tring, 1689

Isaac Tockfield was a young man whose father was dead; he lived with his mother. He had fits, and was 'judged bewitched.' During the fits he sometimes suffered loss of memory. It was the Bible that triggered his attacks. According to Aldridge, who knew the family,

> ...his mother told me, that if she took but a Bible to herself above stairs, when he was below, he would come running up in a fit to tear away the Book from her, crying, 'Do you read? Do you read?' though it was impossible that he should see or hear her, which manifests that he acted by a spirit that knew what his mother did when he neither saw or hear her.

There is no record given of his fate.[14]

David Wright of Offley, 1693

This twenty-seven year old shepherd had suffered from the 'King's Evil,' or tuberculosis of the lymphatic glands, for about fifteen years. In 1693 he was cured after attending a prayer meeting in Hitchin. His previous behaviour ('both wicked and ignorant') was mended too.[15]

Thomas Burridge of Markyate, 1716

Burridge was an apprentice bodice maker. He was 'seized with extraordinary and violent temptations of Satan' to take his own life. One night he tried to hang himself from the foot of his bed, only to be rescued by his landlord's son. He went home to his mother in Dunstable, and was for a while afflicted with fits. Some friends organised a day of fasting and prayer on his behalf on 26 September 1712. He was by then so weak that he had to be 'had to the meeting between two persons.' The prayers were successful: the young man was cured, and his strength restored.[16]

8

JANE WENHAM OF WALKERN
1711-1712

And so we come to Hertfordshire's most famous witch. Jane Wenham gets a chapter of her own, firstly because she was the last witch condemned to death in England, and secondly, because there was an enormous quantity written about the case.

If anyone assumed that the day of the witch believer evaporated with the coming of the eighteenth century, they needed only to look at Wenham's case to find that it was not so; and though most of the events took place in a rural setting, several of the leading players were educated men. Amongst them was Francis Bragge, who in 1712 wrote a detailed booklet on the affair.

At least nine books and pamphlets were published about the case at the time, some for Jane Wenham and some against. Writers defending Wenham generally adopted one of two tactics: the logical approach, in which the claims of Bragge were examined and criticised; and the religious approach, in which the author seeks to demonstrate by reference to the scriptures and to classical authorities that witchcraft is non-existent. I have concentrated on four of them: Bragge's account, and three of the anonymous confutations that appeared. They are entitled:

A full and impartial account of the discovery of sorcery and witchcraft, Practis'd by JANE WENHAM, of Walkerne, in Hertfordshire, upon the bodies of Anne Thorne, Anne Street &c. The Proceedings against Her from Her being First Apprehended, till She was Committed to Gaol by Sir Henry Chauncy. Also her Tryal... London: Printed for F. Curll... 1712. [by Francis Bragge].

The Impossibility of Witchcraft, Plainly proving, From Scripture and Reason, That there never was a WITCH; and that it is both Irrational and Impious to believe there ever was. In which the DEPOSITIONS AGAINST Jane Wenham, Lately

Try'd and Condemn'd for a WITCH, at Hertford, are Confuted and Expos'd. LONDON Printed, and Sold by J. Baker, at the Black-Boy in Pater-Noster-Row, 1712. Price Six Pence.

A Full Confutation of Witchcraft: More particularly of the DEPOSITIONS Against JANE WENHAM, Lately Condemned for a WITCH; at Hertford. In which The Modern Notions of Witches are overthrown, and the Ill Consequences of such Doctrines are exposed by Arguments; proving that, Witchcraft is Priestcraft. A Natura multa, plura ficta, à Dæmone nulla.[1] In a Letter from a Physician in Hertfordshire, to his Friend in London. LONDON: Printed for J. Baker at the Black-boy in Pater-Noster-Row, 1712. Price 6d.

The Case of the Hertfordshire Witchcraft Consider'd. Being an Examination of a book entitl'd, A Full and Impartial Account of the Discovery of Sorcery and Witchcraft, Practis'd by JANE WENHAM, of Walkerne, in Hertfordshire, upon the bodies of Anne Thorne, Anne Street, &c London: Printed for JOHN

'A Full and Impartial Account…'
Francis Bragge's account of the Wenham case set off a war of publications. The book went to four editions in the first few months. This is the third.

PEMBERTON, *at the Buck and Sun against St. Dunstan's Church in Fleetstreet. MDCCXII.*

Francis Bragge was the vicar of nearby Hitchin at the time of the events. He was the grandson of Sir Henry Chauncy, a lawyer who is best known for his Historical Antiquities of Hertfordshire, published in 1700. Bragge was not a particularly popular man. He was short and bombastic, and his parishioners were not sorry when he took himself off to Great Wymondley, leaving Hitchin to his curate. He is buried in St Mary's Church in Hitchin.[2]

The basis of Bragge's account is as follows:[3] Jane Wenham lived in Church End, Walkern, and was already suspected locally of being a witch (see plate 11). She had been married twice; her second marriage, to Edward Wenham in 1697, had ended in separation, when her husband had arranged for the town crier to make it known abroad that he was no longer 'responsible for her proceedings.' He had subsequently died, and his death was attributed by some to bewitchment by Jane. She was at least seventy years of age, and living on the edge of poverty and the charity of her neighbours.

John Chapman, a Walkern farmer, had been concerned for some time over the strange deaths amongst his neighbours' livestock. He had recently lost at least £200 worth himself. He suspected witchcraft, and that Jane Wenham was the culprit.

Jane asked Matthew Gilston, one of Chapman's labourers, for some straw. He refused her, but she took some anyway. Before Sir Henry Chauncy, Gilston swore that

> on the 29 of January last, when this informant was threshing in the barn of his master, John Chapman, an old woman in a riding hood or cloak, he knows not which, came to the barn and asked him for a pennyworth of straw. He told her he could give her none, and she went away muttering. And this informant saith, That after the woman was gone he was unable to work, but ran out of the barn as far as a place called Munder's Hill (which is about three miles from Walkern), and asked at a house there for a pennyworth of straw, and they refusing to give him any, he went father to some dung-heaps, and took some straw from thence, and pulled off his shirt, and brought it home in his shirt; but he knows not what moved him to this, but says he was forc'd to it, he knows not how'.[4]

Other witnesses testified that they had seen Gilston, running at a great pace; when he reached the river, he ignored the bridge and ran through the water. Chapman became convinced the woman in the riding hood

Sir Henry Chauncy, Kt., Serjeant at Law. From the frontispiece of Volume I of his Historical Antiquities of Hertfordshire, *1700. (Alan Millard)*

had been Jane Wenham, and he consequently sought her out. In the altercation that followed he called her 'a witch and a bitch.' Jane's reaction was to apply for a warrant from the nearby justice, Sir Henry Chauncy,[5] of Ardeley Bury.

Chauncy declined to become involved, and recommended that the two disputants should put their cases to an independent neighbour. Jane suggested the Reverend Godfrey Gardiner,[6] the Rector of Walkern; Chapman agreed. If Jane thought that Gardiner would come down firmly on her side she was mistaken. He ordered Chapman to pay her just one shilling, and ordered the two of them to live in peace. Jane was dissatisfied, and 'went away with great heat, saying, 'If she could not get justice here she would have it elsewhere.' As she left the house, via the kitchen, she saw the sixteen-year-old maid, Anne Thorn, who had just returned from the surgeon for treatment for a dislocated knee.

Minutes later the Reverend Gardiner, his wife, and Francis Bragge, who was present at the time, heard a commotion from the kitchen.

Gardiner went to investigate, and found Anne Thorn, 'stripped to her shirt-sleeves, wringing her hands in a dismal manner, and speechless.' At his call, Mrs Gardiner and Bragge came into the kitchen. Mrs Gardiner asked Anne the cause for her distress, and the maid pointed to a pinned bundle on the floor. Mrs Gardiner unpinned it, and found that it consisted of Anne's gown and apron, with a 'parcel of oaken twigs and dead leaves wrapped up therein.'

When Anne recovered, she described how she had felt compelled to leave the house and run to a spot over half a mile away, climbing a five barred gate on the way. Despite her bad knee, she had covered the ground at eight miles an hour. There she met 'a little old woman muffled in a riding-hood, who set her to gather the sticks, made her strip herself and wrap the bundle in her gown, and gave her a large crooked pin to fasten it up with.' Mrs Gardiner advised that they throw the bundle into the fire. As it burned, Jane Wenham came into the room, claiming that she had forgotten to speak to Anne's mother about some washing the two women were to do at Ardeley Bury; to the group however her appearance proved that she was indeed guilty; the destruction of a witch's charm was believed, as we have already seen, to ensure her appearance.

The following morning, as Anne was returning home after delivering a message, she met Jane Wenham, who scolded her for making out that she was a witch. Anne replied that she had told nothing but the truth. According to Anne, Jane threatened her: 'If you tell any more such stories of me it shall be worse for you than it has been yet.' The girl hurried home, and told the Gardiners what had happened.

Once more Anne felt compelled to search for sticks, climbing over gates and, like Matthew Gilston, ignoring bridges, wading through streams and ditches. She began to suffer from fits, and tried to visit Jane, but she fell into a ditch and put her knee out again. Another visit to the surgeon followed, but no sooner was Anne mobile once more than she reverted to her by now usual practise of running and vaulting over gates. This time, though, amongst the witnesses was Sir Henry Chauncy's son, Arthur.[7] Once more Anne met with the old woman in the riding hood, who gave the girl a large bent pin. All the while denouncing Jane Wenham, Anne finally attempted to drown herself. There seemed to the occupants of the rectory only one solution; Jane Wenham must be summoned and forced to remove the spell. Unsurprisingly Jane declined to comply, and locked herself into her cottage.

Sir Henry Chauncy now became involved once more. He signed a warrant authorising the parish constable to arrest Jane. The constable called on her on 13 February, but she refused to open her door to him, and he therefore broke it down, seized her and took her to the rectory to face her alleged victim.

As Jane came into the room and spoke to Anne, the girl cried, 'You are a base woman, you have ruined me. I must have your blood or I shall never be well.' Anne threw herself at Jane, scratching at her face 'with such fury and eagerness that the noise of her nails seemed to all that were present as if she were scratching against a wainscot, yet no blood followed.' Jane kept her head still, and said 'Scratch harder, Nan, and fetch blood of me if you can.' Even though Jane's forehead was wounded, no blood flowed.[8]

On the 14 February, Sir Henry Chauncy came to Walkern to hear depositions; he summoned Jane to appear before him, and ordered that she be searched for witch marks and teats. For an hour four women searched Jane's body, but had to report that they could find nothing. Chauncy adjourned the proceedings to the following day at his home, Ardeley Bury. Anne Thorn suffered more fits, but 'she was recovered by Prayer.' The following day Jane Wenham offered to be swum, but Chauncy vetoed the idea as being illegal.[9] Instead she attempted another extra-legal test – she would recite the Lord's Prayer before the Reverend Strutt, the vicar of Ardeley.

> She... attempted several times to do it, going on very readily till she came to Forgive us our Trespasses, &c., which she could not repeat, not these Two Sentences together, Lead us not into Temptation, but deliver us from Evil, but would thus express 'em, Lead us not into no Temptation and Evil, or Lead us into Temptation and Evil, or Lead us not into no Temptation, but deliver us from all Evil, and thus she was try'd Six or Seven Times together.

Further evidence was heard. Susan Aylott deposed that Jane had, twelve years before, murdered the wife of Richard Harvey, a friend of Edward Wenham, who had helped him at the time of his separation from Jane. According to the examinant, Mrs Harvey was sick in bed when Jane Wenham 'went under the window where the sick woman lay, and said, 'Why don't they take her and hang her out of the way?' and that night the sick woman aforesaid died.' Susan Aylott claimed too that Jane was responsible for the death her child.

Thomas Adams, Junior, of Walkern, told of a dispute he had with Jane over some turnips, three weeks or a month before Christmas. He had refused to let her have any, though 'she had had no victuals that day or money to buy any.' On Christmas morning one of his best sheep died; he later lost three more. 'He also saith, that his Shepherd tells him, that one of his other Sheep was taken strangely, skipping, and standing upon its Head, but in half an Hour was well, and continues so.' Jane having 'the Common Fame of a Witch,' he was sure she was responsible.[10]

THE CASE

OF THE

Hertfordshire

WITCHCRAFT

CONSIDER'D.

Being an

Examination of a BOOK,

ENTITL'D,

A Full and Impartial Account of the Discovery of Sorcery & Witchcraft, *Practis'd by* JANE WENHAM *of* Walkern, *upon the Bodies of* Anne Thorne, Anne Street, &c.

LONDON:

Printed for JOHN PEMBERTON, at the Buck and Sun against St. *Dunstan*'s Church in *Fleetstreet.* MDCCXII.

The Case of the Hertfordshire Witchcraft Consider'd... *A substantial refutation of Francis Bragge's book. The comtent suggests that the author was a local man, well acquainted in the details of the case and the personalities involved.*

On 16 February the Reverend Strutt visited Jane and tested her on the Lord's Prayer once more, and again she failed to repeat it correctly. Strutt, convinced of her guilt, questioned the old woman for some time, eventually getting her to make some damning admissions. Asked if she had a familiar spirit, she agreed that she had; asked if it took the form of a cat, she admitted that it did. She had been a witch for sixteen years, due to her 'Malicious and Wicked Mind.' She named three other Walkern women as confederates. Strutt asked Jane whether she had a pact with the Devil, and was anxious to establish the nature of it. But, he said, 'we could make nothing of her answers, save that an old man did spit upon her.'

Sir Henry Chauncy was told of the confessions, and he issued warrants for the arrest of the three women Jane had named. On examination, however, he could 'fix no one particular Fact upon any of those whom she accused.'

Anne Thorn now reported that 'she saw Things like Cats appear to her.' One of them was said to have a face similar to Jane.

> A dismal Noise like Cats was heard… about the House, sometimes their cry resembled that of Young Children, at other times they made a Hellish Noise to which nothing can be resembled; this was accompanied by Scratchings heard by all that were in the House, under the Windows, and Doors.

Many of the animals were seen by members of the household; when chased away they made off in the direction of Jane Wenham's cottage. Anne fell into a comatose state, but revived when Jane was brought to see her. During this visit, Arthur Chauncy carried out experiments in pricking. He thrust a pin up to its head into the flesh of Jane's arm a great many times; 'and, seeing no blood come, he ran the pin in several times more; at last he left it in her arm that all the company might see it run up to the head; and when he plucked it out before them all, there just appeared a little thin watery serum, but nothing that you can call blood.' On 17 February Arthur Chauncy, who was coming to play an increasingly important part in the affair, found a number of bent pins in the vicinity of Anne Thorn, which prompted recourse to an anti-witch charm:

> This Evening they were advised to take some of the Girl's Urine, and put it into a Stone Bottle, tye the Cork down, and set it over the Fire, which they did, and sent to the House where the Witch was, one that should observe whether she shew'd any more than ordinary Uneasiness; it was found that exactly at the Time she seem'd in great Pain, and shed Tears

plentifully, (which she was never observed to do before or since,) and continued seemingly in Misery and Torture, till the time that the Bottle flew, with a Report as great as that of a Pistol; and then she was very Merry, Singing and Dancing, as before.[11]

It was noted that at the same time that pins were turning up around Anne Thorn, Jane's pincushion, which was full of pins at night, was by the following morning empty. Cats continued to harass the Gardiner household, and Mrs Gardiner sent her children to stay with a neighbour. A warrant was issued committing Jane Wenham to Hertford Gaol to await trial at the Lent Assizes of 1712. Before her escorts, Uriah Wright and Thomas Harvey, took her to Hertford, the Reverends Bragge, Gardiner and Strutt, together with Arthur Chauncy, urged her unsuccessfully to make 'a full and sincere Discovery [confession].' Wright and Harvey later claimed under oath that Jane had confessed to them on the way to gaol that she had been a witch for ten years – a contrast to the supposed confession to the Reverend Strutt on 16 February, when she claimed to have been a witch for sixteen years.

Meanwhile Anne continued to suffer. Pins turned up in and around her bed, and her pillow was stuffed with cakes of feathers. The cakes were described as being round, and a little larger than a crown piece (38mm, or 1.5 inches); they were arranged in a circle, with the small feathers placed so that the quill ends met in the centre. Each cake contained thirty-two feathers. Francis Bragge wanted to retain one of these feather cakes as evidence, but he was overruled and they were burned: once they were destroyed, Anne's fits ceased until the assizes were held. The feline visits continued however, until Arthur Chauncy killed one of them 'that knocked at the door, and after that the dismal cries ceased.'

The trial of Jane Wenham took place at Hertford in March 1712, before the Honourable Sir John Powell.[12] The charge was restricted to 'conversing familiarly with the Devil in the shape of a cat.' To the Reverend Bragge's disgust, Anne Thorn was not mentioned in the indictment. The Grand Jury found a true Bill, and the trial proper began. Mrs Gardiner, the Reverend Gardiner, the Reverend Strutt, Arthur Chauncy and Anne Thorn testified to the events in the Gardiner household, and the bewitchment of Anne herself. Francis Bragge gave details of the cakes of feathers (Justice Powell was disappointed that none had been preserved for examination by the court). William Borroughs had seen Anne's fits, as had Thomas Ireland, who also mentioned cats with Jane Wenham's face. James Burvile saw such a cat too. John Chapman told of arguments with Jane, and the death of his livestock. Matthew Gilston and Thomas Adams told of their clashes with Jane, and their subsequent misfortunes. Elizabeth Field introduced an allegation that Jane had killed another child about nine years before. Jane Wenham said little in her defence other than that she was a 'clear woman.'

Justice Powell summed up. Within the bounds of the law, he invited them to acquit the accused. The court adjourned until the afternoon, when, after a short period of consideration, the jury returned a verdict of guilty. Justice Powell asked them 'whether they found her guilty upon the charge of conversing with the Devil in the shape of a cat,' to which the foreman replied, 'We find her guilty of that.'

The relevant part of the Act of 1604 was unambiguous:

> If any pson or persons… shall use practise or exercise any Invocation or Conjuration of any evill and wicked Spirit, or shall consult covenant with entertaine employ feede or rewarde any evill and wicked Spirit to or for any intent or purpose… that then everie such offendor or offendors… shall suffer pains of deathe as a Felon or Felons…

Justice Powell was therefore left with no choice but to sentence Jane Wenham to death, though he reprieved her execution pending the outcome of an application on her behalf for a pardon.

Frances Bragge hurried into print with his first booklet. It described the events recounted above, and was extremely hostile to the accused. In the preface he stated that

> As for Mother Wenham, I hear she has found out a way to get plenty of money while she is in prison. She says she was prosecuted out of spite, only because she went to the Dissenting Meetings: and by this means, she gets contributions from the party: and of a wicked old witch, is in a sudden become a precious saint. This story puts me upon enquiring of Mr Gardiner whether she had ever been counted a Dissenter, and he declared that he never before heard that she us'd to go to any place of divine worship, and that he never took her to be of any religion at all; however, we are very willing to part with her, and wish the fanaticks much joy of their new Convert. I shall only take notice of one thing more to the Reader, viz., to assure him that neither Mr Gardiner nor Mr Strutt had any Hand in writing this Narrative of the Proceedings against Jane Wenham, altho' they are both Witnesses to the Truth of it; so that some Gentlemen (who in Justice and Gratitude, as well as good Manners, ought to have held their tongues) might as well have spar'd their personal Reflections.

However, he saved his real vitriol for later in the tract:

> As for the Character of Jane Wenham, I would not foul my Paper with it, were it not industriously reported by some People that know nothing of

her, only to discredit a Story, they are unwilling to believe that she is a very good Woman. If a continued Course of Idleness and Thievery, for many Years together, if the Character of a Whore, and the Practice of Common Swearing and Cursing will denominate a good Woman, we are willing to allow Jane Wenham to be one... the Truth of the Business is, that her nearest Relations think she deserves to die, and on other Accounts than Witchcraft.

Bragge's booklet contains an appendix containing 'an Account of the Sufferings of Anne Street, by the Witchcraft of Jane Wenham.' The connection between Anne Street and Anne Thorn is unclear. According to Bragge, on Sunday, 17 February, Street was struck speechless. Convulsions followed, during which strange noises were heard. She felt the urge to run from the house. The following day she attempted suicide, and suffered further convulsions. She said that she had seen the Wenham-faced cat, which told her to take her own life.

Bragge's account finishes with the text of a certificate of a surgeon, William Green, who stated that he set Anne Thorn's knee on Monday, 11 February and Wednesday, 13 February. She was, he said, lame and could not walk, much less run.

Bragge's satisfaction with the verdict was short-lived. Powell's appeal on Jane's behalf was successful, and she was pardoned. Return to Walkern was not an option open to the convicted witch; a home[13] was therefore found for her on the estate of Colonel Plumer of Gilston.[14]

Meanwhile the war of words hotted up. Bragge's pamphlet went into five editions, four of them within a month. It was followed by 'Witchcraft Farther Display'd,' also by Bragge. Refutations followed, then counter refutations. Advertisements appeared in the press; the *Protestant Post-Boy*, for example, carried the following items:

24-27 May 1712
Just Publish'd, the 4th Edition in two Parts, of
A Full and Impartial Account of the Trial and Proceedings against Jane Wenham of Walkerne in Hertfordshire, was found Guilty of Witchcraft, and receiv'd Sentence of Death for the same by Mr. Just. Powell, at Hertford Assizes, March 4. 1711-12. The Second Part containing an Account of the Witchcraft practis'd by the said Jane Wenham since her Condemnation, and the deplorable Condition in which the two poor Maids still remain: With an Answer to the most general Objections against the Being and Power [of] Witches; and some Remarks upon the Case of Jane Wenham, in particular. To which are added, The Tryals of Florence Newton, a famous Irish Witch, Anno 1661. and of two Witches, who were condemn'd at St Edmunds-Bury Assizes, by Sir Matt Hale, and executed Ann. 1664. Printed for E. Curl at

the Dial and Bible against St. Dunstan's Church in Fleet-Street, and sold by B. Berington at Essex-Stret End in the Strand. Price 1s or 6d each.[15]

24-27 May 1712

The Belief of Witchcraft vindicated: Proving, from Scripture, there have been Witches; and from Reason, that there may be Such still. In Answer to a late Pamphlet, Intituled, The Impossibility of Witchcraft; plainly proving, from Scripture and Reason, That there never was a Witch, &c. By G.R.A.M. Printed for J. Baker, at the Black-Boy in Pater-noster row. price 6d.

31 May-7 June 1712
This Day is Publish'd

The Impossibility of Witchcraft further Demonstrated. Both from Scripture and Reason, wherein several Texts of Scripture relating to Witches are prov'd to be falsly Translated, with some Cursory Remarks on two trifling Pamphlets in Defence of the Existence of Witches. By the Author of the Impossibility of Witchcraft, &c. Sold by J. Baker at the Black-Boy in Pater-Noster-Row, Price 6d. Where may be had the Tryal of the Hertfordshire Witch, and all the other Tracts for and against Witchcraft, at Six Pence each.[16]

Jane lived on in Gilston for some years, where Francis Hutchinson visited her. In his Historical Essay Concerning Witchcraft he said:

> I will take leave to add, That as I have had the Curiosity to see the good Woman her self, I have very great Assurance that she is a pious sober Woman. She is so far from being unable to say the Lord's-Prayer, that she would make me hear her say both Lord's-Prayer and Creed, and other very good Prayers besides; and she spake them with an undissembled Devotion, tho' with such little Errors of Expression, as those that cannot read are subject to. I verily believe, that there is no one that reads this, but may think in their own Minds, that such a Storm as she met with, might have fallen upon them, if it had been their Misfortune to have been poor, and to have met with such Accidents as she did, in such a barbarous Parish as she lived in.[17]

On Colonel Plumer's death Jane moved to a cottage on the Cowper estate at Hertingfordbury. She died on 11 January 1730, and was buried at Hertingfordbury churchyard.

According to the diary of Lady Sarah Cowper, representations to Queen Anne for Jane's pardon were made jointly by Mr Justice Powell, Colonel Plumer and Earl Cowper. Lady Cowper went on to say that Jane Wenham claimed that the main evidence against her was the result of malice, because she refused to bestow her favours upon that person. A note in *The*

Gentleman's Magazine[18] suggests that the person referred to was none other than Francis Bragge.

On Jane's death, Mr Squire, the curate of Hertingfordbury, preached a sermon referring to her tribulations. The church was full and the congregation silent and respectful.

The Impossibility Of Witchcraft...

This anonymous pamphlet seeks to demonstrate that witchcraft is non-existent, and goes to considerable length in proving so by reference to the scriptures and to classical authorities. A few extracts will give its flavour:

> UPON the repeated Solicitations of many Letters from my Correspondents, who have approv'd of the following Papers, and been urgent for Publishing them together in one Pamphlet for the General Good, they make their Appearance after this Manner. But because some have been pleas'd to observe, That it is a very odd Thing that our Laws Impower Judges to put People to Death For Witchcraft, if there is no such Thing as a Witch in the World; and others affirm, That the Records of Justice are full of Instances, in all Ages, of the Truth of Witchcraft, which, in their Opinion, amounts to a Demonstration. I shall, for the Satisfaction of the First, have Recourse to such Laws as have been Enacted here in England concerning it, as also those that have been made in Foreign Countries; and to quiet the Minds of the last, shew them how far off their Surmises are from any Thing that bears the Face of Reality.
>
> I... shall Content my self, with bringing some Arguments to prove in the first Place, That this strange Notion of Witchcraft, has its Foundation in Heathen Fables. Secondly, I shall take upon me to affirm, That it has been improv'd by Papal Inquisitous for the sake of Private Interest. Thirdly, I shall prove, That there is no such Thing, as a Witch in Scripture. Fourthly, I shall endeavour to make appear, There is no such thing as a Witch at all; and produce several Arguments against the Affirmers of Witchcraft. Fifthly, I shall answer other Arguments to the contrary. Sixthly and Lastly, I shall shew by what means this Opinion of Witchcraft came into the World.
>
> ...our Translators of the Bible, in the Eighteenth Chapter of Deuteronomy, call a Conjecturer an Enchanter, which why they should, I cannot at all imagine, there being not the least Hint of such a Signification in the Hebrew Word Mankesh, which is far better render'd in the old Translation, a Regarder of the Flying of Fowls; for that is Truth, tho' it be not all the Truth, the Flight of Fowls being but One way of Many, which Conjecturers made use of. A Second Mistake of our Translators, in the same Chapter, is, their calling a Miracle-monger a Witch: The Hebrew

Word is Mickshaph, which the Septuagint renders by the Greek word pharmakos, meaning an Impostor, not a Poisoner. For it is Ridiculous to think, that Pharaoh's Magicians, Jezabel the Queen, and King Manasses did exercise the Art of Poisoning. Thus in the Eighteenth Chapter of the Revelations, and the Twenty third Verse, the Word pharmakeiai, is neither taken for Witchcraft or Poisons, but for Impostures, tho' our Translations have render'd it Witchcraft.

This is an attack on the belief in witchcraft as a whole, not any one case, and there is no detail of the Wenham case; apart from the title, the only reference to Wenham is as follows:

...The Discourse of the Town having been very much taken up for some Days past, with a Trifling pamphlet,[19] in Vindication of the Tryal of one Jane Wenham, a Reputed Witch, whom that Enemy to Superstition, the very Worshipful Sir Henry Chauncy, gravely Committed, without Laughing, to Hertford Goal; where she was Try'd and found Guilty (against the Judge's Will) of Conversing with the Devil in the shape of a Cat, making a Maid that could not Walk without Leading, leap over a Five-Bar Gate, and run as swift as a Grey-hound, with several other Incredibles...

A Full Confutation Of Witchcraft: More Particularly Of The Depositions Against Jane Wenham...

This pamphlet attacks Bragge by means of logic. Each aspect of the case is considered, and Bragge's interpretation refuted. Here are several extracts:

...I shall... directly fall upon examining the Absurdity and Inconsistency of the late Depositions against Jane Wenham. 2dly, Shew that all our Proofs of Witchcraft, are very fallacious, and consequently ought never to extend to Life. And in the last place, That the pretended Exorcisms practised on Anne Thorn, are meer spiritual Juggles, and the very Spirit of Priest-craft.

...I pass by a Hurdle of Follies, much of the same Nature, till Jane Wenham is brought to Anne Thorn, who long'd to satiate her self with her Blood: Accordingly Jane Wenham comes to her, and Anne Thorn's Colour and Speech returns, and she scratches Jane Wenham's Forehead, but could fetch no Blood, which occasioned a very sage Remark. Now, who but a pack of Idiots, could have expected a Torrent of Blood, or indeed but a few Drops, from a shrivell'd Old Forehead, which, if squeez'd and collected, would not yield half an Ounce? and even in its most florid State, is but a dry Muscle, and the Vein a rowling one, not easily to be launch'd by a Finger-Nail.

After this, we find Jane Wenham submitting to be search'd, and willing to undergo all those Trials that never fail of discovering a Witch, according to the Country Probations; but this we find pass'd by as unnecessary at that time, but afterwards try'd to no purpose; tho' if any of those Persons concern'd in her Arraignment, had from their Souls believ'd her as they represented her, I am apt to believe, they would have been likewise satisfied in that Point, as well as given to other ridiculous Notions and Experiments, as burning the Bundle of Sticks, and the Pin, and the Feathers, &c. But now comes on the famous Trial of Skill, about repeating the Lord's-Prayer. The Reverend Mr. Strut, the chief Champion in the Lists, and his Fellow Labourer Mrs. Gardiner, against a poor ignorant Old Woman. Impar congressus: And great Stress is laid upon her repeating, 'Lead us not into Temptation,' with two Negatives. Now I would venture a small Wager upon it, take England round, and there are 3 Parts in 4 of the Country People pronounce that Sentence generally after this manner. But not putting this infallible Touch-stone upon so uncertain an Issue, as coming from the Mouth of a Reverend Divine; It may be worth the while to enquire, whether too many of the Auditors were not very curious in watching every Lapse of her Tongue, or preventing her Repetition of those Words, with too many impertinent Questions, or alarming her with the suppos'd Impossibility of repeating them. But drawing off from Conjectures, I would fain know how the false Pronunciation of that Sentence particularly, came to be the Criterion of a Witch; I think none of our Rubricks enjoin it as a specifick Trial, and I hope, no learned Divine has borrow'd it either from a Popish Legend, or found it amongst some Country Receipts for a Strain, a Quaking-Pudding, or a Cut Finger: No, we cannot think so meanly of any Branch of the sacred Body. Then let's come a little closer to the Point, and try it by dint of Reason. It would be some Satisfaction to know, why a Witch, &c. as the Reverend call poor old Jane, should boggle at one Sentence more than another. The Reason assign'd, I presume, is, that they being conscious of running voluntarily into Temptation, have not the Face to pray that God would prevent them from falling into it; whereby the Reverend allow their Witch some Grace. But pray then, with what Front can such a Creature say, Our Father, &c. when she has renounc'd God, and resign'd her self up to the Devil by Contract? How can she say, 'Thy Will be done,' when she is continually employ'd in the Devil's Service? In fine, How can she pray, 'Thy Kingdom come', or for the second Coming of Christ to Judgment, when she must expect by that Judgment to be irreversibly damn'd?

...In the next place, we meet with an enchanting Pin, which young Chauncy takes out of Jane Wenham's Hand, and pricks her with, and at last fetches out a Watry Serum; by which, I presume, they mean a Serous Blood. And truly, no more could be expected from a Woman advanc'd in Years, who liv'd low, and perhaps might have some other reason for such a Scarcity of florid Blood.

...After this, these Witch-hunters make use of an infallible Secret of proving Jane Wenham a Witch, by putting some of Anne Thorn's Urine into a Stone Bottle, tying the Cork down, and setting it over the Fire. I presume this Experiment, was made at the Instigation of Mrs. Gardiner, who was the prime She-Undertaker in this great Affair. If the Clergy were concern'd with the Maid's Urine, they would oblige the World with giving them a Rationale of its working such surprising Effects.

...Passing by the two sensless Depositions of Isaiah Wright, and Thomas Harvey, we are next presented with an enchanted Pillow, with a great many Cakes of small Feathers; which, how great a Wonder soever the Priests made of it, is no surprize to the Upholsterers, who meet with such Prodigies every Day, in the ordinary Course of Business. As to the Maids being better after the burning the Feathers, it's no wonder, People in Anne Thorn's Condition being always reliev'd by the Smell of such Volatiles.

...If any Mischief befals a Person, or his Family, after the passionate, but impotent threats of an Old Woman, it's a sure Argument of her being a Witch; as if the Muttering of a few Words should conceal in them the occult Malignity of an immediate Poison, or that a Wish should be able to infect Cattle with the Murrain, or that God, whose Omnipotence but very rarely transcends the Laws of Nature, should allow them to be violated continually, to oblige a petulant peevish old Woman, and the Devil be still at her Devotion.

...A learned Man at Paris was accus'd of Magick, for printing a Commentary on the Tenth Book of Euclid; and a Norman Gentleman observing from the Barometer, that it would not be long be fore it rain'd, got his Hay mow'd whilst the fine Weather lasted, which made the Country People report, he held a Correspondence with the Devil. The Water Experiment to try Witches, is the most fallacious of any, so is that of Marks about the Body: A Mole or Wart, or any Excrescency, passing current for the Stamp of the Devil. It would be endless to recount the several idle Tokens the Country People have of Witchcraft, and not one of them with the least Shadow of Reason.

...Before we take our leave of this Subject, we must examine a little into this Exorcism by Prayer... I fear our modern Exorcists will find as little Credit amongst the Judicious, especially if all the Exorcisms are perform'd like that upon Anne Thorn. Here is a poor Maid Epileptick, Hysterical, Lunatick by turns: The Priest comes and prays by her in one of her Fits, which lasts more or less, according to the Disposition of her Animal Spirits. The Fit goes off in its due Course, and this is call'd an Exorcism. I do say, any one that sprinkles Water in a Person's Face that's going to swoon, has a better Claim to an Exorcist, than these. I thought in all true Exorcisms, the Evil Spirit was cast out and entirely banish'd, and left the Patient with some Struggles; still we find him returning into this Exorcis'd Person at Pleasure: But perhaps it was not the same Devil, and 'twere more for the Priests Credit to give out it was a fresh Demon every time: So having a Legion upon their Hands, they would have the Reputation of the greatest Kill-Devils in the Kingdom…

The Case of the Hertfordshire Witchcraft Consider'd. Being an Examination of a book entitl'd, A Full and Impartial Account of the Discovery of Sorcery and Witchcraft…

This substantial refutation is another 'logical' one. The author is clearly a local man, and acquainted with some of the people involved in the case. His identity is however a mystery.

He says that, for Jane Wenham to be considered guilty, there are two things to be proven: (a) did anything preternatural actually happen? and (b) if it did, was Jane Wenham responsible? Each aspect of Bragge's pamphlet is considered in turn. The book runs to eighty-six pages.

> Mr Bragge… has at the end of his Narrative given us a Certificate from one William Green, whom he is pleased to call the Surgeon that set Anne Thorn's Knee, which tells us that it was really out of Joint. But who is this William Green who attests this? By Mr. Bragge's calling him a Surgeon, the Reader may perhaps look upon as some considerable Body; that he has served Seven Years at St. Thomas's Hospital, and understands what he pretends to very well. But it is fit he should be informed here, that he is an ignorant Pretender; one who does not understand the Business of Chirurgery half so well as he does Farming, which I am told is his proper Employment…
>
> But there is one Circumstance in this very Story… that Anne Thorn's Knee was not really out of Joynt. Mr. Green tells us, that after he had set this Knee, Anne Thorn was very lame, and not able to walk: and yet Mrs. Gardiner, by the very next Morning, could think her well enough to go to a Neighbour's House to fetch Pease.

Following the incident when Anne Thorn was found in the kitchen, semi-clad, with her bunch of sticks,

> ...here comes a very strange and surprising Accident. We will burn the Old Witch, cries Mrs. Gardiner, and then throws Sticks, Pin and all into the Fire. Immediately in comes Jane Wenham with a Lye in her Mouth... how does Mother Wenham's coming in with a Lye in her Mouth, prove her to be a Witch?
> ... a little after we are told there were more Sticks burnt upon the same Occasion, and yet no Jane Wenham appeared...

When the author reaches the tales of the supernatural cats, he has this to say:

> ...but hark! I am call'd away by a Legion of foul Monsters like Cats: They speak to me; they tell me I must go... They must be the Imps of Mother Wenham, their Features do so exactly resemble her! 'Tis certainly so! They are armed too with Knives and Razors, and tempt me to stab myself, or to cut my Throat. Oh where is Mr. Chauncy, that Scourge of Devils, and of Cats! Look, look, Sir! That, that's Mother Wenham; kill her, and the Charm is broke! But wither am I going? Let me recover my Senses a little, lest I grow mad too, and furnish Mr. Bragge with materials for a Second Narrative. To be serious then: This Story of the Cats is so ridiculous, that methinks I know not who to pity most, whether the poor distracted Creature, or Mr. Bragge, who has thought it worth his while to insist upon it, as a Proof of his pretended Witchcraft.

Several of the witnesses who testified concerning the cats first mentioned them in court, which seems suspicious; even more so is the fact that two of them were

> Those very Fellows that were Married to the two Wenches [Anne Thorn and Anne Street] some time after.

Even if the cats did have Jane Wenham's face, it does not make her a witch – surely the Devil can take on any form he pleases, innocent or guilty.

> The story of the Bottle of Urine... I shall leave to be answer'd by those more merrily disposed than I am at present. All that I shall remark concerning it is, that if they had a mind to have made the World believe, that there was anything wonderful in this Experiment, they ought to have repeated it several times, and seen whether or no the same Effect always followed.

The matter of the cakes of feathers is of concern: the material holding the feathers together

Mr Bragge tells us puts him in mind of that Oyntment made of dead Men's flesh, which Mr. Glanville mentions as often used by Witches.[20]

The author of this pamphlet urges Bragge to look for an explanation for the adhesion of the feathers to one another in 'Magnetism or Electricity.'

The question of Anne Thorn's fits comes in for a good deal of attention. Not all of them were necessarily feigned; but until a means to distinguish between the real and the supposed fits can be found, 'Disputes about Anne Thorne's being recovered out of her Fits by Prayer will be to very little purpose...' In the pamphlet author's view, 'there is but one Fit in this whole Book... but what may, for anything Mr. Bragge has told us to the contrary, to be pure Cheat and Imposture...' The fit in question 'must be supposed to be some real Distemper...'.

The author next addresses Jane's confession. The Reverends Gardiner and Strutt are 'both of them Men of too much Integrity, to attempt by any outward violence to make her confess ... Mr Strutt told me himself not long ago, that when endeavouring to bring Jane Wenham to a Confession he did tell her, that he would prevail upon Sir Henry Chauncy, if he could, to defer putting the Mittimus[21] into execution...' thus putting pressure on Wenham to confess.[22] Equally, it may be that after spending many years as a pariah in Walkern, suspected of being a witch, she might become 'sick of the World, and desirous of being removed out of reach of these Misfortunes...'

Regarding the scratching of Jane Wenham, and her failure to bleed, we are told that the author has seen many similar examples, and does not think they were all witches. Perhaps the most interesting (and damning) revelation is in regard to Anne Thorn's reliability as a witness:

> That as to her character, whatever it might have been formerly, it will now be of little Service to her, in securing her from the Imputation of Ill Designs, which may be charged upon her. Mrs. Gardiner, who at that time seem'd so fully persuaded of her Innocency, and who all along spoke so favourably of her, has by this time so much Reason to alter her Opinion, that I dare believe, she will not now say any thing in her Defence. Her Fidelity, which is the only Virtue which is able to support and give Credit to the greatest Part of these Relations, is now entirely lost, and she is at last found to be so arrant a Lyar, that there is no manner of heed to be given to anything she says. I do not by this mean, that she is a known and common Lyar; that, I must confess, is more than I can affirm: But thus much I can say, and that upon the Credit of one whom I can rely on, and who heard it from Mrs. Gardiner's own Mouth; That she has (since these Accidents have happen'd) caught her in so many gross and palpable Lies, that she has now entirely laid aside that good Opinion that she once entertained of her.

What really happened in Walkern in 1711-12 can only be speculated upon. Was Anne Thorn acting on her own initiative? Were her symptoms genuinely felt, or were they a sham? It is possible that she was no more than an attention seeker. Arthur Chauncy and the Reverends Gardiner, Strutt and Bragge, all educated men, were apparently convinced of the reality of the bewitchment, unless the story of Jane's rejection of Bragge and his subsequent enmity is true; even then it seems unlikely that the other two clergymen would lie for him in order to get petty revenge.

Anne Street's behaviour smacks of imitation. Anne Thorn was receiving a great deal of attention from important people; what is more natural than that Anne Street should imitate her behaviour? That she did not figure more significantly in the case suggests that some people might have been suspicious.

As a postscript, in December 1968 a letter appeared in *Hertfordshire Countryside* in response to a short article on Jane Wenham in the previous issue:

> Jane Wenham was by no means a misjudged woman. Long before her trial she was regarded in her area as a woman possessed of certain 'powers,' and evidence of a quite startling nature was produced that she used these 'powers' at will... Although Jane was later reprieved, the initial evidence was strong against her, and it is an indication of complete lack of sympathy with the past to maintain after all these years that she was undoubtedly innocent, the victim of cruel superstition and unfriendly neighbours.

Both the original article and the subsequent letter contain several errors of fact; but it is interesting that the writer of the latter apparently felt that Wenham was guilty, if not of the offence with which she was charged, certainly of witchcraft.

9

UNOFFICIAL ACTION

We have already noted that those fearing themselves bewitched sometimes took matters into their own hands. Occasionally such action landed them in trouble.[1]

Scoring Above the Breath

1652/6 Information, Hertford Sessions Rolls: Joane Whillocke
Information of Joane Whillocke, that Mary, wife of George Asser, made an assault upon her, scratching her face and 'drawing blood upon her,' and that George Asser threw a kettle of hot water at her, Mary Asser also saying that the deponent had but one eye, and that she would pull out the other. Further documents depose that the face of Joane Whillocke was 'all over with gore blood.'

The witchcraft connection in this case is speculative, but the nature of the injuries sustained may indicate a likely attempt to break a bewitchment. The exact year is unknown, as the undated documents are bound in a volume that covers a five-year period. The outcome of any prosecution is also a mystery.

1661 Depositions, Hertford Sessions Rolls: Goodwife Bailey
Elizabeth Godfrey, wife of Richard, of Broxbourne, deposed that on 21 January 'her girl came in to her crying and told her that Andrew Camp was dragging Goodwife Bailey out of her house,' and that his wife was scratching her as she went out. When they were asked why they were attacking the old woman, they said that she had bewitched their child. Elizabeth told them that if she were guilty, the law would punish her, upon which they released her. Goodwife Bailey, a widow, deposed that

Andrew Camp had 'dragged her out of her own house into the street over a stone that bruised her and kneeled upon her breast, and when he had her so under him his wife came and clawed her by the face and said she would claw her eyes out of her head, and her tongue out of her mouth, and called her a d——d w- old witch.' Had it not been for the interference of Elizabeth Godfrey she feared that the Camps would have done her more harm.

Like the assault on Joan Whillocke, the outcome of the case is unknown.

Slander

1669 Hertford Sessions Rolls: John Allen
An accusation of witchcraft was a serious matter. The Reverend Knightly of Guilden Morden proceeded against Elizabeth Lane of Walsworth; and Jane Wenham went to Sir Henry Chauncy when she was abused by John Chapman. Here is a third example:

> Indictment of John Allen the Elder, of Stondon, for using false and scandalous words about Joan, wife of Richard Mills, to wit 'Jone Mills is a witch and did bewitch the ale of Matthew Parnell,' by means of which words he has taken away her good name and fame.

Once again, the outcome is unknown.

Swimming

1700: Amey Townsend
In some instances unofficial action led to tragic consequences. *The Post-Boy* of Thursday the 18 January 1700 carried the following item:

> London, January 18-
> We are inform'd from St Albans, that one Amey Townsend, who lay under the misfortune of being a reputed witch, about ten days since going by a watchmaker's shop in that corporation, ask'd the price of a watch; the apprentice snapt her up short, saying, What's that to you, forty shillings is more than you are worth; upon which 'twas observ'd, that she only pointed at the boy with her finger, and trudg'd about her business. Her character struck the lad with such frightful apprehensions of danger from the reputed hagg, that next day he fell sick in good earnest; keeps his bed, cries out, Amey Townsend had bewitch'd him, and he should dye, if he did not

immediately fetch blood from her. The poor old creature was brought in the lad's chamber, he, in a great fury, leaps out of bed, sets his nails in her face, made her bleed, and the boy recovered, while the poor wretch was turn'd out of doors to seek her remedy for being severely scratch'd. The mob learnedly debating this affair, concluded that the boy was bewitch'd by Townsend, and they in justice ought to inflict the punishment by making an experiment. Immediately they seize the poor soul, force her into a river near the town, and drag her so often through it, till she was like to expire by their barbarous usage: which some of the brutes perceiving, had the humanity to put her into a warm bed, where she lay in a hopeful way of recovery. Some of the more judicious inhabitants discanting upon her being duck'd, averr'd they saw her swim, ergo, she was a witch, and scandalous to that corporation. This further enrages the mob (who always are bewitch'd and tumultuous), they assemble again in a body, haul the miserable creature out of her bed, and setting her in a chair, hoist her upon their shoulders, and carried her about the town in triumph, shouting and bauling out a Townsend, a Townsend: after which they had her before a justice of the peace, who to appease them, sent her to the town-house, where she died in two hours. And we hear that several are taken up to answer it at the next assizes for Hertfordshire, where no question but some of them will decently swing for it.

I have been unable to trace any further reference to Amey Townsend. The details in the account sound plausible however, and it may well be true.

1751: Ruth and John Osborne[2]

The case of the Osbornes is one of the best-known examples of unofficial action in England. The following account is drawn from several sources: reports in *The Gentleman's Magazine*,[3] two contemporary pamphlets, *The Tryal of Thomas Colley*, and *The Remarkable Confession and Last Dying Words of Thomas Colley*, and documents held at Hertfordshire Archives and Local Studies (formerly Hertford Record Office).

At the time of the events described, John Osborne was fifty-six years of age, thirteen years younger than his wife, Ruth. The lived in the Long Marston area, close to the border between Hertfordshire and Buckinghamshire. Other than that they seem to have been poor, little more is known of them.

John Butterfield was a dairy farmer from whom, 'a little before the defeat of the Scotch in the late rebellion,'[4] Ruth Osborne attempted to beg some buttermilk; he refused her in no uncertain terms. He had, he said, 'not enough for his hogs.' Ruth walked off, muttering that 'the Pretender would have him and his hogs too.' Her remarks would later be recalled.

Not long afterwards, several of Butterfield's calves fell ill, 'upon which some ignorant people, who had been told the story of the buttermilk, gave out that they were bewitched by old mother Osborne.'

Further misfortune followed. Butterfield suffered a recurrence of fits that had plagued him on and off for many years. He left his dairy, and took a public house, the Black Horse, near Gubblecote Brook. He became convinced that Ruth Osborne had bewitched him, and was advised to consult with a cunning woman from Northamptonshire. She confirmed the diagnosis. She ordered that six armed men should watch his house day and night, and gave them protective charms to hang round their necks. Rather embarrassingly, nothing happened.

At about this time, one Daniel Nicholls, of Long Marston, arranged for the following notice to be cried by William Dell, the town crier, at Hemel Hempstead: 'This is to give notice That on Monday next there is to be at Long Marcon in the Parish of Tring towo Hill Desposed porsons to be Ducked by the neighbours Cosent'[5]

Dell complied, and the notice was duly cried on Thursday, 18 April 1751. The same information was broadcast at Winslow and Leighton Buzzard. On Saturday 20 April John Osborne was warned of the impending 'trial' and he and his wife sought refuge in the workhouse at Tring. The master of the workhouse, John Thompkins, did not believe that their safety could be guaranteed in his establishment, and at about three o'clock on the morning of Monday 22 April he had them taken to the vestry of the church.

Thompkins was right in his assessment of the security of his institution. The crowd that assembled that morning was estimated by some to be between 4,000 and 5,000 strong. The first port of call was the Osbornes' house, and not finding the elderly couple there, they moved on to the workhouse, arriving at between eleven o'clock and midday. They demanded that the Osbornes be handed over. Such was the press that the garden fence was damaged and one wall of the building collapsed, injuring several people. The local constable, Sebastian Green, a blacksmith, told the crowd to desist, but they threatened his life, and he could do nothing to control them.

On being told that their victims were not there, the ringleaders insisted on searching the building. They did so, but without success. Presumably believing in the power of witches to transform themselves into smaller creatures, they even searched spaces where the Osbornes could not possibly be, including the salt box.

The crowd threatened to drown Thompkins, and to set fire to the town – they even gathered straw to carry out the threat. Thompkins gave way, and told them that the Osbornes were in the church. The crowd

This depiction of witches being 'swum' is purported to represent the Osbornes. The costumes are of the right period, but the origin of the picture is unknown; this copy came from Witchcraft in Hertfordshire *by Lewis Evans, an item that appeared in* Bygone Hertfordshire, *William Andrews & Co, 1898.*

dragged their victims from the building to Marston Mere. Henry Archer later testified that Ruth was beaten on the way, and that she cried out 'for God's sake don't murder me!' The pair were partially stripped and tied in the prescribed manner – left thumb to right toe, and right thumb to left toe.

According to Robert Gregory, the ducking pool was artificially created by means of a dam. The water was some two feet deep. Thomas Colley, a chimney sweep, asked for volunteers to help him drag Ruth into the pond. Amongst those who responded were 'Doctor' William Umbles, of Leighton Buzzard, and a broom seller, Charles Young, alias Leigh, also known as 'Redbeard.' John Worcester of Tring said that a rope was tied to Ruth in such a manner that a man standing on the opposite bank could pull her through the pool. She was ducked several times, being pushed around with a pole, and then laid out on the bank whilst her husband was subjected to the same ordeal. In all, each of them was 'swum' three times. During the swimming, Colley stripped Ruth Osborne naked, and used his pole to hold her underwater.

According to some witnesses, the Osbornes were not only swum, but kicked and beaten again as well; Ruth 'got her head above the water and cried out and got hold of Colley's stick but he wrenched it from her...' Eventually they were laid on the bank, and it was clear that Ruth Osborne was dead. Colley meanwhile was moving amongst the crown collecting money, though from some all he received was abuse.

John Foster, the local surgeon, examined Ruth. He found no wounds that would have caused her death, and concluded that she had died 'by being suffocated with water and Mudd and suffering to lye on the cold ground for a considerable time.' One account says that John Osborne meanwhile was in a poor way. He was put to bed, but the barbarity was not done yet; Ruth's dead body was put into bed with him, and they were tied together.

Somewhat belatedly the authorities acted, though it is possible that their concern was as much the riotous assembly as the murder of Ruth Osborne.[6] The inquest on the body of Ruth Osborne was held at the Half Moon public house in Wilstone (see plate 12). A number of witnesses appeared, and a number of culprits identified. In addition to those already mentioned, Benjamin Price of Chesham, Francis Hopton of Ivinghoe, Henry Worcester of Pitstone and Richard Symmonds of Aldbury were accused of 'riotous and unlawful acts.' Later, John Eastoffe, alias East, John Walters, alias Waters, and John Mayor were accused of involvement in the damage to the workhouse.

Colley was indicted for murder, and locked up in Hertford Gaol. At the Summer Assizes, before Lord Chief Justice Lee, he was one of ten accused. The Grand Jury found a true Bill against only three: Umbles, Young and Colley; Umbles and Young had absconded however, and only

Colley was tried. Convicted of the wilful murder of Ruth Osborne, he was sentenced to death. Worcester was in custody, and warrants were issued for Price, Hopton, Symmonds, Eastoffe and Walters. The six were charged with 'Demolishing or beginning to Demolish any Dwelling House' under an Act passed in the first year of the reign of George I. The intention was to try them together at the next assizes, but it didn't happen; the whole affair was allowed to let slide.

It has been claimed in some accounts that Colley was executed at Hertford, but there is so much detail concerning his execution near the scene of his crime that the latter seems more likely. On 23 August 1751, Colley was taken from Hertford to St Albans. There had been rumours of an attempt to free the condemned man, and he was therefore escorted by seven officers and 108 men from the Oxford Blues. From there, at five o'clock the following morning, he was taken to Tring, where his wife and daughter were allowed a few moments with him. As the procession moved through the town, one of the troopers accidentally discharged his pistol, causing some alarm.

At about eleven o'clock Thomas Colley was hanged at Gubblecote Cross, though the people in the Marston Mere area petitioned against hanging him near their houses. According to *The Gentleman's Magazine*, 'many thousands stood at a distance to see him go, grumbling and muttering that it was a hard case to hang a man for destroying an old wicked woman that had done so much mischief by her witchcraft.'

Colley's body was left hanging in chains at Wilston Green as a warning to others, though that part of the sentence had been kept secret 'that the Sheriff may not be interrupted with too great a mob at the Erecting [of] the Gibbet and Suspending the Body therein.'[7]

At that time considerable effort was put into inducing condemned men to confess. The chaplains who attended them in their last days were particularly anxious that they should do so, in order that they unburden their souls to God (and perhaps to reassure the authorities that a miscarriage of justice had not taken place). The confession was frequently published as part of a pamphlet describing the crime.

The convicted man usually expressed penitence, and exhorted his readers to avoid the dreadful path he had trod. Colley's confession followed the same pattern. Hertfordshire Archives and Local Studies hold a document that might be the original document. The handwriting of the text does not match that of the signature, and the language is not that which one might expect from a chimney sweep. If it is the original, it seems likely that it was written for him. Whether he either knew or cared what he was signing we shall never know – it was 'Signed at Hertford augst the 23 1751,' the very day that the condemned man began his journey to the scaffold.

Good People I beseech you all to take Warning by an Unhappy Man's Suffering, that you be not deluded into so absurd and wicked a Conceit, as to believe that there are any such Beings upon Earth as Witches.

It was that Foolish and vain Imagination, heightened and inflamed by the strength of Liquor, which prompted me to be instrumental (with others as mad-brained as myself) in the horrid and barbarous Murther of Ruth Osborne, the Supposed Witch; for which I am now so deservedly to Suffer Death.

I am fully convinced of my former Error And with the Sincerity of a dying Man declare that I do not believe there is such a Thing as a Witch: and I pray God that None of you, through a contrary Persuasion, may hereafter be induced to think that you have a Right in any shape to persecute, much less endanger the Life of a Fellow-Creature.

I beg you all to pray to God to forgive me and to wash clean my polluted soul in the Blood of Jesus Christ my Saviour, and Redeemer.

So Exorteth you all the Dying.

(Signed at Hertford augst the 23rd 1751
by Thomas Colley, just after Receiving the Sacrament
In Presence of Edwd Bouchier Minister of All Saints
Robt Keep – Parish Clerk).   *Thomas Colley, of All Saints*

The Osborne case has raised some interesting queries about the motives for the ducking. There are several possibilities: the whole business was orchestrated by John Butterfield and his friends, and was intended to bring large numbers of customers into his public house, the Black Horse; Colley, Young, Umbles and others organised the ducking, partly for entertainment and partly to raise money from the crowd; the whole mob, including the ringleaders, genuinely believed they were doing the right thing, and that one or both of the Osbornes were witches.

Which motive is correct is a matter for speculation.

10

Appearances of the Devil

We have several alleged diabolic appearances in Hertfordshire. As in the case of possession, the historical interest lies in what the tales tell us about the period in question, rather than as a description of real events. With the possible exception of the first, they seem to be apocryphal stories, told for the moral benefit of the audience. In this respect, they hark back to the exemplars of the medieval church.

1648: The Devil in St Albans

I am uncertain as to whether the pamphlet recording the appearance of the Devil in St Albans in 1648 is written 'tongue in cheek'. There are in fact two tales in the pamphlet. I have included the full text.[1]

THE
Devill seen at St Albons
BEING A TRUE
RELATION
HOW
The Devill was seen there in a Cellar, in the likenesse of a Ram;
and how a Butcher came and cut his throat; and sold
some of it, and dressed the rest for
himselfe, inviting many to Supper, who eat of it.
Attested by divers Letters, of men of very good credit in the Towne.
Whereunto is added a Comment, for the better
understanding of the unlearned,
or ignorant.
Printed for confutation of those that beleeve there
are no such things as Spirits or Devils.
Sunt mala, at tu non meliora facis
Printed in the yeare, 1648.

THE WITCHES OF HERTFORDSHIRE

The description of that goodly Town St Albons, with the distance thereof from London

Saint Albons is a goodly Towne, scituate in the County of Hertford; and of distance from London (according to the compute of the ablest Carriers of that Roade) some twenty miles. This Town is very ancient, or as I may so say, a Borough Town, sending Burgomasters to the Parliament. It is likewise a Corporation, having yearly a Maior of Worship elected for the better administration of Justice. The Church belonging to this Towne is of a curious structure, and very large, famous for the tomb of Humphrey, called the good Duke of Glocester, sonne of King Henry the fourth, brother to King Henry the fifth, and uncle to King Henry the sixth, in whose raigne the said good Duke was murthered, and was buried in this Church of Saint Albons. This Duke leaving behind him the best monument, a good name, had his memory much reverenced, insomuch, that many (those being superstitious times) held him for a Saint. Now it fortuned that an old man, having been long impotent in his feet, could not be cured; but after he had spent all he had on Chirurgions and Doctors, was at last faine to be content with this unreasonable salve, You are past cure. This old man I say, after all this, yet despaired not, but calling to minde this good Duke of Glocester, he resolved to make him his particular Saint, and imposing unto himselfe a confidence, that by going to this good Dukes Tombe, and invoking him for help, that thereupon he should be cured.

The Maior

The Church

Tombe of Duke Humphrey

See Hollenshead, Martin, Stow, Speed and Shakspeare in the second part of Henry the Sixth

The Duke a Saint

Here begins the story of the old man, Shakspeare, ut supra

He makes the Duke his particular Saint

He goes to his Tombe

Infandum

This poore soule went unto the Tombe, rejoyceing as he went, with a conceit of being made whole; but (a thing not to be spoken) the old man no sooner offered up his hands in the Orrisons to the Duke, but the Duke sent downe such an Almes into his legs, that the old man went away frisking and skipping like a young colt.

Here begins the Devils story

Note Reader

But now, Reader, from the Tombe of Saint Humphrey, turne thee to the Bull at Saint Albons, which Inne is as famous as the Tombe wee spoke of, only Reader I pray thee observe, that these two memorable accidents should happen in the two most memorable places of the Towne; for who hath not heard of the Tombe of Saint Humphrey, and who hath not heard of the Bull at Saint Albons? but how the Devill appeared there in the likenesse of a Ramme, I shall now relate.

Description of the Bull at Saint Albons, with the commodities thereof

Description of the Cellar, where the Devill was seen

This Inne called the Bull at Saint Albons, hath not only good victuals of all sorts, as flesh, fish, and fowle, to entertaine travellers withall, but also good store of refreshing wine, viz. Sack, Claret, and white wine. This wine lieth in a large Cellar that is cut under ground, a great way from the house, and having no cealing but the earth, out of which it is taken. Now it fortuned that an old acquaintance of the Hoasts travelling that way, came to lodge with his good friend the Hoast on munday night last, being the 27. of November last past; the good joviall Innekeeper was very glad to see his ancient acquaintance, and as a testimony thereof, he commands one of his Drawers to goe downe, and pierce a fresh But of Sack that stood at the furthermost end of all the Cellar.

 The Drawer takes a candle in his hand, and very nimbly flits downe the staires, goes to the appointed vessell, and pierces it but whiles the wine was running into the pot, he casts his eyes aside, and saw a huge black thing like a Ramme, having glassie eyes, shag haire, wreathed hornes, and (which assured him it was the Devill) cloven feet. The Drawer stood so long amazed at this horrid apparition, that the pot overflowd even to the ground, at least a gallon, and the Drawer being so wise, as to take care for himselfe in the first place, for his better lightnesse, flings wine and pot away, and leaving the vessell running, with a strange alacrity mounts the staires, appearing to his Master and Mistris, and many other beholders, very pale, and distracted with some strange chance that had happened. At last his feare burst out into these words, Oh Master! the Devill is in the Cellar, and appeaed to me, and I was so frighted, that I left the vessell running, and came up as you see; the Hoast answers him with a box on the eare, which he felt, calling him faint-hearted rogue, and that it was nothing but feare which made him conceit such a thing: but the Hoasts wife saying, husband, though you venture your selfe with the Devill, yet, let us not lose our wine; the Hoast obeys his wife, and taking a candle, he valiantly descends the staires, running with all hast towards the further end of Cellar, to stop the vessell, the Devill with his hornes meets him full butt in the midst of the way, the Hoast not being used to see the Devil, knew not how to look on him, but casting himselfe backward, like an active tumbler, never left playing the Sommerset, till he mounted the staires: and shaking and quaking, swore that he had seen the fearfullest, ugliest Devill that ever he saw in his life, and that he should have all his wine, before he would venture to stop a drop of it. These outcries bring all the neighbors into the Inn, & amongst the rest a Butcher, worthily deemed, and taken to be the stoutest man, both of heart and hands, within the jurisdiction of the Maioraltie, he had broke two armes the last football playing, and woud knock down an Oxe with an Axe 7 pound lighter at the helme then any other could; briefly, he was the very George of Green of St Albons. The said Butcher manfully

The drawer goes downe into the cellar

He sees the Devill

Hereafter, for shame, let none deny that the Devill hath cloven feet

Note the policy of this Drawer in the extremity of his feare

The Hoast descends the staires, and after he had seen the Devill, sommersets them up again

Note that to Sommerset is to tosse heels over head, and to light on heeles again, the word is frequent amongst tumblers at this day

The Butcher with his indowments described

Note that the Sack run all this while of its own accord

looking on these affrighted ones, couragiously asked what was the matter, or what could make them so fearfull; the Hoast replys that the devill was in the Cellar, and had appeared to him and his man in the likenesse of a black Ram, telling him withall, how they had left a But of Sack running, and promising the Butcher, that if he would venter downe and stop the vessell, he would give him a gallon of the best Sack he had; the Butcher looking somewhat surly, as being angry they should make a doubt of his prowesse; snatches up a candle, and swears that he would fetch up the devill Ram, stick him, and quarter him, to make amends for the black Ram he had lately lost. Armed with this resolution, down he goes, and nothing regarding the devill, he goes first and stops the vessell, & suddenly turning himself about, he casts his angry eye upon the devill, and after he had looked so long, as to perceive how his hornes grew, he steps to the devill, and seiseth on his hornes with his approved hands. The cunning devil, knowing by instinct, that he could not prevaile against true valour, meek as a sheep, suffers himself to be dragged up the staires, the noise whereof makes all retire to their ground, at the furthermost end of the roome, but the Butcher no sooner come up with his infernall captive, but thus he speakes, Loe here is that fiend of darknesse, which shall dearly pay for frighting you, for I vow to manacle his feet, and carry him to my slaughter house, cut his throat, flea off his skin, & sell his flesh, & this by Lucifer his Prince, I sweare to performe. All applauded the Butcher, and the Hoast thanked him for saving his Sack. But the butcher intending to prosecute his revenge against the now silly quiet devill, hales him to his slaughter house, cuts his throat, fleas off his skin, sells all of him but a hinde quarter he had reserved for his owne supper, to which supper he invites many of his friends, who eate heartily of his flesh, and pickt his bones, whilst the Butchers story of this his atcheivment, together with his hoasts wine, made excellent sauce to this hellish foode, so that merrily downe it went the Devill and all, at which mirth I leave them.

Claudite jam Rivos, pueri sat prat a biberunt.

I might have inlarged this discourse with a querie, whether cuckolds go to hell or no, since it appears by this story, the devill himself hath hornes, but I affect brevity, especially when the question depends not on the thing related.

Curteous Reader, I thought good according to Brittanicus custom, to add a Comment to this my concise relation, this being (as most of the learned will avouch) of equall validitie with anything he ever writ.

Marginalia:

The Butcher goes downe into the Cellar

Note that none went downe without a candle

He stopt the vessell

He vanquisheth and bringeth up the Devill

The Butchers speech after he had brought up the Devill

Some incredulous people seeking to deceive the truth, impudently give it out, that the earth falling into the Cellar, a black Ram fell in therewith, which Ram the Butcher had lost the day before, *sed benigne lector utere sapientia tua*

That the Devill may, and hath often appeared, Read Frier Rush, Dr Faustus, Dr Lambe and that man of men, and glorie of the black art, the famous Lilly now living

APPEARANCES OF THE DEVIL 167

Here, the Devil is depicted as gullible and foolish. If a butcher is capable of killing and eating him, he does not appear to be much of a threat to anyone. The obvious explanation of the events (if they happened at all) is given in the side note: the ram discovered in the cellar was that lost by the butcher, and it came to be in the cellar by falling through the earth 'cealing.' Nonetheless the pamphlet emphasises several points worthy of note: The Devil was believed to have horns and cloven feet. By the mid-seventeenth century, at least for some, he has become a suitable target for fun, and the idea of miraculous cures at the tombs of saints had not disappeared, more than 100 years after the Reformation.

1678: The Mowing Devil

The tale told in the Mowing Devil has two morals: it condemns greed, and demonstrates that frivolous use of the name of Satan is a dangerous exercise. It appeared in two editions, one with a woodcut of the Devil's activities and one without.

THE MOWING-DEVIL:
OR, STRANGE NEWS OUT OF
HARTFORD-SHIRE.

Being a True Relation of a Farmer, who Bargaining with a Poor Mower, about the Cutting down Three Half Acres of Oats; upon the Mower's asking too much, the Farmer swore That the Devil should Mow it rather than He. And so it fell out, that very Night, the Crop of Oat shew'd as if

The Mowing Devil at work, from the original pamphlet. This illustration has been used in recent years as evidence of an early crop circle. However in the pamphlet the oats in question are described as having been cut down by the devil, not flattened as in modern crop circles.

it had been all of a Flame; but next Morning appear'd so neatly mow'd by the Devil or some Infernal Spirit, that no Mortal Man was able to do the like.

Also, How the said Oats ly now in the Field, and the Owner has not Power to fetch them away.

Licensed, August 22nd, 1678.

Men may dally with Heaven, and criticise on Hell, as Wittily as they please, but that there are really such places, the wise Dispensations of Almighty Providence does not cease continually to evince. For if by those accumulated circumstances which generally induce us to the belief of anything beyond our senses, we may reasonably gather that there are certainly such things as DEVILS, we must necessarily conclude that these Devils have a Hell; and as there is a Hell, there must be a Heaven, and consequently a GOD; and so all the Duties of Christian Religion as indispensable subsequents necessarily follow.

The first of which Propositions, this ensuing Narrative does not a little help to Confirm.

For no longer ago, than within the compass of the present Month of August, there hapned so unusual an Accident in Hart-fordshire, as is not only the general Discourse, and Admiration of the whole Country; but may for its Rarity challenge any other event, which has for these many years been Produc't in any other Country whatsoever. The story thus.

In the said County lives a Rich industrious Farmer, who perceiving a small Crop of his (of about three Half-Acres of Land which he had Sowed with Oats) to be Ripe and at for Gathering, sent to a poor Neighbour whom he knew worked commonly in the Summer-time at Harvest Labor, to agree with him about Mowing or Cutting the said Oats down. The poor Man as it behoov'd Him endeavour'd to sell the Sweat of his Brows and Marrow of his Bones at as dear a Rate as reasonably he might, and therefore askt a good round Price for his Labour, which the, Farmer taking some exception at, bid him much more under the usual Rate than the poor Man askt for it; So that some sharp Words had past, when the Farmer told him he would Discourse with him no more about it. Whereupon the honest Mower recollecting with himself, that if he undertook not that little Spot of Work, he might thereby lose much more business which the Farmer had to imploy him in beside, ran after him, and told him, that, rather than displease him, he would do it at what rate in Reason he pleas'd; and as an instance of his willingness to serve him, propos'd to him a lower price, than he had Mowed for any time this Year before. The irretated Farmer with a stern look, and hasty gesture, told the poor man That the Devil himself should Mow his Oats before he should have anything to do with them, and upon this went his way, and left the sorrowful Yeoman, not a little troubled that he had disoblig'd one in whose Power it lay to do him many kindnesses.

But, however, in the happy series of an interrupted prosperity, we may strut and plume our selves over the miserable Indigencies of our necessitated Neighbours, yet there is a just God above, who weighs us not by our Bags, nor measures us by our Coffers; but looks upon all men indifferently, as the common Sons of Adam; so that he who carefully Officiates that Rank or Station wherein the Almighty has plac't him, tho' but a mean one, is truly more worthy the Estimation of all men, than he who is prefer'd to superior dignities, and abuses them: And what greater abuse than the contempt of Men below him: the relief of whose common necessities is none of the least Conditions whereby he holds all his Good things; which when that Tenure is forfeited by his default, he may justly expect some Judgment to ensue; or else that those riches wherby he prizes himself so extravagantly may shortly be taken from him.

We will not attempt to fathom the cause, or reason of, Preternatural events; but certain we are, as the most Credible and General Relation can inform us, that that same night this poor Mower and Farmer parted, his Field of Oats was publickly beheld by several Passengers to be all of a Flame, and so continued for some space, to the great consternation of those that beheld it.

Which strange news being by several carried to the Farmer next morning, could not but give him a great curiosity to go and see what was become of his Crop of Oats, which he could not imagine, but what was totally devour'd by those ravenous Flames which were observed to be so long resident on his Acre and half of Ground.

Certainly a reflection on his sudden and indiscreet expression [That the Devil should Mowe his Oats before the poor Man should have any thing to do with them] could not but on this occasion come into his Memory. For if we will but allow our selves so much leisure, to consider how many hits of providence go to the production of one Crop of Corn, such as the aptitude of Soyl, the Seasonableness of Showers, Nourishing Solstices and Salubreous Winds, &c., we should rather welcome Maturity with Devout Acknowledgments than prevent our gathering of it by our profuse wishes.

But not to keep the curious Reader any longer in suspence, the inquisitive Farmer no sooner arriv'd at the place where his Oats grew, but to his admiration he found the Crop was cut down ready to his hands; and as if the Devil had a mind to shew his dexterity in the art of Husbandry, and scorn'd to mow them after the usual manner, he cut them in round circles, and plac't every straw with that exactness that it would have taken up above an Age, for any Man to perform what he did that one night: And the man that owns them is as yet afraid to remove them.

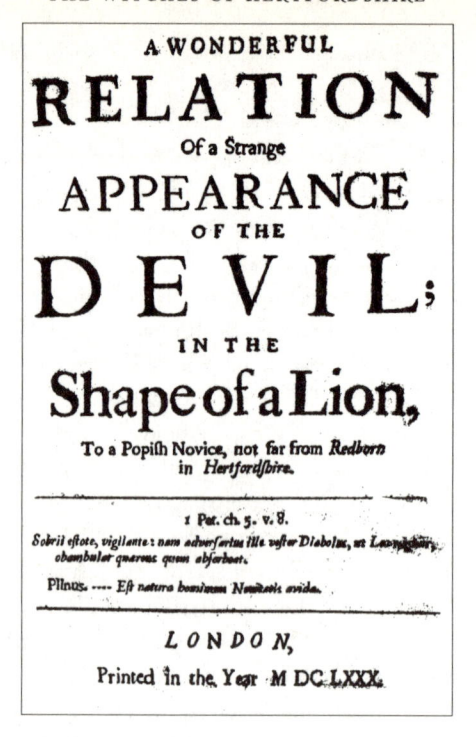

> A WONDERFUL
> RELATION
> Of a Strange
> APPEARANCE
> OF THE
> DEVIL;
> IN THE
> Shape of a Lion,
> To a Popish Novice, not far from *Redborn*
> in *Hertfordshire*.
>
> 1 Pet. ch. 5. v. 8.
> *Sobrii estote, vigilante: nam adversarius ille vester Diabolus, ut Leo rugiens, obambulat quaerens quem absorbeat.*
>
> Plinus. ---- *Est natura hominum Novitatis avida.*
>
> LONDON,
> Printed in the Year MDCLXXX.

The front page of this cautionary tale about the dangers of 'popery.'

Cautionary tales of this type hark back to the medieval exempla, and have much in common with them; not least in that the story is at best a substantial exaggeration of events, and may well never have occurred at all.

1680: The Devil in the Shape of a Lion

This is another exemplary tale, in this case warning of the dangers of Papism. The chief character (apart from the Devil) is portrayed sympathetically; he is, after all, misguided, not evil.

> Kind Reader,
> *Our Age doth so swarm with Lebells and Lies, and Pamphlets of Falshoods, and Fictions of mens Brains, that it is become a thing next to impossibility for ought that is strange and miraculous, (although truth) to find entertainment among men, or to get any room in their Credit or belief. Yet when those things that are only Fictions and Lyes are thouroughly sifted, and narrowly looked into, they prove to be void of Verity, and wanting Truth to uphold them, they fall to the ground, and are soon set at naught; whereas, when things that are not onely strange but true, are searched*

out, they prove real and unfeigned; and when through disclosed, they are better entertained, and more freely received than before: so that 'tis the issue of things that proveth whether they are worthy of reception or not and not the fairness of their Face, or the plausibleness of the Words they are presented in. These things being premised, I subject the following Relation into the hands of the diligent Inquirer into things to prove, and try it, to see whether it be truth or not.

Onely note, that it hath been concealed now for some time, by reason (at least partly) of the failure of those from whom the publication hereof was expected: now at length, our expectations being frustrated, we now do undertake to give a brief account of a wonderful Transaction.

The Relation take as followeth:
One Mr Michael Benyon, Brother to a Per'on of the same name in Redborne in the County of Hertford, having purposed and fully determined to take his Journey into the Country to place himself in a Knights house (who was, as I am informed, a Roman Catholick) there to be a Tutor to the said Knights Children, he being a Scholar. And in the prosecution of this his said purpose and intent, he had accomplished one dayes journey, and had taken an Inn for his residence that night, being the seventh day of December.

At which very juncture of time, came into the same Inn a Servant of the afore-mentioned Knight; Now when they had taken knowledge of eachother, and the aforesaid Michael Benyon had acquainted him with his Design, the Servant doth intreat his stayance until his return, (himself being engaged in a farther Journey) that so he might accompany him to his Master's house; This Proposition being consented to, they parted each with other. Then the said Michael Benyon betook himself to his Bed, and did enjoy good rest and quietness in sleep until about two of the Clock in the morning; at which time, (being awake) he cast up his eyes on the wall, where appeared to his view a very bright and shining light darting it self up and down, to and fro upon the wall, at which sight he arose immediately out of his Bed with great fear, and went to his accustomed Prayers (which he called the Rosary), to the Virgin Mary, and all the Saints, and his earnestness was such, that he reiterated his Prayer, and said the Rosary over and over. After which he went to his bed again, and took quiet rest until morning. The next day he told the People of the House, that he would not have them expect him, nor think it strange if he came not down to them the next day until Evening, or while the Sun was set, for he purposed to give himself up to Prayer and Fasting: because he thought he had seen an Angel, to confirm him in his Principle, (viz. in Popery, for that was his Principle.) But for the first Night thus much.

Now when the next Evening came (which was the close of the eighth day of December,) he went to Bed again, and took quiet rest as before, until three or four of the clock in the morning; then he felt an heaviness upon his Breast, and saw the Light upon the Wall, but notwithstanding, being heavy with sleep, he turned himself from the Light, and purposed not to mind it, but immediately he thought something with a small blow smote him on the shoulder, and heard a low Voice say to him SLEEP NOT. Upon that he sate up in his bed, and saw an Appearance, as it had been of a little Child, very beautiful, at his Beds feet, and being much astonished, he arose to Prayer, and prayed as before: and after his Prayer was ended, the Appearance being vanished, he went to bed, as before: and when the morning came, he kept the day very strict in Fasting and Prayer, as before-minded, and after the Sun was Set, he went down and eat and drank for the refreshment of his Body.

And when the next Night came, he betook himself to bed again, as in the two former Nights, he took good rest until towards morning, then felt something lye very heavy upon his feet; now thinking it had been some part of his wearing Clothes, he lift up his feet, and immediately heard something (as it were) grabble down behind his Beds-head, but looking, found nothing, but was again surprised with the Light upon the Wall, which strook him with such an amazement, that he could get nothing on save his Breeches, and so upon his Knees by the Beds-side he went to Prayer with his Beads in his hand, and was very earnest, and said four parts of five of his Prayer again; then there appeared unto him a great LION, and a Chain about him, and Appearances like DOGS surrounding him, and he thought they would have sucked his Breath from him, and pressed so hard upon him, that he durst not arise off his knees, but drew back upon his Knees: But now at this time, when he was so sorely pressed upon, and had no relief from his Prayers, his heart failed him, and he cried out to Jesus Christ for Help and Deliverance, so that after a little time he had that Confidence, that he told the LION (the DEVIL) that he should have no power over him, neither should he stay until day-light; he further told him, if he had any thing to do with any Sinner, let him do it, for Jesus Christ had pardoned his Sins. He continued praying two hours, insomuch that the Neighbours and the People of the House heard, and brought up a Light, but they could not perceive the Appearances. Thus he continued until morning, then the Appearances left him, according to his expectation. After his deliverance out of the paw of this Lion, he burn'd his Pardons and his Beads; and at his return he burn'd a Book, much esteemed by him before, which is affirmed that he himself brought from Rome, and entirely renounc'd the Communion of the Whore of Babylon.[2]

II

THE PHYSICAL EVIDENCE OF WITCHCRAFT

Ritual Hoards and Witch Bottles

Deposits in buildings of personal items, witch bottles and suchlike and small animals such as cats are not uncommon across England. Hertfordshire is no exception. I am sure that there are other examples in the county than those recorded here; but they often go unrecognised for what they are. Then again, it is clearly not the case that every dried-up rat found in a building is an example of a ritual deposit; such a find was made at Purwell Mill in the Parish of Wymondley – in this case it is more likely to be one of the many rodents that infested such buildings, and died a natural death.[1]

Nor does the practice seem to be completely extinct – Brian Hoggard[2] points out that he has several instances in his records of pet owners who believe that their cats have been deliberately walled up by builders. Some of the spaces in which they were discovered were so small that accidental entombment can be ruled out; and some builders denied any knowledge of the entire incident. This seems to demonstrate a pagan tradition that is alive if not kicking today.

In the case of cats, which are sometimes found with rat companions, the creatures were probably a sacrifice, though it is possible that the dead cat was thought to act as a deterrent to rodents. As we have already discussed, witches in Britain were believed to use familiar spirits, frequently in the form of small animals; perhaps the spirit of the deposited cat was intended as a defence against witches' imps.

The purpose of the inanimate objects is more uncertain. Shoe deposits are particularly common, sometimes alone, though they are often associated with other objects. It has been suggested that they are 'essentially a male superstition connected with the building trade,' and that it is unlucky to remove such deposits from their resting places.[3] If so, it reinforces the claims of the pet owners recorded above. It must be said that such an association is speculative, and does not hold true for all such collections. Some are positioned where any household member might have access – for example beneath floorboards. Such collections are often termed 'spiritual middens'. Scissors are included in several finds. According to E. and M.A. Radford, they were thought to be a protection against witchcraft, along with other iron objects and implements.[4]

The following list contains examples of various types of deposit, but it is not by any means exhaustive:

Anstey	A hand-blown green glass bottle discovered in the tower of the church.
Ashwell	A dried brown rat found behind plaster at 28, Hodwell.
Baldock	A dried cat is said to have been found in roof space of 83, High Street.
Baldock	A dried brown rat found between roof rafters at 11, High Street.
Baldock	A dried brown rat found behind a lath and plaster wall in a former bookshop in Church Street.
Caldecote	A complete donkey was buried in a barn. It is thought that this was to ward off a beast which, according to local folk belief, roamed the area.
Great Hormead	Shoes found dating to 1700.
Hitchin	A dried rat found in a house in Tilehouse Street in 1982.
Hitchin	The stretched hairless skin of a rabbit (or a young hare) on a stick was found embedded in the wall of a house near Hitchin.
Tewin	A shoe was found at Queen Hoo Hall, dating to 1700.
Walsworth	At 'the Long House,' the owners found a dried cat and a dried rat together above a ground floor fireplace; they also found a shoe, a shoe iron, three marbles, two buttons, two coins and a pair of scissors in the ceiling of a ground floor room (see plates 13 & 14).[5]
Water End, North Mimms	A hoard including shoes, a hat, scissors, shells, bottles, lace, bird skulls, an ox tooth and newspapers dating from 1895, found hidden in a fireplace and a wall near the door. The late date of this example demonstrates the survival of the belief that led to such deposits.
Weston	In Howells Farm, Halls Green, Weston, a large hoard of objects was discovered behind an inside wall of a

bedroom. The list is as follows; a red ceramic costrel with basketry cover; a hair comb; a cheek snaffle horse bit created from two different bits, cheek pieces have been cut with sharp knife; sword scabbard, mis-assembled with hangars twisted; slipware sherd; black leather shoe of adult male dated between 1695-1720; two small pieces of white fabric block printed in red with floral design - dated 1675-1690; fragments of woman's corset in white linen with wooden bones, 1650-1750; red ware shards; other sherd; two stones; stoneware shards; deep green-black glass bottle with deep conical frog; blue ceramic bead; fragment of leather jacket, 1600-1700; blade of metal knife. Probably a spiritual midden as apparently the objects accumulated over time having been deposited through a hole in the attic (see plates 15, 16 and 17).[6]

Stones with holes in them — frequently, though not exclusively, flint — were thought to be lucky. According to Aubrey they were in wide use in the seventeenth century:

...in the West of England (and I beleeve, almost everywhere in this nation), the Carters and Groomes, and Hostlers doe hang a flint (that has a hole in it) over horses that are hagge-ridden for a Preservative against it'.[7]

A particularly fine example is on display in Ashwell Museum. Where it was originally found is unknown, but it was kept for many years at Dixie's Farm, where it was thought to protect the horses in the barn where it hung from the 'glanders.'[8] As late as the 1930s strong objections were expressed by the horse-keeper to its removal.

Doris Jones-Baker was warned that another example she had in her garden was unlikely to remain there for long if it remained on open display.[9]

But stones with holes in them (sometimes called hag stones) were not the only variety thought to have special powers. Hertfordshire puddingstone was also believed to be lucky, and to be able to divert evil.[10] Puddingstone is a glacial conglomerate, and has the texture of concrete, though somewhat more attractive in appearance. It consists of rounded pebbles cemented together in a silica matrix, ranging in colour from brown to pink. Though the largest deposits are in Hertfordshire, it crops up in other counties as well — Buckinghamshire, Bedfordshire, Middlesex and west Essex all have deposits.

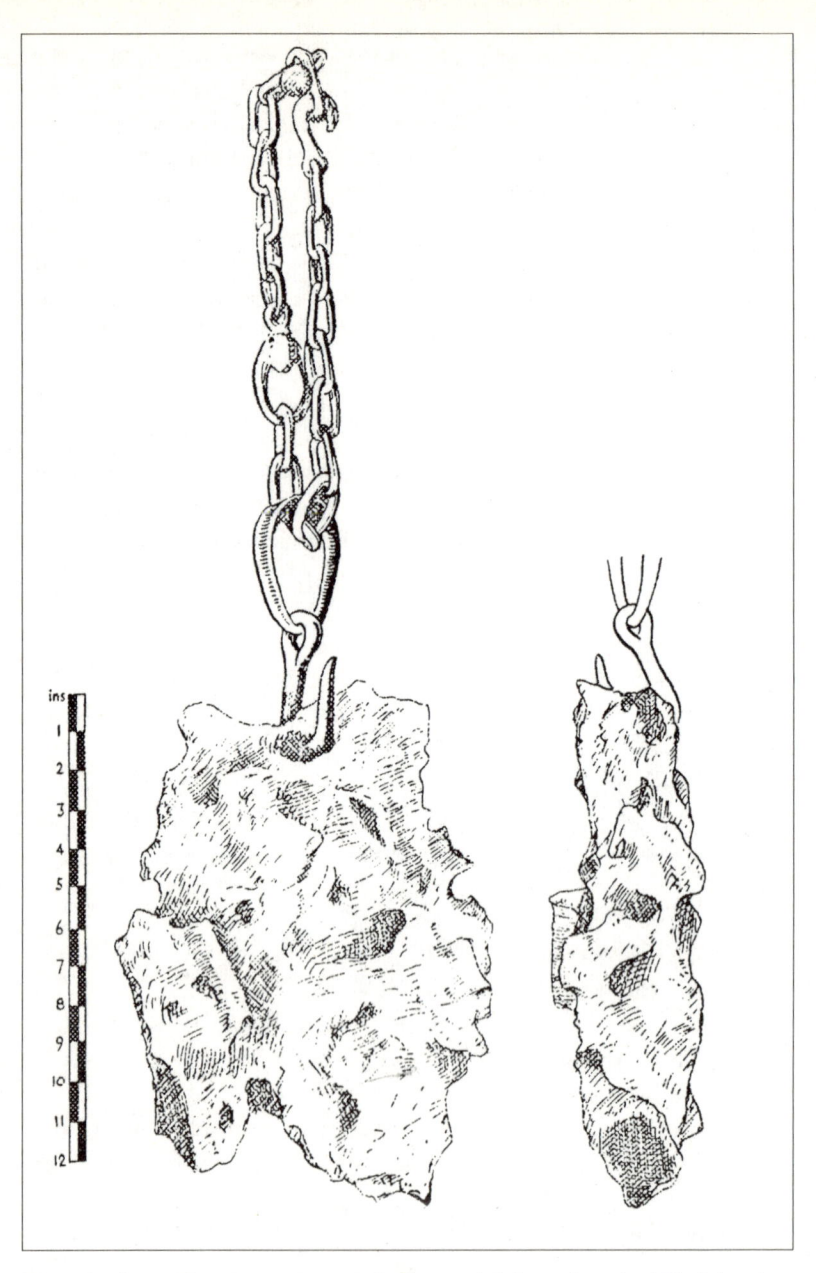

The Ashwell stone from Dixie's Farm. Why flints with holes in them should be believed to have special powers is not clear. It may be nothing more than their scarcity.

Puddingstones can be found in the foundations of many churches[11], leading to speculation that they were the object of pagan worship, and were therefore incorporated into Christian churches. Though most English churches are Norman or later, many of them were built on the site of earlier Saxon structures, and it is possible that stones were re-used either as objects of superstition or, more prosaically, as a good, hard, building material.

According to a leaflet published by the Museum of St Albans[12], a parish record of 1662 states '…that a hagstone be placed on the coffin, for her bodie within be bewitched.' Unfortunately my attempts to trace the reference have so far failed.[13] 'Hagstone' might refer to puddingstone, or it might mean no more than a stone with a hole in it. Nor is the reason for the deposit of the stone clear. Was it because the deceased was a victim of witchcraft, as the quotation implies, or was because she was a suspected witch, as the leaflet claims?

Graffiti

Graffiti are sometimes ritual in their nature, and many buildings contain examples; but churches are often a good place to look, especially if they are built of soft stone, if only because of their age and accessibility. There is room here only to scratch the surface.[14] I must emphasise that rubbings must not be taken without permission, as serious damage can result.

Graffiti take many different forms. Some are of the 'name and date' variety; some record events.[15] Illustrations are often difficult to interpret unless they clearly represent known objects; examples include hobbyhorses (see plates 18 and 19), buildings, ploughs, and human portraits and figures, but the reasoning behind many of them, other than perhaps boredom, is unclear. Others are thought to be of a ritual nature.

Symbols include crosses, bells and daisywheels. All three were thought to repel evil. The cross is an obvious example; church bells were thought to drive away evil spirits and devils. The daisywheel is a symbol that appears in secular as well as ecclesiastical buildings, and is thought to have been a general protection against witchcraft, as well as being a good-luck charm (see plates 20, 21 and 22).[16] The butterfly-shaped dagaz is thought to have the same purpose (see plate 24).

On the southeast column of the transept in St Helens Church, Wheathampstead, is an interesting graffito that has been interpreted as a witch's head with the body of a swan.[17] Whether the interpretation is accurate is difficult to say; it is certainly an interesting piece of work, measuring some 10 inches (25.4cm) from nose to tail (see plate 25). At some stage in its life it has been defaced with a diagonal cross, much more

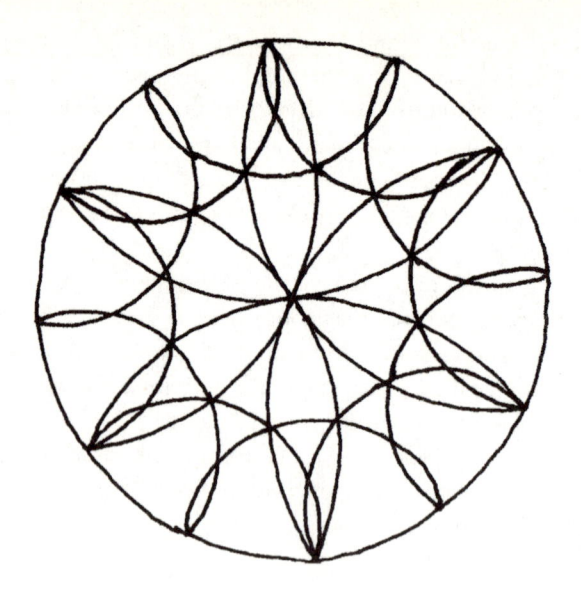

Good luck marks: a complex form of daisywheel from Ashwell parish church. (Author)

deeply incised than the figure itself. It is possible, but unlikely, that the cross is contemporary with the engraving. The date of the figure is unknown, but it is clearly of some antiquity.

A second interesting graffito can be found on the south-east column in the tower of St Mary's Church, Gravely (see plate 25). It depicts an animal head with antlers, beneath which are a row of dots said to represent bells. In many ways it is reminiscent of a mummer's mask, or the antlers worn by the Abbots Bromley deer men, which in turn takes us back to the seventh-century *Liber Pœnitentialis*.

Witch bottles

Witch bottles are covered in Chapter 3, but I would like to say a few words about how they (or any other find) should be dealt with:
Do not clean the item; its contents should be analysed.
Record the location of the find, and take photographs.
If possible, contact your local museum for assistance.
Contact the author, or Brian Hoggard (See Notes, Chapter 11 (2), pg 214).

12

MISCELLANY

The following cases cannot be verified and must, at present, be considered of little or no historical value. I have been unable to find any evidence that the persons named ever existed, though of course they may have done. There are, I am sure, many folk legends in the county, but these few will suffice to give a flavour of the sort of tales that were once common.

John and Joan Newell

All we know of this couple comes from the title of a contemporary pamphlet, listed in William Lowndes' *Bibliographer's Manual of English Literature*, the many volumes of which were published between 1834 and 1864. The pamphlet was listed as: *The Arraignment and Execution of 3 detestable Witches, John Newell, Joan his wife, and Hellen Calles, two executed at Barnett, and one at Braynford, 1 Dec., 1595.*

No example of the pamphlet is known to exist, and neither of the Newells, nor Hellen Calles, appear in the assize records, though records for that year, and for several years before and after it, still exist; nor are any of those that appear in the records from Barnett, or a couple.

It may be that the pamphlet relates to cases for which the individual indictments have been lost, both for Hertfordshire and Essex; but it is more likely to be fictitious, or based upon some other, unrecognisable prosecution. There is very little to go on, unfortunately.

Mother Haggy

Old Mother Haggy is said to have been a witch in the time of James I (1603-25). Originally she was a white witch, a healer, and married to a yeoman of St Albans. In her advancing years however she turned to evil, and delighted in playing 'mighty pranks' on the townsfolk. She would fly on her broomstick through the town's streets in broad daylight, and used a kettle-drum to cross the River Ver (though why she didn't simply fly over it is a mystery!). She had the power to change herself into a cat, a lion or a hen.

Though the country folk were terrified of her, and there was talk of prosecuting her as a witch, nothing came of it, and she died a natural death. Her ghost is said to haunt Battlefield House, in Chequers Street.[1] She leaves behind her no record that I am able to find, and must, unless further evidence comes to light, be cast into the realm of folk tale.

Sally Rainbow

Just to the north of Bramfield is Sally Rainbow's Dell, and it is said that a witch of the same name made her home in a cave in the dell. It is in fact a chalk pit, from which local farmers extracted the raw material for making lime for their fields. According to the legend, it was these same farmers that most feared Sally, and they propitiated her by supplying her every requirement. It is also claimed that Dick Turpin relied upon the local fear of the Dell, and used it as a hideaway for the spoils from his many robberies in the area (though it would take a dozen Turpins to have visited all the places that claim a connection with that unsavoury character!). Sally Rainbow appears as Dame Sad in a novel, *Queen Hoo Hall*, by Joseph Strutt,[2] published in the first decade of the nineteenth century.[3] If it is true that Sally was Strutt's inspiration, it at least demonstrates that the legend has some age.

Rosina Massey

This must be a very tentative item, as the source is completely unknown. Rosina Massey is said to have had a three-legged stool, which she had run errands for her. One day she asked a woodman for some off-cuts. When he refused, she caused his axe to attach itself firmly in a tree trunk.[4]

Mary Cocker

According to Reginald Hine's *History of Hitchin*, Mary Cocker of Temple Dinsley was examined by Thomas Sadleir in 1587 concerning 'a vision or ghost that had appeared to her in the night season, and warned her to tell the Queen [Elizabeth I] that there was a jewell in making for her, which if she received would be her destruction.'[5]

If correctly reported, Mary Cocker was little different to most people of her time. Dreams were genuinely believed to provide warnings of forthcoming events, and the art of their interpretation, orniromancy, was widely practised throughout recorded history. Mary Cocker was taking a considerable risk, because since 1580 it had been a felony punishable by death for diviners to attempt to discover 'how longe her Highnes should lyve, and who should raigne after her Decease.' Presumably she believed in what she told the justice, and felt that it was her duty to report her dream to the authorities.

Captain James Hind and the Cunning Woman[6]

According to *The English Gusman*, by George Fidge, 1652, Captain Hind the highwayman had an encounter with a cunning woman in Hatfield. *The English Gusman* purports to be a biography of a famous highwayman, James Hind, who was still alive (though in gaol) at the time it was written. In fact, like many such publications, the book is mostly fiction.

How Hind was inchanted by a cunning woman, who after some discourse switched him with a Charmed Rod, not to be taken or harmed during the time this Charm should last; which was for Three years.

After Hind had robbed the High-way-men of their money; It was his chance to ride to Hatfield, lying at the George-Inn, being then the Posthouse; where he very merrily spent the evening with some Gentlemen that were there: In the morning very early Hind cals for his horse, to be gon; being now mounted he takes leave of all those Gentlemen that were stirring; as he rod along Hatfield, at the Towns end, an old Ill-favoured woman asked an Almes of him: his horse presently staid, and would go no further; Sir, said the old woman, I have something to say to you, and then you shal be gon; Hind not likeing her Countenance, puld out five shillings and gave her, thinking she would but like a Gipsee, tell his fortune: Said, good woman I am in hast: Sir, said she, I have staid all this morning to speak to you; and would you have me lose my labour: speak your mind, said Hind'.

The old woman began thus:

Captain Hind, You ride and go in many dangers; wherefore by my poor Skill, I have thought on a way to preserve you, for the space of Three Years: but that time being past, you are no more then an ordinary man, and a mischance may fall on you as well as another: but if you be in England, come to me, and I will renew the Vertue of this Charm again: in saying these words, she puld out of her bosom, a little box, almost like a *Sun Dyal and gave it Captain Hind, and said to him, When you are in any distress, open this, and which way you see the Star turn, ride or go that way, and you shall escape all dangers: so she switched him with a white Rod that was in her hand, and strook the horse on the buttocks, and bid him farwell: the horse presently leaped forward with such courage, that Hind could not turn him to give her thanks; but guessing it was her will it should be so, rod on his way. The time of this Charm was expired in Ireland about some two months before Youghall was surprised by the Inhabitants for the Commonwealth of England, where Hind was wounded: as hereafter you shall hear in his Voyage to Ireland.

* This Star was at the end of a needle, like a dyal.[7]

Unnamed Witch from Brent Pelham

A report from Mist's Weekly Journal, *Saturday, 30 April 1726*[8]
St Alban's, April 23.
On Saturday last an old woman of the Parish of Burnt-Pelham in this county, was, by virtue of a warrant of a Justice of the Peace, apprehended for a witch; but being brought, in order to her commitment, before another Justice, when several Gentlemen were in his company, he acquitted her at first sight, having the opinion of all the Gentlemen present to back him, that she was too old and too homely for a witch. The report, however, was immediately spread about the country, and it being the opinion of the learned, that none but the young and the handsome are capable of being witches, it is said, that several pretty young ladies of the said Parish were so alarm'd that they absconded upon it, as apprehensive of being taken up for bewitching several of the King's subjects.

Burnt Pelham is the modern Brent Pelham in north-east Hertfordshire. It was so named after the village was seriously damaged by fire, reportedly in the twelfth century. Brent Pelham has a fine set of stocks, which stand outside St Mary's Church.

I know of no other mention of this somewhat whimsical item, and it may be the equivalent of an eighteenth-century urban myth. Unfortunately we have no names which we might investigate. It seems unlikely that all the pretty girls in the area would flee, believing themselves in danger of being accused as witches.

13
Conclusion

What conclusions can we draw about witchcraft and magic in England, and more specifically, Hertfordshire? Firstly, the scale of the persecutions throughout Europe was far less significant than popular wisdom would have it; and England had fewer witchcraft prosecutions than most other countries in Europe. Hertfordshire had fewer trials than some other counties, notably its eastern neighbour, Essex.

Because of the practice of destroying indictments thrown out by the Grand Jury; the destruction or loss of depositions presented to the Courts of Assize; and the lack of record keeping by Justices of the Peace, we cannot know how many suspicions there were, or how many unsuccessful prosecutions. The cases we do know of in Hertfordshire never seem to have caused the panic that occurred in some areas of Continental Europe and, in the 1640s, in other parts of East Anglia.

The chief reason for England's low number of trials must be the illegality of torture under Common Law. In Scotland, where torture was used, the casualty list was higher, at about 1,500 executions, and for a smaller population. On the whole England got off lightly.

Occasionally prosecutions were the result of the zeal of an individual, or small group of individuals, such as Matthew Hopkins, concerned with hunting down witches as enemies of society as a whole; but the Hopkins entourage did not visit Hertfordshire (though they came close). The majority were private actions, instigated by people believing themselves to be victims of witchcraft, or under threat from it.

In most cases neighbour prosecuted neighbour – in very few instances did accused and accuser live more than a mile or two apart. Witchcraft accusations were personal matters in predominantly small communities.

The reasons for the witch-hunts are complex. Many cases were brought by people sincere in their belief that they had been bewitched. After all, the

Church said that witches existed, and the law of the land agreed; the reality of demons and evil spirits was widely accepted by many of the leading thinkers of the time. But in some instances the prosecutions were malicious, the result of ill feeling between members of the same community. A wayward reputation increased the likelihood of being accused of witchcraft, and a reputation as a witch was even more likely to prompt a formal accusation.

There is no evidence to suggest that a co-ordinated anti-female plot existed – too many of the witnesses were women, and too many of the accused were men. The whole affair was too haphazard to be a strategic operation. But the majority of victims were women. For the most part, this was because people expected witches to be women.

Whether the English Civil War was a cause of the rise in prosecutions between 1640 and 1650 is uncertain. It was probably the cause of an increase in convictions, as a result of a breakdown in the court system, but we cannot tell whether there was an increase in the number of accusations. The prosecutions that occurred at Hertford Assizes in the 1640s may have been a result of a knock-on from Hopkins' activities in neighbouring counties, but we cannot say for sure.

Though Hertfordshire was comparatively lightly affected by the purges, belief in the county was strong; and whilst the laws against witchcraft were repealed in 1736, many people remained convinced that witches were real and dangerous. The last witch condemned to death in England came from Hertfordshire, and the witnesses included educated people, including several clergymen.

This book began with the story of a divided family – the Rayes of Berkhamsted, in southern Hertfordshire – and the question, 'How could it be that family members could turn against one another in such a way, with the result that a wife and mother lost her life at the end of a rope?' In view of the beliefs and society in which those events took place, perhaps we should not be quite so surprised after all.

The future of the study of witchcraft prosecutions in Hertfordshire lies in two areas. Firstly, the investigation of Ecclesiastical Court records,[1] and secondly a search of local newspapers. Before the Witchcraft Act of 1542 witchcraft accusations, as well as cases involving folk magic, were most likely to be heard in an Ecclesiastical Court. After 1736, local newspapers reported assaults and such offences, justified by the accused on the basis of bewitchment.[2]

Neither source is likely to reveal further executions for witchcraft however. The punishments open to the Ecclesiastical Courts were extremely limited – abjuration, penance or excommunication. The newspapers are most likely to reveal cases of unofficial action (assaults, swimmings), defamation and prosecutions under the Act of 1736 for what was in effect fraud.

APPENDIX A

TABLE OF WITCHCRAFT PROSECUTIONS IN HERTS

The tables include all known Hertfordshire prosecutions in assize sessions and quarter sessions for witchcraft and related offences from 1542-1736. Where the same name appears more than once, there was more than one indictment (for example Mary Burgis of Bengeo was indicted in 1590 on three counts of murder by witchcraft, one of bewitching a horse to death and one of causing illness by bewitchment. She therefore has five entries). In some cases the indictment is missing, and only a gaol calendar or a recognisance remains (for example Joan Edmonds and Mary Bushe in 1595).

The majority of cases are drawn from the Assize records for the Home Circuit, and it is important to realise that not all have survived. Unfortunately, it has often been the earliest records that have been lost: for the period summer 1563 to Lent 1573, of the twenty sessions held records of thirteen are missing entirely, whilst others may be incomplete. Later years are not so bad: from summer 1573 to Lent 1625 we have some or all of but nine of the 104 sessions.[1]

In addition, there are a number of records held at Hatfield House, details of which are available at Hertfordshire Archives and Local Studies, County Hall, Hertford. They include for example the indictments for Helen Browne of Aspenden, Midsummer Sessions 1589. This is probably the same Ellen Browne of Buntingford who was tried and acquitted in 1593 – Aspenden and Buntingford are next door to each other. Elizabeth Lane also appears in these records.[2]

In some cases the victim's town of domicile is given, for example John Skelton of Flamstead. In others, only the place where the alleged offence took place is recorded: 'Alice Crutch, wife of Thomas Crowtch of Grt. Trynge, labourer, on 26 Dec., 38 Eliz., at Grt. Trynge, bewitched 1 horse valued at £4 the goods and chattels of Barnard Mychell.' One might reasonably assume that Mychell lived in Tring, where his horse was bewitched; but this is not certain.

186

YEAR	ALLEGED WITCH/SUSPECT'S NAME AND DOMICILE	OFFENCE	VICTIM/OWNER OF GOODS, PLACE OF BEWITCHMENT OR DOMICILE OF VICTIM	VERDICT/SENTENCE
1573	Thomas Heather, Hoddesdon	Conjuration and invocation of Evil spirits	None	Guilty – pardoned?
1576	Alice Sparke, Buntingford	Bewitching two cows	John Harvey, of Buntingford	Acquitted
1579	Alice Cowle, Therfield	Bewitching a brewing vat full of water at which two cows were drinking	Henry Gynne	Pillory x 4, and probably 1 year in gaol
1580	Joan Danne, Hitchin	A common sorceress and enchantress, causing illness by witchcraft	John Sympson, of Hitchin	Acquitted
1582	Margaret Bonner, Flamstead	Murder by witchcraft	John Skelton, of Flamstead	Acquitted
1587	Agnes Morris, Stevenage	Murder by witchcraft	Richard Jenkinson, of Stevenage	Guilty – remanded
1587	Agnes Morris, Stevenage	Bewitching a cow	John Clark, at Stevenage	Guilty – remanded
1589	Helene Browne, Aspenden	Causing illness by witchcraft	Robert Snowe, of Aspenden	Acquitted
1589	Helene Browne, Aspenden	Causing illness by witchcraft	Joan Sewell, of Aspenden	Acquitted
1589	Helene Browne, Aspenden	Causing illness by witchcraft x2, bewitching a cow to death	William Sewell, of Aspenden	Guilty – 1 yr gaol and pillory x4
1590	Mary Burgis, Bengeo	Murder by witchcraft	William Noble, probably of Hertford	Acquitted
1590	Mary Burgis, Bengeo	Murder by witchcraft	Elizabeth Noble, probably of Hertford	Acquitted
1590	Mary Burgis, Bengeo	Murder by witchcraft	Susan Hill, probably of Bengeo	Acquitted
1590	Mary Burgis, Bengeo	Bewitching a horse to death	George Grave, at Stapleford	Guilty – 1 yr gaol and pillory x4

1590	Mary Burgis, Bengeo	Causing illness by witchcraft	George Grave, at Stapleford	Guilty – 1 yr gaol and pillory x4
1590	Thomas King, Barkway	Causing illness by witchcraft	James Moyses (or Mayster), at Barkway	Acquitted
1590	Thomas King, Barkway	Murder by witchcraft	John Watson, at Barkway	Acquitted
1590	Margery King, Barkway	Murder by witchcraft	John Watson, at Barkway	Acquitted
1590	Joan White, Bushey	Murder by witchcraft	Marion Mann, of Bushey	Acquitted
1592	John Sely, Stanstead	Bewitching 40 hogs to death	John Spencer, at Stanstead	Acquitted
1592	Mary Hamont, Walkern	Bewitching a horse to death	William Walby, at Walkern	Guilty – 1 yr gaol and pillory x4
1592	Mary Hamont, Walkern	Bewitching hogs to death	William Bramfield, at Walkern	Guilty – 1 yr gaol and pillory x4
1592	Mary Hamont, Walkern	Bewitching a horse and a cow to death	William Bramfield, at Walkern	Guilty – 1 yr gaol and pillory x4
1593	Ellen Browne, Buntingford	Causing illness by witchcraft	Margaret Dellew, at Buntingford	Acquitted
1593	Ellen Browne, Buntingford	Causing illness by witchcraft	John Gates, at Buntingford	Acquitted
1593	Joan Garrett, Hatfield	Murder by witchcraft	Margery Hawkes, at Hatfield	Acquitted
1593	Joan Garrett, Hatfield	Murder by witchcraft	Christopher Penifather, at Hatfield	Acquitted
1593	Joan Garrett, Hatfield	Murder by witchcraft	Agnes Clark, at Hatfield	Acquitted
1593	Joan Garrett, Hatfield	Murder by witchcraft	Susan Clark, at Hatfield	Acquitted
1593	Joan Garrett, Hatfield	Bewitching a horse	William Marshall, at Hatfield	Guilty – 1 yr gaol and (probably) 4x pillory
1594	Alice Eames, Little Gaddesden (?)	Bewitching cattle	Unknown	Guilty – 1 yr gaol and 4x pillory
1595	Joan Edmonds	Unknown – indictment missing	Unknown	Guilty – hanged
1595	Mary Bushe	Unknown – indictment missing	Unknown	Guilty – hanged
1595	Joan White	Bewitching goods	Unknown	Guilty – 1 yr gaol and (probably) 4x pillory

YEAR	ALLEGED WITCH/SUSPECT'S NAME AND DOMICILE	OFFENCE	VICTIM/OWNER OF GOODS, PLACE OF BEWITCHMENT OR DOMICILE OF VICTIM	VERDICT/SENTENCE
1596	Katherine Dewxburie, Ware	Causing illness by witchcraft	Agnes Wattes, of Ware	Acquitted
1596	Katherine Dewxburie, Ware	Causing illness by witchcraft	Thomas Bromley, at Ware	Guilty – 1 yr gaol and (probably) 4× pillory
1596	Katherine Dewxburie, Ware	Murder by witchcraft	Robert Cock, at Ware	Acquitted
1596	Alice Crutch, Great Tring	Murder by witchcraft	Hugh Balden, at Great Tring	Guilty – hanged
1596	Alice Crutch, Great Tring	Bewitching a horse	Thomas Grave (or Grace), at Great Tring	Guilty – hanged
1596	Alice Crutch, Great Tring	Bewitching a horse	Barnard Mychell, at Great Tring	Guilty – hanged
1598	Mary Taylor, Hertford	Murder by witchcraft	Simon Grubb, at Hertford	Guilty – 1 yr gaol and (probably) 4× pillory
1598	Mary Taylor, Hertford	Bewitching 7 hogs	Ralph Willowbye, at Hertford	Acquitted
1599	William Browne, Buntingford	Causing illness by witchcraft	Thomas Hantler, of Buntingford	Acquitted
1599	Alice Fulwood, Chipping Barnet	Murder by witchcraft	Marion (or Mary) Harwood, of Chipping Barnet	
1600	Joan Vaughan, Cheshunt	Murder by witchcraft	Alice Slowden (or Slowen), of Cheshunt	Unclear: probably acquitted
1600	Alice Bockett, Great Gaddesden	Bewitching a cow to death	Thomas Wells, of Great Gaddesden	Acquitted
1600	Elizabeth Turlogg, Cheshunt	Murder by witchcraft	Alice Havers, at Cheshunt	Acquitted
1600	Elizabeth Turlogg, Cheshunt	Causing illness by witchcraft	Alice Twygg, at Cheshunt	Acquitted
1601	Sara Assar, Little Munden	Murder by witchcraft	Mary (or Mercy) Irelande, at Little Munden	Acquitted
1601	Mercy Hill, Barley	Murder by witchcraft	Grace Ollivere, at Barley	Guilty of trespass[3] only. Sentenced 'according to Statute'

1601	Mercy Hill, Barley	Murder by witchcraft	Anne Ollivere, at Barley	Guilty of trespass only Sentence unknown
1601	Mercy Hill, Barley	Bewitching a cow	Roger Braine, at Barley	Guilty – probably 1 yr gaol and 4x pillory
1603	Agnes Whittenbury, Aston	Causing illness by by witchcraft	Joice Newland, at Aston	Guilty – hanged
1603	Agnes Whittenbury, Aston	Bewitching two piglets	Francis Combes, at Aston	Guilty – hanged
1603	Agnes Whittenbury, Aston	Causing illness by witchcraft	Thomas Hills, at Aston	Guilty – hanged
1605	George Adownes, Flamstead	Suspected of witchcraft	Unknown	Unknown
1605	Sarah Adownes, Flamstead	Suspected of witchcraft	Unknown	Unknown
1606	Joan Vaughan, Cheshunt	Causing illness by witchcraft	Alice Cheare, at Cheshunt	Acquitted
1606	Alice Stokes, Royston	Murder by witchcraft	Richard Bland, at Royston	Guilty – hanged
1606	Alice Stokes, Royston	Causing illness by witchcraft	John Rumbold, at Royston	Pardoned or acquitted
1606	Christian Stokes, Royston	Murder by witchcraft	Roger Gybbons, at Royston	Guilty – hanged
1606	Christian Stokes, Royston	Murder by witchcraft	John Peirse, alias Hogg, at Royston	Guilty – hanged
1606	Christian Stokes, Royston	Causing illness by witchcraft	Jane Wakefield, at Royston	Pardoned or acquitted
1607	Alice Eames, Little Gaddesden	Suspected of witchcraft, indictment missing	Unknown	Unknown
1608	Agnes Smith, Ashwell	Murder by witchcraft	John Barley, at Ashwell	Acquitted
1608	Agnes Smith, Ashwell	Causing illness by witchcraft	Susanna Warren, at Ashwell	Acquitted
1609	Alexander Lewis, probably of St Albans	Practising enchantments and poisoning	Unknown	Unknown

189

YEAR	ALLEGED WITCH/SUSPECT'S NAME AND DOMICILE	OFFENCE	VICTIM/OWNER OF GOODS, PLACE OF BEWITCHMENT OR DOMICILE OF VICTIM	VERDICT/SENTENCE
1610	Margery Raye, Berkhamsted	Murder by witchcraft	Elizabeth Humfrey, at Barkhamstead	Guilty – hanged
1610	Elizabeth Raye, Berkhamsted	Probably murder by witchcraft	Probably Elizabeth Humfrey, at Barkhamstead	Probably acquitted
1610	Agnes Sutton, Eastwick Manor	Murder by witchcraft	Bewitched Audrey Sewell, at Eastwick	Acquitted
1610	Agnes Sutton, Eastwick	Causing illness by witchcraft	Elizabeth Munke, at Bishop's Hatfield	Guilty – thought to be 1 yr gaol and pillory x4, but but possibly hanged
1611	Woolmer Lane, Hitchin	Suspected of witchcraft, indictment missing	Unknown	Unknown
1612	Agnes Smith, Ashwell	Bewitching two horses to death	George Arnold, at Ashwell	Acquitted
1612	Elizabeth Baker, Cheshunt	suspected of witchcraft, indictment missing	Unknown	Unknown
1613	George Adownes, Flamstead	Murder by witchcraft	Hugh Adownes, at Flamstead	Guilty – hanged
1613	Sarah Adownes, Flamstead	Murder by witchcraft	Hugh Adownes, at Flamstead	Acquitted
1613	Thomas Hamond, Appesden (Aspenden)	Murder by witchcraft	Henry Chapman, at Appesden (Aspenden)	Discharged by Grand Jury
1613	Agnes Hamond, Appesden (Aspenden)	Murder by witchcraft	Henry Chapman, at Appesden (Aspenden)	Unknown
1613	Thomas Hamond, Appesden (Aspenden)	Bewitching horses	Edward Parker, at Appesden (Aspenden)	Acquitted
1613	Agnes Hamond, Appesden (Aspenden)	Bewitching horses	Edward Parker, at Appesden	Reprisoned without bail on suspicion of witchcraft. Eventual fate unknown
1613	Lyon Gleane	'Suspected for a cunjurer'	Unknown	To be set in the stocks, whipped and sent to Boston

1613	Richard Frisbye, Bennington	Suspected of witchcraft, indictment missing	Unknown	Unknown
1614	John Parrat, Wheathampstead	Suspected of witchcraft, indictment missing	Unknown	Unknown
1614	Elizabeth Parrat, Wheathampstead	Suspected of witchcraft, indictment missing	Unknown	Unknown
1614	Agnes Hutten, Hoddesdon	Murder by witchcraft	Unknown	Unknown
1615	Anne Smith, Ashwell	Causing illness by witchcraft	Frances Ashelyn, at Ashwell	Acquitted
1615	Anne Smith, Ashwell	Bewitching a horse to death	Clement Gunnill, at Ashwell	Guilty (probably 1 yr gaol and pillory x4
1616	Anne Smyth, at Ashwell	Murder by witchcraft	Thomas Wrangle, at Ashwell	Reprisoned (final fate unknown)
1618	Joan Messenger of Barkhamstead Mary	Murder by witchcraft	Elizabeth Poope, at Barkhamstead Mary	Acquitted
1618	Joan Messenger of Barkhamsted Mary	Murder by witchcraft	William Cocke, at Barkhamstead Mary	Acquitted
1618	Joan Messenger of Barkhamstead Mary	Bewitching two horses to death	Miles Wodd, at Barkhamstead Mary	Acquitted
1618	Alice Nash, Barkway	Murder by witchcraft	Margaret Bishopp, at Barkway	Acquitted
1618	Margaret Hullett, Barkway	Murder by witchcraft	Heny Braie, at Barkway	Acquitted
1618	Edward Whitenbury, Cottered	Suspected of witchcraft, indictment missing	Unknown	Unknown
1621	Francis Catlyn, Bengeo	Suspected of witchcraft, indictment missing	Unknown	Unknown
1641	Elizabeth Peacock, Berkhampsted St Peters	Murder by witchcraft	Ellen Webb, probably of Barkeway	Acquitted, but returned to gaol pending sureties
1647	Margaret Burby, Barley	Murder by witchcraft	Thomas Skepp, probably of Barley	Acquitted
1647	Margaret Burby, Barley	Causing illness by witchcraft	Robert Pattin, at Barley	Acquitted

YEAR	ALLEGED WITCH/SUSPECT'S NAME AND DOMICILE	OFFENCE	VICTIM/OWNER OF GOODS, PLACE OF BEWITCHMENT OR DOMICILE OF VICTIM	VERDICT/SENTENCE
1647	Elizabeth Browne, Cheshunt	Murder by witchcraft	Mary Addams, at Cheshunt	Guilty; returned to gaol pending sentence. Fate unknown
1647	Margaret Cotterell, Little Munden	Causing illness by witchcraft	Lady Anne Holmes, Little Munden	Discharged by Grand Jury
1649	William Litchfield, Ardley	Bewitching a black cow	William Halfehead, Yardley (Ardley)	Discharged by Grand Jury
1649	Prudence Litchfield, Ardley	Bewitching a black cow	William Halfehead, Yardley (Ardley)	To remain in gaol pending surities. Fate unknown
1649	Anne Man, Ashwell	Bewitching four horses to death	Thomas Plumer, Ashwell	Unknown – no verdict or sentence recorded
1650	Elizabeth Balden, Knebworth	Bewitching a horse to death	Richard Milton	Acquitted (tried in Essex)
1658	Agnes Gardiner, Bennington	Did feed, employ and entertain two evil spirits; one in the likeness of a black cat, and the other in the likeness of a toad	Unknown	Acquitted
1658	Agnes Gardiner, Bennington	Causing illness by witchcraft	Marcy Spencer, at Bennington	Discharged by the Grand Jury
1674	Susan England, West Berkhamsted	Murder by witchcraft	Thomas Gold the younger, at Westbarkhamsted	Guilty but discharged
1712	Jane Wenham, Walkern	Conversing with the Devil in the form of a cat	None listed in the indictment	Guilty, sentenced to death but pardoned

QUARTER SESSION RECORDS

YEAR	ALLEGED WITCH/SUSPECT'S NAME AND DOMICILE	OFFENCE	VICTIM/OWNER OF GOODS, PLACE OF BEWITCHMENT OR DOMICILE OF VICTIM	VERDICT/SENTENCE
1590	Thomas Harding, Ickleford	Fraudulent cunning man	See PART II above	Unknown
1590	Joan White, Bushey	Murder by witchcraft	Marion Man, Bushey	referred to assizes, acquitted, see above
1598	Elizabeth Lane, Walsworth	Cunning woman. Accused clergyman of bewitching her clients	See PART II above	Unknown
1652	Joan Whillocke	Probable assault over suspected witchcraft	Unknown	Unknown
1659	Alice Free, Little Hadham	Murder by witchcraft	Frances Rustat, of Little Hadham	Probably did not proceed beyond Quarter Sessions
1661	Goodwife Bailey, Broxbourne	Assault over alleged bewitchment of child	The child of Andrew Camp	Unknown
1669	Joan Mills	Accused of bewitching ale	Matthew Parnell, probably of Stondon	Unknown
1676	Joseph Haynes, London	Fraudulent fortune telling	See PART II above	Unknown
1676	James Domingo, London	Fraudulent fortune telling	See PART II above	Unknown
1676	Sarah Domingo, London	Fraudulent fortune telling	See PART II above	Unknown
1703	Thomas Ingroom	Fraudulent fortune telling	See PART II above	Unknown
1703	Margaret Ingroom	Fraudulent fortune telling	See PART II above	Unknown
1703	Easter Joanes	Fraudulent fortune telling	See PART II above	Unknown
1703	Susan Wood	Fraudulent fortune telling	See PART II above	Unknown

APPENDIX B

STATISTICS FOR HERTFORDSHIRE

A 'case' is defined in this section as a charge or group of charges tried at the same time – Sarah Adownes was charged on two occasions, 1605 and 1613, and so is counted twice. Agnes Whittenbury was charged with three offences, but all at the same time, and so appears only once. A probable outcome is included as though it were definite.

The fate of the suspects breaks down like this (figures in brackets are total accusations/indictments):

	Hanged	Gaol and pillory	Acquitted	Unknown/ Other
Men	1 (1)	0 (0)	7 (9)	6 (6)
Women	8 (13)	12 (15)	31 (44)	14 (17)

There are a total of sixty-five females and fourteen males indicted; that is to say, 82.3 per cent of those accused were women.

About 65 per cent of all indictments ended in acquittal, a little lower that the average for the Home Circuit as a whole (67 per cent). The acquittal rate for women for Hertfordshire was about 61 per cent; this is in line with the experience elsewhere – not only were women more likely to be accused of witchcraft, they were more likely to be convicted once accused.

When we look at the indictments analysed by offence, we find that murder by witchcraft is by far and away the most common:

OFFENCE	MALE DEFENDANTS	FEMALE DEFENDANTS
Murder by witchcraft	3	39
Causing illness by witchcraft	2	21
Bewitching livestock	2	24
Other (excludes unknown offences)	3	3

APPENDIX B

The geographical spread of the cases is interesting. Hertfordshire follows the trend of the rest of Europe: witchcraft was predominantly a rural offence. Each individual instance represents a single case, whether there is one indictment against the accused or more. The locations are the places given as the home settlements of the accused.

Ardley	1	Great Gaddesden	1
Ashwell	3	Hertford	1
Aspenden	2	Hitchin	2
Aston	1	Hoddesdon	2
Barkway	2	Knebworth	1
Barley	2	Little Gaddesden	1
Bengeo	2	Little Munden	2
Bennington	3	Stanstead	1
Buntingford	2	Stevenage	1
Bushey	2	Therfield	1
Cheshunt	4	Tring	1
Chipping Barnet	1	Walkern	2
Eastwick	1	Ware	1
Flamstead	2	Wheathampstead	1

Of the identifiable witnesses, 66 are women and 108 are men. The women are in the minority, but it is a substantial one – slightly less than 38 per cent.

Recognisances given by or on behalf of those accused of witchcraft display an interesting feature. Of the thrity-one instances of which we have records, only nine are given by the accused or an obviously close relative. In twenty-two cases, the person putting their money down is apparently unrelated. In some cases, for example that of the co-accused Alice Nashe and Margaret Hullett, in which Margaret's husband entered into recognisances for Alice as well, we can see the connection. In others we cannot. Were Michael Wilkinson and Richard Spede no more than friends of Elizabeth Lane? Why did William Browne, whose occupation is given as 'gentleman,' support Thomas and Agnes Hamond of Aspenden? Thomas was a husbandman, and might be considered beneath the station of Browne. Perhaps he was a sceptic who disapproved of witchcraft prosecutions in general and felt obliged to support the accused. Perhaps Thomas or Agnes were employees; Aspenden is only a mile or so from Westmill.

Of the forty-two cases where it is possible to identify the home town or village of both the alleged witch and her victim, in all but four instances they are the same place. Those that differ are:

Witch	Victim
Bengeo	Hertford
Ashwell	Newnham
Flamstead	Caddington
Berkhamsted	Barkway

Bengeo and Hertford are cheek by jowl; from Ashwell to Newnham is about two miles, and it is about three miles from Flamstead to Caddington. From Berkhamsted to Barkway is more than thirty miles. Elizabeth Peacock of 'Barkhampsted St Peeters' bewitched Ellen Webb on 24 July, 1641, at 'Barkhampsted St Peeters;' she died at 'Barkwaie.' We assume that Ellen Webb lived in Barkway, but she may have lived elsewhere, and travelled to Barkway where the 'bewitchment' caught up with her. That she died at home seems more likely, however.

Thus in only one case is the distance between witch and victim significant. An accusation of bewitchment was apparently an extremely personal affair, and this should cause no surprise; most cases were

The spread of cases across Hertfordshire. The eastern half of the county seems to have suffered worst. It is possible that this is due to its proximity to Essex, for which there are more recorded cases that anywhere else in England. The figures indicate the number of cases in each location.

APPENDIX B

probably the result of ill feeling or the desire for revenge for a perceived wrong, and long distance travel was, for most people, unknown.

When looking at those who were believed to be the victims of witchcraft, it would be interesting to know their ages. Unfortunately the courts rarely recorded the ages of either the defendants or their victims. In only two cases from the Hertfordshire Assize indictments is this information available, and one of those is from another source.[1] In some instances, though, their status gives a very broad clue. Adult males are recorded under their own name, often giving their town or parish of residence and trade: 'William Browne of Buntingford, in the parish of Leyston, locksmith...' Married women are recorded almost as a possession: 'Alice Crutch, wife of Thomas Crowtch of Great Trynge, labourer...' Children are recorded in a similar manner: 'Elizabeth Noble, daughter of Thomas Noble...' Thus we might infer that those recorded as daughter of, or son of, are younger than the age of majority, though it may mean no more than that they were still living with their parents.

The casualty list for Hertfordshire looks like this:

	Adult males	Juvenile males	Adult females	Juvenile females
Killed by witchcraft	18	1	13	6
Bewitched, lamed etc	8	2	10	1
Totals	26	3	23	7

It is interesting that the total number of males killed is identical to the total for females (nineteen). On average the females seem to have died younger than the males – there are more 'daughters' than 'sons' recorded. This may be an illusion however, because it is possible that unmarried females were more frequently recorded in this manner, whatever their age was. The differences between the sexes in bewitchment, laming and so on in a sample this small are not significant.

Unfortunately the status or trade of victims is frequently omitted. In only a handful of cases do we have this information: wives (five) and yeomen (four) top the list; there is one mercer (merchant) and one husbandman.

The length of time between bewitchment and death varies a great deal. Marion Harwood died instantly, whilst Mary Addams lingered for almost three years. Discarding these two extremes, the average is around 100 days. Eight victims lasted a week or less, and fifteen held out for longer than the 100-day average.

Animal casualties are also interesting:

	Cows	Horses	Hogs
Killed by witchcraft	2	12	43
Bewitched, lamed, etc.	8	6	2
Totals	10	18	45

Cattle seem more resilient than horses, though horses are more often the victims than cattle. The high total for hog mortality is distorted by a single case in which forty of them died.

Glossary

abjure, abjuration
: To renounce a (usually heretical) action or belief, often under oath. A common sentence of Church Courts for cunning folk.

Agnus Dei
: Latin, Lamb of God. A Catholic icon.

ague
: A severe fever, sometimes malaria.

alchemy
: The art of turning base metals into gold, and the discovery of the Philosophers' Stone. Most alchemists would be offended by the suggestion that alchemy was magic.

almanac
: A book providing predictions, lucky and unlucky days etc. as well as calendars of tide tables, phases of the moon, celestial events and so on.

amulet
: An item worn as a general defence against bad luck or bewitchment.

assize sessions or courts
: Courts dealing with serious or capital cases, presided over by senior justices. They heard civil as well as criminal cases.

astrology
: Divination by the stars and planets. Claimed to be a science.

bewitchment
: A fairly hazy term. Loosely, anyone or anything suffering from the attentions of a witch.

black witch
: A malignant witch.

blessing witch
: A white witch.

bot
: Payment of atonement to the victim.

canon
: A law of the church.

changeling
: It was believed that sometimes fairies or elves stole human children and left changelings in their place. Changelings were backward, fractious and sickly.

charm
: An item carried or worn to ward off the attentions of evil witches or spirits; or to bring good fortune.

coney
: Literally, a rabbit. Slang expression for the target of a conman or couzener.

coney catcher
: A conman or couzener.

conjurer
: Literally, one who summons spirits or the souls of the dead.

couzener, cousener
: A conman, a trickster.

coven
: Group of witches. The term came into use very late and was very uncommon during the period of suppression of witches.

cunning folk
: White witches, dealing in a wide range of services.

curse
: A malignant spell.

demon
: A spirit or creature from Hell, subservient to the Devil.

deposition
: A statement given before a justice by a witness or a prosecutor.

Devil
: The Lord of Hell; Satan.

devil's mark
: See witches' mark.

diviner
: One who seeks magical aid to tell the future, find lost goods, detect thieves and so on.

Ecclesiastical Court
: A church court, with limited powers (abjuration, penance, etc.) The powers of Ecclesiastical Courts declined throughout the period of the witch-hunts in England.

enchantment
: Under the influence of a charm or spell.

evil eye
: The power to curse with a glance.

exemplar
: A book of exemplary tales, or parables, often for use in sermons. Such stories were often later quoted as being true.

exorcism
: Forcing a demon to relinquish control of a person or thing by use of prayer.

familiar
: A small personal spirit or imp, used by a witch to carry out her evil deeds.

fascination
: Bewitchment, enchantment.

Grand jury
: A preliminary jury that decides whether the person or persons named in an indictment have a case to answer.

hagstone
: A special stone, usually with a hole in it, thought to be lucky, or to have the power to protect the owner from bewitchment.

heresy
: religious opinion opposed to that of the established church.

husbandman
: A person who cares for livestock.

ignoramus
: The decision of a grand jury that there is no case to answer.

image magic
: Use of an image, or dolls of wax, clay or some other material, to which an action is applied, in the belief that it will be replicated in the original.

incubus
: A male sexual demon that visits women at night.

indictment
: A formal document declaring the nature of an accusation in court.

Inquisition
: The Holy Inquisition was an Ecclesiastical Court. The word 'inquisition' was also used to describe secular courts, and this may be the origin of the belief that the Church was responsible for most of the witch-hunts.

Justice of the Peace
: A lay magistrate, usually drawn from the upper classes.

lay on the ten commandments
: Use one's hands to draw blood from a suspected witch in order to break a curse or spell.

liberty court
: A liberty was a manor or a lordship with a charter making it quasi-independent, including the power to hold its own court hearings.

love magic
: Magic used to engender love, change the object of a person's affections, or to interfere with the sexual act (e.g. to cause impotency).

lycanthropy
: The ability to change into another creature, usually a wolf.

maleficium
: Evil or malignant witchcraft.

medium
: A person who gets in touch with the dead. A nineteenth-century term.

necromancy, negromancy
: Raising the souls of the dead, or spirits, for interrogation.

obsession
: Influence of a person by a demon from outside their body.

penance
: Self-punishment to atone for a sin or crime.

penitential
: A book specifying punishments to atone for a sin or crime.

philtre
: A potion, usually designed to raise sexual passion.

piscina(e)
: A stone basin in a church into which water used in Mass is poured away.

possession
: Influence of a person by a demon from within.

pricker, pricking
: A test for a witch. Witches were thought to have witch marks that were insensitive to pain and which did not bleed.

quarter sessions
: A court dealing with less serious, non-capital cases.

quicksilver
: The metal mercury in its liquid form.

recognisance
: A payment made to guarantee appearance in court, or good behaviour.

relic
: Part of the corpse of a saint or holy person, believed to be imbued with divine power.

Roman law
: A legal system based on the Roman pattern. It permitted torture of suspects.

sabbat, sabbath
: A meeting of witches, where they worshipped the Devil, indulged in cannibalism, murdered children, had sex with demons and so on.

sawyer
: A worker in wood, a cutter of timbers.

score above the breath
Draw blood from above the nostrils in order to break a curse or spell. See 'laying on the ten commandments.'

scryer
A magician or diviner who uses a crystal ball, or a mirror, pool or other reflecting device.

serjeant
A lawyer. The word comes from the same root as military 'sergeant'.

sessions
A court sitting, for example the Lent Sessions of the Assize Court.

sigil
A sign, image or charm believed to have magical power.

sorcerer
A person that uses the power of the occult to affect the real world. In the past a sorcerer was not necessarily considered evil.

speculum
A mirror or polished surface used in divination.

Star Chamber
A criminal court, originally dealing with violation of royal proclamations.

succubus
A female sexual demon that visits men at night.

superstition
An irrational belief, sometimes associated with the supernatural.

swimming
A trial by ordeal for suspected witches involving immersion in water. If the suspect floated she was guilty; is she sank, she was innocent. Trial by ordeal was banned by the Fourth Lateran Council of 1215 by Pope Innocent III.

sympathetic magic
A magical system in which an action is applied to an item connected to the target in some way, for example the use of a person's toenails on a wax doll to identify it with the victim.

talisman
A charm designed for protection against a specific threat.

true bill
The decision of a grand jury that there is a case for the accused to answer.

veneficium
Witchcraft or poisoning. The use of the word could cause considerable confusion.

walking
A form of torture in which the suspect is 'walked' up and down for a protracted length of time, eventually causing disorientation and leading to confessions.

watching
A form of torture in which the suspect is deprived of food and and sleep, causing disorientation, in order to extract a confession, and to force the witch's familiar to appear.

werewolf
A person who changes into a wolf. Often connected with witchcraft in continental Europe.

white witch
A good witch.

witch
A person using magic for good or evil purposes. Usually female, but not exclusively so.

witch bottle
A ceramic or glass bottle containing the victim's urine and other ingredients. Intended to break a spell or harm the witch.

witch's mark
The mark made upon a witch's body by the Devil. Similar in purpose to a brand mark on cattle.

witch's teat
A supernumerary nipple for feeding a witch's familiar.

witchfinder
A man or woman who detects witches professionally.

wizard
Originally a wise man or woman. By the time of the witch-hunts, normally a high magician.

yeoman
A farmer of his own land, who could both vote and sit on juries.

BIBLIOGRAPHY

Archer, Fred, *Country Sayings*, Alan Sutton, 1990.
Ashe, Geoffrey, *Mythology of the British Isles*, Guild Publishing, 1990.
Aubrey, John, *Miscellanies Upon Various Subjects*, 1696.
Bennett, H.S., *Life on the English Manor, a Study of Peasant Conditions*, 1150-1400, Alan Sutton Publishing, 1987.
Blundell, Nigel, *The World's Greatest Crooks and Conmen*, Octopus Books, 1982.
Bodin, Jean, *De la démonomanie des sorciers*, (1580), CRRS Publications, 2001.
Boguet, *Henri, Discours des sorciers*, 1602, (published as *An Examen of Witches*), Portrayer Publications, 2002.
Chauncy, Sir Henry, *The Historical Antiquities of Hertfordshire*, 1700.
Cockayne, the Rev. Oswald, *Leechdoms, Wortcunning and Starcraft in Early England*, 3 vols., HMSO, 1864/5/6.
Cockburn, J.S., *Calendar of Assize Records, Herts Indictments*, Elizabeth I, HMSO, 1975.
Cockburn, J.S., *Calendar of Assize Records, Herts Indictments*, James I, HMSO, 1975.
Cooper, Quentin & Sullivan, Paul, *Maypoles, Martyrs and Mayhem*, Bloomsbury Publishing Inc., 1994.
Coward, Barry, *The Stuart Age, England 1603-1714*, Longman, 1994.
Dalton, Michael, *The Countrey Justice*, edn. 1699.
Davies, Owen, *A People Bewitched*, published by the author, 1999.
– , *Cunning-folk, Popular Magic in English History*, Hambledon & London, 2003.
– , *Witchcraft, Magic and Culture 1736-1951*, Manchester University Press, 1999.
de la Porta, John Baptista, *Natural Magick*, 1558.
Dickens, A..G., *English Reformation*, B.T. Batsford Ltd., 1989.
Drage, William, *Physical Experiments Being a Plain Description Of the Causes, Signes and Cures of most Diseases incident to the body of Man. To which is added a Discourse on Diseases proceeding from Witchcraft*, 1668.
Ellis, Peter Berresford, *The Druids*, Constable & Co Ltd., 1994.

Ellis, William, *The Country Housewife's Family Companion or Profitable Directions for whatever relates to the Management and good Economy*, 1750. Prospect Books edition, 2000.
Ely Episcopal Records, Gibbons, 1891.
Evans, Lewis, *Witchcraft in Hertfordshire*, William Andrews & Co., 1898.
Ewen, C. L'estrange, *Witch Hunting and Witch Trials*, Kegan, Paul, Trench, Trubner & Co. Ltd., 1929.
Ewen, C. L'estrange, *Witchcraft and Demonianism*, Frederick Muller Ltd., 1970.
Foulsham's Original Old Moore's Almanack for the Year 2002
Foulsham's Original Old Moore's Almanack for the Year 2003
Gerish, W.B., *Hertfordshire Folklore*, S.R. Publishers Ltd., 1970.
Guazzo, Francesco Maria, *Compendium Maleficarum* (1608), Dover Publications, 1988.
Harrison, G.B., *A Jacobean Journal, Being a Record of Those Things Most Talked of During the Years 1603-1606*, George Routledge & Sons Ltd., 1941.
Hazlitt, W.C., *Dictionary of Faiths and Folklore*, Bracken Books, 1995.
Hine, Reginald, *History of Hitchin*, 2 vols., Eric T. Moore, 1972.
– , *Hitchin Worthies*, George Allen & Unwin Ltd., 1932.
– , *Relics of an Uncommon Attorney*, J.M. Dent, 1951.
Hole, Christina, *Witchcraft in England*, two editions: Collier Books, 1966, BCA, 1977.
Hopkins, Matthew, *The Discoverie of Witches: in answer to severall Queries, lately Delivered to the Judges of Assize for the County of Norfolk, and now published by Matthew Hopkins, Witchfinder. For the Benefit of the Whole Kingdome*, 1647.
How, Anne, *Jane Wenham of Walkern* by Hertfordshire Past and Present, 3rd Edition, issue 1 (Spring 2003).
Howlett, Bridget, *Survey of the Royal Manor of Hitchin, 1676*, Hertfordshire Record Society, 2000.
Hoyland, John, *A Historical Survey of the Customs, Habits and Present State of the Gypsies*, 1816.

BIBLIOGRAPHY

James I, *Daemonologie, in Forme of a Dialogue, Divided into three Bookes.* 1597.

Jones, Arthur, Ed., *Hertfordshire 1731-1800 as Recorded in The Gentleman's Magazine*, Hertfordshire Publications, 1993.

Jones-Baker, Doris, *The Folklore of Hertfordshire*, B.T. Batsford Ltd., 1977.

Kittredge, George Lyman, *Witchcraft in Old and New England*, Russell & Russell, 1958.

Le Hardy, W., *Quarter Session Rolls (Hertfordshire County Session Rolls, 1581-1698)*, Hertfordshire County Council, 1905.

Levack, Brian, *Witch Hunt in Early Modern Europe*, Longman, 1995.

Macfarlane, Alan, *Witchcraft in Tudor and Stuart England*, Routledge & Kegan Paul, 1999.

Martin, Ruth, *Witchcraft and the Inquisition in Venice, 1550-1650*, Basil Blackwell, 1989.

Martin, Ruth, *Witchcraft, Medicine and the Inquisition in Sixteenth Century Venice*, The Society for Social History of Medicine Bulletin 47, 1987

Merrifield, Ralph, *The Archaeology of Ritual and Magic*, B.T. Batsford Ltd., 1987.

Munby, Lionel, *The Common People are not Nothing*, Hertfordshire Publications, 1995.

Muskett, Paul, *A Late Instance of English Witchcraft*, Hertfordshire's Past, Issue 48, 2000.

Page, Dr F.M., *History of Hertford*, Hertford Town Council, 1993.

Perkins, William, *A Discourse of the Damned Art of Witchcraft*, 1608.

Phillips, Roger, *Mushrooms and Other Fungi of Great Britain and Europe*, Pan Books, 1981.

Porter, Enid, *Folklore of East Anglia*, B.T. Batsford Ltd., 1974.

Porter, Roy, *The Greatest Benefit to Mankind*, Harper Collins Publishers, 1997.

Pound, John, *Poverty and Vagrancy in Tudor England*, Longman Group Ltd., 1986.

Pound, John F., ed., *The Norwich Census of the Poor, 1570*, Norfolk Record Society, 1971.

Pritchard, Violet, *English Medieval Graffiti*, Cambridge University Press, 1967.

Radford, E. & M.A., *Encyclopaedia of Superstitions* (Christina Hole, ed.), Hutchinsons & Co., 1974.

Read, Carveath, *Man and his Superstitions*, Cambridge University Press, 1925.

Rosen, Barbara, *Witchcraft in England, 1558-1618*, University of Massachusetts Press, 1991.

Russell, Jeffrey B., *History of Witchcraft*, Thames & Hudson, 1980.

Ruthven, Malise, *Torture: the Grand Conspiracy*, Weidenfeld & Nicholson, 1978.

Salgâdo, Gâmini, *The Elizabethan Underworld*, Alan Sutton Publishing Ltd., 1992.

Scot, Reginald, *The Discoverie of Witchcraft*, (1584), Dover Publications, 1972.

Sharpe, James, *Witchcraft in Early Modern England*, Longman, 2001.

Sherwood-Taylor, F., *The Alchemists*, Barnes & Noble, 1992.

Sibley, *The Popular Fortune Teller, Contains Never Failing Means for Ladies to Obtain Good Husbands, and Husbands Good Wives, Etc., by Sibley, the Great Astrologer.* Reprinted by Senate in 1994.

Somerset, Anne, *Unnatural Murder – Poison at the Court of James I*, Weidenfeld & Nicolson, 1997.

Spalding, T.A., *Elizabethan Demonology*, Chato & Windus, 1880.

Spraggs, Gillian, *Outlaws and Highwaymen*, Pimlico, 2001.

Sprenger & Kramer, *Malleus Maleficarum* (1486), Braken Books (Summers edition), 1996.

Stearne, John, *A Confirmation and Discovery of Witchcraft* (1647), The Rota, University of Exeter, 1973.

Stuart, Malcolm, ed., *The Encyclopaedia of Herbs and Herbalism*, Caxton, 1989.

Stubbs, William, *Select Charters and Other Illustrations of English Constitutional History*, Clarendon Press, 1884.

Summers, Montague, *History of Witchcraft & Demonology*, Castle Books, 1992.

Swain, John, *Witchcraft in Seveneenth Century England*, Stuart Press, 1994.

Thomas, Keith, *Religion and the Decline of Magic*, Penguin Books, 1991.

Thompson, C.J.S., *Mysteries and Secrets of Magic*, Senate, 1996.

Thurston, Robert R., *Witch, Wicce, Mother Goose*, Longman, 2001.

Trevelyan, G.M., *English Social History*, Longman, 1978.

Vaughan, E., *Witchcraft in the Eastern Counties*, Home Counties Magazine, 1910, 1912.

Walker, Simon, *Crime In Hertfordshire: Volume I, Law and Disorder from Anglo-Saxon England to the Present*, The Book Castle, 2002.

Walker, Simon, *Crime in Hertfordshire: Volume II, Murder and Misdemeanours*, The Book Castle, 2003.

Wheeler, C.B. Ed., *Six Plays by Contemporaries of Shakespeare*, Oxford University Press, 1929.

Wooley, Benjamin, *The Queen's Conjuror: the Science and Magic of Doctor Dee*, Harper Collins Publishers, 2001.

Wrightson, Keith, *English Society 1580-1680*, Hutchinson, 1982.

Youings, Joyce, *Sixteenth Century England*, Penguin Books, 1984.

Zadkiel & Sibley, *Handbook of Dreams & Fortune-Telling*, Senate, 1994.

NOTES

ACKNOWLEDGEMENTS
1 Ming (urinate) is changed to sing, and reference to a Gentleman Usher (penis) is deleted; the intended meaning is therefore lost. The version printed in Part II of this book is the original.

INTRODUCTION
1 Michael Dalton, *The Countrey Justice*, 1618 (edition 1699), p.383.
2 England and Sweden were the only countries in Europe that forbade torture under their domestic laws. Malise Ruthven, *Torture: the Grand Conspiracy*, Weidenfeld & Nicholson, 1978, p.7.

PROLOGUE
1 The procedure for prosecutions was different from today. There was no central prosecutor – it was up to an aggrieved party to prosecute. The first step was to gather witnesses, and make statements (depositions) before a local Justice of the Peace. The Justice would, if he felt the case merited it, issue a warrant for the arrest of the accused. The prosecutor, witnesses and accused (or others on their behalf) gave recognisances (payments) to guarantee their appearance in court. When the case came to trial at the assizes (or for lesser offences the quarter sessions), the case was assessed by the Grand Jury – a group of between twelve and twenty-four local worthies – who decided whether there was a case to answer. If they thought there was not, they returned a verdict of not found (ignoramus in legal jargon, literally, we do not know), and the accused was discharged. If they thought a case had been made, they returned a true bill (billa vera). The accused was then tried before the Petty Jury in a similar manner to modern practice; though early courts were rowdy affairs, and rules somewhat flexible. Provided all those giving recognisances turned up, their money was returned to them – this appears in the record as 'discharged recognisances.'
2 No indictment survives for Elizabeth Raye. In cases where the Grand Jury threw the case out, the document was usually discarded as well, especially before the reign of Charles I.
3 The possession of goods was an important issue. For many crimes the convicted persons goods were forfeit to the authorities.
4 Hanging during the period of the witchcraft suppressions was a brutal business. The condemned person was forced to mount a ladder and the rope placed around his or her neck. The ladder was twisted to 'turn off' the criminal, who was left hanging for up to an hour to ensure that life was extinct. No effort was made to break the spine and make a swift end to the whole business.

PART ONE
CHAPTER ONE
1 *Oxford English Dictionary*, 2001.
2 *Collins Concise English Dictionary*, 1990.
3 *Pocket Oxford Dictionary*, 1946.
4 White witches were believed to carry out benign magic; black witches were evil.
5 Reginald Scot, *The Discoverie of Witchcraft, 1584*. Scot was a sceptic, and believed all witchcraft was in reality a 'cozening art' practised at the expense of the gullible.
6 William Perkins, *A Discourse of the Damned Art of Witchcraft*, 1608, p.9.
7 William Drage, *Physical Experiments Being a Plain Description Of the Causes, Signes & Cures of most Diseases incident to the body of Man. To which is added a Discourse on Diseases proceeding from Witchcraft*, 1668 edition, p.16.
8 These examples are evidence of some form of ritual activity and supernatural belief. They are not evidence for a horned god dating from prehistoric times, who was still worshiped as late as the 18th century, as has been suggested by some New Age adherents.
9 Peter Berresford Ellis, *The Druids*, Constable & Co

Ltd., 1994, p.152.
10 Ergot is a fungus found on grain crops and grasses, and is classified as deadly poisonous. Symptoms of ergot poisoning are hallucinations, psychotic behaviour and convulsions, though it can also cause gangrene. It contains chemicals related to LSD. Roger Phillips, *Mushrooms and other fungi of Great Britain and Europe*, Pan Books, 1981.
11 The Lindow man has been radiocarbon dated to the first or second century AD. Other remarkably well-preserved examples have been found in Tollund and Grauballe in Denmark, some from the fourth century BC. P. V. Blog, *The Bog People*, 1971.
12 Translation from Ralph Merrifield, *The Archaeology of Ritual and Magic*, B.T. Batsford, 1987, p.139.
13 The curse is now held by Letchworth Museum.
14 Vivian Crellin, *Baldock's Middle Ages Volume I*, Egon Publishing, 1995, p.15.
15 Ralph Merrifield, *The Archaeology of Ritual and Magic*, p.141/2.
16 Ralph Merrifield, *The Archaeology of Ritual and Magic*, p.142.
17 The charm begins with the words of the square, not reversed, and then invokes various Biblical entities. It ends with the words 'Be ye all present in my aid, and for whatsoever I shall desire to obtain.' Ralph Merrifield, *The Archaeology of Ritual and Magic*, p. 146.
18 As with the adoption of Christianity by the Romans, the coming of the Anglo-Saxons cannot have resulted in the conversion of all of the indigenous population, and many of those that had embraced Christianity must have continued to practise that religion.
19 From Gotfrid Storm's *Anglo-Saxon Magic*, quoted by Jeffrey Russell, *A History of Witchcraft*, Thames and Hudson, 1980, p.45.
20 Rev Oswald Cockayne, *Leechdoms, Wortcunning and Starcraft in Early England*, Vol. II, HMSO, 1854/5/6, p.323.
21 Doris Jones-Baker, *The Folklore of Hertfordshire*, B.T. Batsford, 1977, p.98, mentions the same cure for warts in the Harpenden area. It seems to work, too; I have seen it used on several occasions. In fact the real reason is most probably no more than coincidence – warts are not long lived, and usually disappear within a few months anyway.
22 William Ellis, *The Country Housewife's Family Companion or Profitable Directions for whatever relates to the Management and good Economy*, 1750, p366.
23 Bede, *Historia Ecclesiastica*, quoted by H.S. Bennett, *Life on the English Manor, a Study of Peasant Conditions, 1150-1400*, Alan Sutton Publishing, 1987, footnote, p.35.
24 Kalends – the first day of each month in the Roman calendar.
25 Quoted by, amongst others, by Montague Summers, *The History of Witchcraft and Demonology*, and Margaret Murray, *The Witch Cult in Western Europe*. Similar restrictions appear in other penitentials, for example the Penitential of Halitgar (*c.* 830, France).
26 Quoted by Jeffrey Russell, *A History of Witchcraft*, p.45.
27 C. L'Estrange Ewen, *Witch Hunting and Witch Trials*, Kegan, Paul, Trench, Trubner & Co. Ltd., 1929, p.4. Bot was atonement to the victim of a crime.
28 Christina Hole, *Witchcraft in England*, BCA, 1977. Being outlawed was a serious affair; it meant that the individual received no protection from the law, and his goods and life were fair game for anyone to take.
29 William Stubbs, *Select Charters and Other Illustrations of English Constitutional History*, Clarendon Press, 1874, p.76.
30 *Leechdoms, Wortcunning and Starcraft in Early England*, Vol. I p.xxxii.
31 *Leechdoms, Wortcunning and Starcraft in Early England*, Vol. II p.139. Alpha and Omega are the first and last characters of the Greek alphabet, and appear in the Book of Revelations 1:11, 'I am Alpha and Omega, the first and the last.' Beronikh is thought to mean 'bringer of victory.'
32 According to *De Gestis Herewardi Saxonis*, chap. XXV, anyway. Whether the account is accurate is open to question.
33 Francesco Maria Guazzo, *Compendium Maleficarum* (*Compendium of Witchcraft*), 1608 (Dover edn, 1988), Book I, chap. 5
34 C. L. Ewen, *Witchhunting and Witch Trials*, p.5.
35 The ordeal of iron was one of several forms of trial by ordeal. The defendant had to walk a specified number of paces carrying a heated bar. The burns were bound, and inspected after three days. If there was evidence of infection, a guilty verdict was reached. Other forms of ordeal included water (later to be found in the 'swimming' of witches), and wager of battle. All but wager of battle, which was introduced to England by the Normans, were Frankish in origin. D.W. Rollason, *Two Anglo-Saxon Rituals: Church Dedication and the Judicial Ordeal*, Vaughan Paper no. 33. Trial by ordeal is also covered in some detail by Sir Henry Chauncy in his *Historical Antiquities of Hertfordshire*, 1700.
36 According to Richard L. Hale, *St Mary the Virgin, a Short History of the Church*, 1994, the painting owes its preservation to a coat of lime

wash at the time of the Reformation; it was not uncovered until 1972. He refers to the depiction as a 'Doom' painting, and with good reason.
37 Quoted by H. S. Bennett, *Life on the English Manor, a Study of Peasant Conditions, 1150-1400*, p.33.
38 See W. Le Hardy, *Hertfordshire County Session Rolls, 1581-1698*, Hertfordshire County Council, 1905.

Chapter Two

1 *Malleus Maleficarum*, 1486, (Braken Books edition, 1996), Part II Question 1 Chapter 13.
2 *Malleus Maleficarum*, Part II Question 1 Chapter 3.
3 It is interesting to note a lull in editions of the *Malleus* between the mid-1520s and 1570s, a period when there was a lull too in prosecutions.
4 Jean Bodin, French lawyer and political philosopher. Despite his rationality in other spheres, he was a firm believer in the satanic witch cult, and his *De la démonomanie des sorciers* of 1580 was widely read throughout Europe. He is perhaps best known however for his *De la Republique*, in which he recognised that false accusations of orgies and child murder had been levied against several groups in the past; unfortunately, he seemed not to remember this when writing the *démonomanie*.
5 Reginald Scot, *The Discoverie of Witchcraft*. James Sprenger and Henrie Institor are Jacob Sprenger and Heinrich Institoris.
6 Francesco Maria Guazzo: cleric, author of the *Compendium Maleficarum*, Milan, 1608. The book is well known for its illustrations of witches and their activities.
7 Jean Bodin: French lawyer, political theorist, and author of *De la démonomanie des sorciers*, 1580. A firm believer in witchcraft and the satanic pact.
8 Pierre de Lancre: French lawyer, author of *Tableau de l'inconstance des mauvais anges et démons où il est amplement traité des sorciers et de la sorcellerie*, 1612. De Lancre was involved in mass prosecutions in the Basque region of south-west France, though claims that hundreds were executed as a result are thought to be exaggerated; less than a hundred is a more likely figure.
9 Nicolas Rémy: French lawyer, author of *Daemonolatreiae libri tres*, Lyons, 1595. A fierce prosecutor of witches, who claimed that in sixteen years 'no less than eight hundred have been clearly proved guilty, and condemned to death' by the Provosts in the Duchy of Lorraine.
10 Henri Boguet, French lawyer, author of *Discours exécrable des sorciers*, 1590. The book is subtitled 'drawn from various trials of many of this sect in the district of Saint Oyan De Joux commonly of Burgundy, including the procedure necessary to a judge in trials of witchcraft.'
11 Henry Cornelius Agrippa von Nettesheim (1486-1535). In 1518 Agrippa successfully defended a woman on trial for witchcraft under the Inquisition.
12 Ruth Martin, *Witchcraft and the Inquisition in Venice 1550-1650*, Blackwell, 1989, gives an interesting insight both to the Inquisition and the practices of witches and magicians of that city. Of particular interest is the similarity in the offences to those committed in other parts of Europe, including the British Isles.
13 Henri Boguet believed that whole fields could be transported from one place to another. *Discours exécrable des sorciers*, 1602, chapter 34. (published in translation as *An Examen of Witches*, Portrayer Publications, 2002).
14 *Malleus Maleficarum*, Part II Question 2. Easily said by those not doing the suffering.
15 A German mile was a somewhat elastic unit of measurement, depending upon the region concerned. It is generally given as 4.68 English miles (7.532 kilometres).
16 *Malleus Maleficarum*, Part II Question 2.
17 *A true Discourse Declaring the damnable life and death of one Stubbe Peeter, a most wicked Sorcerer, who in the likeness of a Wolf committed many murders, continuing this devilish practice 25 Years, killing and devouring Men, Women, and Children. Who for the same fact was taken and executed the 31st of October last past in the town of Bedbur [Bedburg] near the City of Collin [Cologne, Köln] in Germany. Truly translated out of the high Dutch, according to the copy printed in Collin, brought over into England by George Bores ordinary post, the 11th day of this present month of June 1590, who did both see and hear the same. AT LONDON Printed for Edward Venge, and are to be sold in Fleet Street at the sign of the Vine.*
18 Henri Boguet, *Discours exécrable des sorciers*, chapter xlvii.
19 *Malleus Maleficarum*, Part I Question 10.
20 Paul Grilland – Paulus Grillandus: author of *De Sortilegiis*, published in 1533. Until 1524 he doubted the reality of the Sabbat, when he heard the confession of an accused witch and changed his views.
21 Wolves were common in England until the thirteenth century, but regular hunting reduced their numbers rapidly. There is a mention that Richard III hunted wolves in 1486, but there were very few left by then. In Scotland, the last one is thought to have been killed in 1684.
22 From the *Otia Imperialia*, 1211, quoted by

Christina Hole, *Witchcraft in England*.
23 Of the witnesses from the existing Assize records relating to Hertfordshire, whose sex can be identified, just under 38 per cent were women (66 out of a total of 174). This figure is not unusual.
24 Matilda Gage, *Woman, Church And State*, 1893, p.247. Gage does not give the source for this computation. In end notes to the same chapter, she gives modern examples of successful rain making: 'Some very strange stories of such power at the present time have become known to the author, one from the lips of a literary gentleman in New York City, this man of undoubted veracity declaring that he had seen his own father extend his hand under a cloudless sky and produce rain.' (note 28). Such an assertion damages the author's credibility.
25 A. Dworkin, *Woman Hating: A Radical Look at Sexuality in New York*: Feminist Press, 1973.
26 Brian Levack, *Witch Hunt in Early Modern Europe*, Longman, 1995, p.24-25.
27 Robert Thurston, *Witch, Wicce, Mother Goose*, p.3-4.

Chapter Three

1 The penalty for treason could be burning or drawing, hanging and quartering. A sentence handed down in 1685 describes the procedure for the latter: 'You must, every one of you, be had back to whence you came, from thence you must be drawn to the place of execution, and there you must severally be hanged by the necks, every one of you by the neck till you are almost dead; and then you must be cut down, your entrails must be taken out and burnt before your faces, your several heads to be cut off, and your bodies divided into four parts, and these to be disposed of at the pleasure of the King; and the Lord have mercy on your souls.'
2 Familiars are sometimes found in Germany, but they were most common in the British Isles.
3 The 1612 trial referred to is that of the Pendle witches. Of the thirty-five witches 'discovered,' ten were hanged and one died in prison. The book referred to by Dalton is probably *The Wonderful Discoverie of Witches in the countie of Lancaster. With the Arraignment and Triall of Nineteene notorious Witches, at the Assizes and Gaole deliverie, holden at the Castle of Lancaster, upon Munday, the seventeenth of August last, 1612. Before Sir James Altham, and Sir Edward Bromley, 1613*.
4 Michael Dalton, *The Countrey Justice*, 1618 (edition 1699), p.383.
5 George Gifford, *Discourse of the subtill Practices of Devills by Witches and Sorcerers*, 1587, p.60.
6 *A Tryal of Witches at the assizes held at Bury St Edmunds for the County of Suffolk; on the tenth day of March, 1664*. The pamphlet was printed in 1682 and again in 1716; it also appeared as an addendum to one of the many Jane Wenham pamphlets. The case referred to actually took place in 1662, not 1664.
7 Statutes of the Realm, vol. iii.
8 The indictment (in translation) reads 'Hertford. The Jurors for our lady the Queen do present that Thomas Heather, late of Hoddesdon in the county aforesaid, yeoman, being a common conjuror and invoker of evil spirits, not having God before his eyes, but seduced by the instigation of the Devil, on 1 Jan., 15 Eliz., at Hoddesdon aforesaid, in a certain wood there maliciously, devilishly and feloniously did employ certain conjuration and invocation of evil spirits with the intent of gaining diverse great sums of money against the form of the statute in this case lately made and provided, and in bad example of all others in like case offending and against the peace of the said lady the now Queen, her crown and dignity…'
9 Benefit of clergy amounted to a reprieve for many felonies. The test of a cleric was the ability to read, in Latin, the first verse of psalm 51, which thus became known as 'the neck verse.' From the late fifteenth century, laymen who had claimed benefit of clergy were branded on the thumb in open court, with an 'M' for manslaughter or an 'F' for felony. Benefit was thus restricted to a single crime only: reoffending brought the full force of the law down upon the culprit.
10 Sanctuary permitted the felon to flee the land after making the claim, though a number of conditions and restrictions applied. Sanctuary for criminal acts was abolished by James I in 1623.
11 E. Vaughan, *Witchcraft in the Eastern Counties*, the *Home Counties Magazine*, 1910-12.
12 E. Vaughan, *Witchcraft in the Eastern Counties*, the *Home Counties Magazine*, 1910-12.
13 Sir Henry Chauncy, *The Historical Antiquities of Hertfordshire*, 1700.
14 John Strype's *Annals of the Reformation in England*, 1709, quoted by W. C. Hazlitt, *Dictionary of Faiths and Folklore*, Bracken Books edition, 1995, p.644.
15 *Articles of the Church of England*, quoted by Ewen, *Witch Hunting and Witch Trials*.
16 *Statutes of the Realm*, vol. iv, pt. i.

17 For more information on imprisonment and other forms of punishment, see the author's *Crime In Hertfordshire: Volume One, Law and Disorder from Anglo-Saxon England to the Present*, The Book Castle, 2002.
18 *Statutes of the Realm*, vol. iv, pt. i.
19 Torture was permitted, and widely used, in Scotland.
20 *Newes From Scotland, declaring the damnable life and death of Doctor Fian, a notable Sorcerer*, 1591.
21 *Statutes of the Realm*, vol. iv, pt. i.
22 Acts of Parliament, vol. xiii.
23 See Appendix B for statistics for Hertfordshire.
24 Whether this is true of Essex compared to other parts of the country is more difficult to say, because many records are lost. It seems likely though.
25 C.L. Ewen, *Witch Hunting and Witch Trials*. Note that a single defendant might be indicted on multiple charges, and some indictments name more than one individual.
26 The Ecclesiastical Court records represent a considerable problem for the researcher as a result of the sheer volume of data (the Public Record Office alone holds several tons of them) and their scattered nature. The ecclesiastical boundaries of Hertfordshire do not match the civil ones, and records for the county can be found as far afield as Lincoln and London, as well as Hertford. Very few have been published.
27 Alan Macfarlane, *Witchcraft in Tudor and Stuart England*.
28 The records for the period in question are lost.
29 Ewen includes an estimate for Borough and Liberty Courts.
30 Alan Macfarlane, *Witchcraft in Tudor and Stuart England*.
31 Robert Steele, *Social England*, 1903, G.P. Putnams & Sons.
32 If the accused was remanded, their name, and sometimes and the offence with which they were charged, was recorded in the Gaol Delivery Rolls.
33 About 65 per cent of the Assize indictments found for Hertfordshire resulted in a 'not guilty' verdict.
34 Roger North, *Lives of the Norths*, quoted by W.C. Hazlitt and Christina Hole. North was a seventeenth-century jurist.
35 Robin Goodfellow was a mischievous spirit, who could, according to Reginald Scot, sometimes be appeased by small offerings, such as a saucer of milk. The earliest mention of him is in the fifteenth century, but he is almost certainly much older. He takes a leading role in Shakespeare's *A Midsummer Night's Dream* as Puck.
36 Christina Hole, *Witchcraft in England*.
37 'A Rehersall both strange and true, of heinous and horrible acts committed by Elizabeth Stile, Alias Rockingham, Mother Dutten, Mother Margaret, Fower notorious Witches, apprehended at winsore in the County of Barks, and at Abbingdon arraigned, condemned, and executed on the 26 daye of Februarie laste Anno. 1579'.
38 Matthew Hopkins, *Discoverie of Witches: in answer to severall Queries, lately Delivered to the Judges of Assize for the County of Norfolk. And now published by Matthew Hopkins, Witchfinder. For the Benefit of the Whole Kingdome*, 1647.
39 *The Divels Delusions or A faithfull relation of John Palmer and Elizabeth Knot two notorious Witched lately condemned at the Sessions of Oyer and Terminer in St Albans*, 1649.
40 John Stearne, *A Confirmation and Discovery of Witchcraft*, 1648, p.21. Stearne was Hopkins' assistant.
41 Gibbons, *Ely Episcopal Records*. This deposition, and three associated ones – two accusing Dorothy Ellis, the third by Robert Ellis, in which he refuses to confess to being a witch though they 'puld him to peeces wth wild horses,' are the only published witchcraft entries amongst the Plea Rolls and Gaol Delivery Rolls for the Episcopal Records of Ely.
42 Matthew Hopkins, *The Discoverie of Witches*, 1647.
43 Helen Bretton, Margery Grew, Anne Leach, Elizabeth Clark, Rebecca Jones, Anne West, Margaret Moone, Anne Cate, Alice Dixon, Ellen Clarke, Sarah Bright, Elizabeth Goodwin, Elizabeth Heare, Mary Wiles, Anne Cooper, Joyce Boones, Margaret Landish, Sarah Hatyn and Mary Hockett.
44 John Gaule later wrote *Selected cases of Conscience Touching Witches and Witchcraft*, in 1646.
45 E. Vaughan, *Witchcraft in the Eastern Counties*, the Home Counties Magazine, 1910-12.
46 John Stearne, *Confirmation and Discovery of Witchcraft*.
47 John Gaule, *Selected cases of Conscience Touching Witches and Witchcraft*, 1646.
48 According to Sir Henry Chauncy, in the original version of the ordeal, if the accused 'began at once to plunge and labour for Breath immediately upon his falling into Liquor, he was condemn'd as guilty of the Crime, and receiv'd his Punishment for it.' Sir Henry Chauncy, *The Historical Antiquities of Hertfordshire*.
49 James I, *Daemonologie, in Forme of a Dialogue, Divided into three Bookes*. 1597. Books in the form of conversations were a popular means of presenting an argument.

NOTES

50 Reginald Scot, *The Discoverie of Witchcraft*, book II, chap. 5.
51 Michael Dalton, *The Countrey Justice*, 1618 (edition 1699), p. 384.
52 John Webster, *Displaying of Supposed Witchcraft*, 1677, p. 96.
53 C.J.S. Thompson, *Mysteries and Secrets of Magic*, Senate Books, 1996.
54 John Gaule, *Selected cases of Conscience Touching Witches and Witchcraft*, quoted by Hazlitt, *Dictionary of Faiths and Folklore*.
55 James I, *Daemonologie*.
56 Part III, questions xv, xxv and xxxiii.
57 I know of no example of a witch being condemned by this method.
58 There are four Oakleys, in Bedfordshire, Buckinghamshire, Staffordshire and Suffolk; a Great and a Little Oakley in Essex, and the same in Northamptonshire. Which of these is the Oakley referred to is not recorded.
59 Hitchin Museum, *Loftus Barham Scrapbook* Volume 6.
60 Christina Hole, *Witchcraft in England*.
61 James I, *Daemonologie*.
62 Quoted by C.L. Ewen in *Witch Hunting and Witch Trials*.
63 Cristina Hole, *Witchcraft in England*.
64 John Aubrey, *Miscellanies Upon Various Subjects*, 1696, under the heading of 'magick.'
65 Reginald Scot, *The Discoverie of Witchcraft*, book XII, chap. 21.
66 Reginald Scot, *The Discoverie of Witchcraft*, book XII, chap. 18.
67 Mother Redcap was said to have five imps, something like white mice, called Bonnie, Blue Cap, Red Cap, Jupiter and Venus. They were given her by a black man who required a signature in a book. She died in 1926. Ralph Merrifield, *The Archaeology of Ritual and Magic*. Mother Redcap was mentioned in the *Sunday Chronicle* in September 1928; the gist of the story is the same, but there are differences in detail. C. L. Ewen, *Witch Hunting and Witch Trials*, and Christina Hole, *Witchcraft in England*.
68 Joseph Blagrave, *Astrological Practice of Physick*, 1671, quoted by Ralph Merrifield, *The Archaeology of Ritual and Magic*, and W. C. Hazlitt, *Dictionary of Faiths and Folklore*.
69 John Gaule, *Select Cases on Conscience Touching Witches and Witchcraft*, 1646, quoted by Hazlitt, *Dictionary of Faiths and Folklore*.
70 For example, if the number of Victorian houses still in existence is higher than the number of survivors from the Elizabethan period (and this must be true), then it is likely that there will be more hoards found in Victorian houses. Or perhaps some hoards in early houses were removed during later building work.
71 Brian Hoggard has records of more than 1,400 examples of hidden shoes, and Northampton Museum has an extensive collection of them.
72 Denise Dixon-Smith, *Concealed Shoes*, from the Archaeological Leather Group Newsletter No 6, Spring 1990.
73 Personal communication, Brian Hoggard. This is the best explanation I have heard.
74 *Astrological Practice of Physick*, 1671, quoted by Hazlitt, *Dictionary of Faiths and Folklore*.
75 William Drage, *Physical Experiments Being a Plain Description Of the Causes, Signes & Cures of most Diseases incident to the body of Man. To which is added a Discourse on Diseases proceeding from Witchcraft*, 1668.
76 *Maleus Maleficarum*, Part I Question XVIII.
77 John Aubrey, *Miscellanies Upon Various Subjects*, 1696, under the heading of 'magick.'
78 Doris Jones-Baker, *The Folklore of Hertfordshire*.
79 John Cotta, *A Short Discoverie of Witches*, 1612, quoted by Hazlitt, *Dictionary of Faiths and Folklore*.
80 Anne Somerset, *Unnatural Murder – Poison at the Court of James I*, Weidenfeld & Nicolson, 1997.
81 Owen Davies of the University of Hertfordshire has written two books on the subject of cunning folk: *A People Bewitched*, published by the author, 1999, and *Cunning-Folk, Popular Magic in English History*, Hambledon & London, 2003. They are both readable and highly informative.
82 The efficacy of love philtres was debated at Oxford University in 1620, 1637 and 1653. Anne Somerset, *Unnatural Murder – Poison at the Court of James I*. I suppose we would now refer to them as aphrodisiacs.
83 A piece of rope that had been used in an execution was especially prized, and the touch from the hand of an executed corpse was believed to cure the 'King's Evil,' tuberculosis of the lymphatic glands. The disease was so-called because it could reputedly be cured by the touch of the monarch. The practice was introduced into England by Edward the Confessor in the eleventh century. Charles II was said to have touched almost 100,000 people during his reign. The custom died out in the eighteenth century.
84 Shortened version of the Hebrew *Attâh Gibbor Leholâm Adonâi*: 'Thou art mighty forever, O Lord.' AGLA appears in other places as a word of power (e.g. the Medieval magic texts *Liber Juratus* and *Lemegeton Clavicula Salomonis*).
85 'I am the Alpha and the Omega, the first and last.'

Revelations of St John, 1:11. Alpha (A) is the first letter of the Greek Alphabet and Omega (Ω) is the last.
86 I have been unable to trace the meaning of 'bhurnon + blictaono.'
87 I am grateful to Bridget Howlett and Richard Walker for this translation.
88 Roy Porter, *To the Greatest Benefit of Mankind*, reports that St Artemis was associated with genital afflictions, St Christopher with epilepsy, St Lawrence with backache and St Fiacre with piles. St Thomas Becket cured blindness, insanity, leprosy and deafness.
89 Agnus Dei: from the Latin, the Lamb of God.
90 The use of Holy Water and the Host of the Communion in charms was widespread. Both were pilfered from churches. Some fonts have marks from locks that once protected the contents from being appropriated, and examples can be found throughout Hertfordshire and other parts of England. The Host was sometimes obtained by sleight of hand during Communion.
91 From John Aubrey's *Brief Lives*, the usual name for his *Lives of Eminent Men*, which was not published until 1823, long after his death in 1697.
92 Fred Archer, *Country Sayings*, Allan Sutton, 1990
93 William Drage, *Physical Experiments Being a Plain Description Of the Causes, Signes and Cures of most Diseases incident to the body of Man*, 1668.
94 Richard Bernard, *A Guide to Grand Jury Men*, Book II chap. 9.
95 William Perkins, *A Discourse of the Damned Art of Witchcraft*, 1608, p.54.
96 Alan Macfarlane, *Witchcraft in Tudor and Stuart England*, records trips from Essex to London to consult a cunning man.
97 Alan Macfarlane, *Witchcraft in Tudor and Stuart England*.
98 A diviner, especially one using a crystal ball.
99 C.J.S. Thompson, *Mysteries and Secrets of Magic*, p. 278.
100 Rudolph II (1552-1612) was interested in chemistry, alchemy, astronomy and astrology. He was a patron of Johannes Kepler, whose work on planetary motion won him an important place in the science of astronomy.
101 The tale is reprinted by W.B. Gerish, *Hertfordshire Folklore*.
102 John Melton, the *Astrologaster, or Figure Caster*, 1620, quoted by Hazlitt, *Dictionary of Faiths and Folklore*.
103 Quoted from *Encyclopædia Britannica*, 1949 edition, Almanac.
104 Mary Croarken, Henry Andrews (1744-1820) *An Astronomical Calculator from Royston* in *Herts Past and Present*, 3rd Series – Issue no. 2, Hertfordshire Association for Local History.
105 Alan Titchmarsh, the television gardener, will be pleased to hear that he has 'the quiet warmth and sensuality of the Sun-Venus link'.
106 Foulsham's *Original Old Moore's Almanack for the Year 2002*. A comparison between the predictions for 2003 and the actual events is interesting.
107 Gâmini Salgâdo, *The Elizabethan Underworld*.
108 22 *Henry VIII*, chapter 10.
109 Quoted by John Hoyland, *A Historical Survey of the Customs, Habits and Present State of the Gypsies*, 1816. If a Gypsy were proceeded against as a thief or a vagrant, he or she might be hanged.
110 A juggler, or jongleur, originally meant any type of street entertainer. Legerdemain is from the French, meaning 'lightness of hand.'
111 Quoted by W.C. Hazlitt, *Dictionary of Faiths and Folklore*.
112 Michael Dalton, the *Countrey Justice*, 1618 (edition 1699), p.386.
113 Hitchin Museum, Hine Box, Folklore. I have been unable to verify this entry, but the language is plausible for the period.
114 Thomas Ingroom, his wife Margaret, Easter Joanes and Susan Wood, the heads of a group of some fifty travelling folk.
115 *A Historical Survey of the Customs, Habits & Present State of the Gypsies*, John Hoyland, 1816.
116 John Gaule, *Selected cases of Conscience Touching Witches and Witchcraft*. Most of the others come from *The Popular Fortune Teller, Contains Never Failing Means for Ladies to Obtain Good Husbands, and Husbands Good Wives, Etc.*, by Sibley, the Great Astrologer. Reprinted by Senate in 1994.
117 *A Treatise of the Interpretation of Sundry Dreames*, 1601 (licensed for the press 1566) quoted by W.C. Hazlitt, *Dictionary of Faiths and Folklore*.
118 Zadkiel's *Dreams and their Interpretations*. Reprinted by Senate in 1994.
119 *The Popular Fortune Teller, Contains Never Failing Means for Ladies to Obtain Good Husbands, and Husbands Good Wives, Etc.*, by Sibley, the Great Astrologer.
120 Nigel Blundell, *The World's Greatest Crooks and Conmen*, Octopus Books, 1982.
121 This form of extortion was still occurring in the late 1960s – I have personal knowledge of an instance when refusal to buy clothes pegs from a person claiming to be a 'genuine Romany' who was selling them door to door resulted in a 'gypsy's curse.'
122 Squier's fraud had a nice twist, in that the

123 Winch later presided over a witchcraft trial at the assizes at Hertford in 1612. Crewe did the same in 1618 and 1621. 'Not guilty' verdicts were returned in all three cases.
124 It may be significant that there seem to have been only five more executions for witchcraft in the remaining nine years of James' reign.
125 More detail of both the Smythe and Robinson cases can be found in many books on witchcraft. George Lyman Kittredge, *Witchcraft in Old and New England*, and Wallace Notestein, *A History of Witchcraft in England*, both give original source information for these cases.
126 Christina Hole, *Witchcraft in England*.
127 William Drage, *Physical Experiments Being a Plain Description Of the Causes, Signes and Cures of most Diseases incident to the body of Man. To which is added a Discourse on Diseases proceeding from Witchcraft.* (1668)
128 The dogs were said to die as well. The story dates from at least the eleventth century. *Leechdoms, Wortcunning and Starcraft in Early England*. An example of a persistent belief despite the lack of canine casualties, clear evidence to its falsehood.
129 John Baptista de la Porta, *Natural Magick*, 1558, Book 3 Chapter XVIII.
130 Malcolm Stuart, ed., *The Encyclopedia of Herbs and Herbalism*, Caxton, 1989.
131 The family fell out with Hartlay, and he was tried as a witch and hanged in 1597.
132 A local prison, originally for confinement of rogues and vagabonds. Also known as a bridewell.
133 The Darrell case generated one book, *A Discovery of the Fraudulent Practises of John Darrel, Batchelor of Arts*, Samuel Harsnett, 1599; and a host of pamphlets, many of them written by Darrel in his own defence. He clearly did not go quietly.
134 The story is told in detail in a contemporary pamphlet: *A true and just Recorde, of the Information, Examination and Confession of all the Witches, taken at S. Oses in the countie of Essex ...by W. W. ...1582.*
135 Reginald Scot, *The Discoverie of Witchcraft*, Book I Chapter 1.
136 Hazlitt, *Dictionary of Faiths and Folklore*.
137 The list was reproduced from Johan Weyer, who had copied it in turn, most probably from the Goetia, the first book of the *Lemegeton*, or *Little Key of Solomon*.
138 *The Daily Telegraph*, December 11th 1867.
139 She had previously been convicted as a fraud in Edinburgh, in 1933.
140 At the time of writing there is a web site dedicated to clearing Helen Duncan's name.
141 John Webster, (1580?-1625). This is not the same John Webster who wrote *The Displaying of Supposed Witchcraft*. *The White Devil* was first performed in around 1608. *Six Plays by Contemporaries of Shakespeare*, ed. C.B. Wheeler, 1915.
142 T.A. Spalding, *Elizabethan Demonology, an Essay*, Chato & Windus, 1880.
143 Quoted by Salgâdo Gâmini, *The Elizabethan Underworld*.
144 Thomas Hobbes, *Leviathan*, Book I.2, 1651.
145 John Gaule, *Selected cases of Conscience Touching Witches and Witchcraft*, 1646.
146 John Webster, *The Displaying of Supposed Witchcraft*, 1677.
147 William Drage, *Physical Experiments Being a Plain Description Of the Causes, Signes and Cures of most Diseases incident to the body of Man. To which is added a Discourse on Diseases proceeding from Witchcraft*, 1668.
148 Joseph Glanvill wrote two works on witchcraft: *Some Philosphical Considerations Touching Witches and Witchcraft*, 1666, and *Sadducimus Triumphatus*, 1681. Glanvill was not alone in his views. Other believers in witchcraft levelled the charge of atheism against sceptics, a serious matter in a society where few openly denied at least some form of Christianity.
149 Francis Hutchinson, *Historical Essay concerning Witchcraft*, 1718.
150 Christina Hole, *Witchcraft in England*.
151 E. Vaughan, *Witchcraft in the Eastern Counties*, the *Home Counties Magazine*, 1910-12.
152 E. Vaughan, *Witchcraft in the Eastern Counties*, the *Home Counties Magazine*, 1910-12.

Chapter Four

1 Ralph Merrifield, *The Archaeology of Ritual and Magic*.
2 Christina Hole, *Witchcraft in England*.
3 Ralph Merrifield, *The Archaeology of Ritual and Magic* p.155, and E. & M. A. Radford's *Encyclopaedia of Superstitions* (edited and revised by Christina Hole) p. 202.
4 Roger Phillips, *Mushrooms and other fungi of Great Britain and Europe*, Pan Books, 1981.
5 In Joan's case, the motive may have included greed – her goods and chattels were confiscated, along with rents and dower.
6 Friar John Randolph, who confessed his guilt,

was imprisoned for life, though he was later murdered by a priest in the Tower of London.

7 The more so as I once met Doctor Murray in about 1960, near the end of her life.

8 According to Brewer's *Dictionary of Phrase and Fable* (1870), there are twelve dancers, including six deermen, a hobbyhorse, a 'maid,' two boys, and two musicians. One of the boys, who is armed with a crossbow, pretends to shoot the deermen. The ceremony is held on the Monday following 4 September, unless it is a Sunday; in which case it is deferred to 12 September. The dance seems to be based on a hunting rite of some antiquity. The September date of the Deermen's activities is not consistent with Theodore's remarks in the *Liber Pœnitentialis* (q.v.).

9 Examples are *The History of Witchcraft and Demonology* and *The Geography of Witchcraft*.

10 For example *Malleus Maleficarum*, *The Discoverie of Witchcraft* and *Compendium Maleficarum*.

11 Both quotes are from Summers' *History of Witchcraft and Demonology*.

12 The demonic pact formed a common part of witchcraft accusations of the Civil War period and later.

Part Two
Note on Sources

1 The Home Circuit for this period consisted of the counties of Essex, Hertfordshire, Kent, Surrey and Sussex.

2 See note 1, Prologue, for a brief description of court procedures.

Chapter Five

1 The date of the offence in this indictment is given as 20 December, 32 Elizabeth, and the Sessions date is July 32 Elizabeth. This is presumably an error on the part of the Clerk of Assize.

2 Full details of this case can be found in *Hertfordshire Folklore* by W. B. Gerish, or Simon Walker, *Crime in Hertfordshire: Volume II, Murder and Misdemeanours*, Book Castle, 2003.

3 The 'Scotch Boote' consisted of a metal boot that was strapped to the victim's leg and foot. In some versions a screw compressed the calves, in others wooden wedges were then driven down the sides, breaking tissue and bones. The strappado involved lifting the victim from the ground on a rope, by his arms, which were tied behind him.

4 The name is variously spelt in the records as Downes, Addownes, Adowns, Adownes and Adowins.

5 ratsbane: rat poison, normally arsenic compounds.

It is colourless, odourless, and tasteless. The symptoms are similar to acute food poisoning, with abdominal cramps, vomiting and diarrhoea. The fatal dose could be as small as the size to a pea.

6 George Adownes was recorded as being known as 'Clothier' in his indictment.

7 A husbandman looked after farm animals. On occasion the expression was used to describe a small-scale cattle farmer.

8 Probably a reference to William Lilly (1602-81), a famous and influential astrologer and writer of almanacs.

9 W.B. Gerish, *Hertfordshire Folklore*, S.R. Publishers Ltd, 1970. Gerish collected a number of pamphlets, and did valuable background research; for example, it was he that investigated the alleged accomplices of Palmer.

10 John Aubrey, *Miscellanies*, 1696, under the heading 'Converse With Angels And Spirits.'

11 William Drage, *Physical Experiments Being a Plain Description Of the Causes, Signes and Cures of most Diseases incident to the body of Man. To which is added a Discourse on Diseases proceeding from Witchcraft*, 1668

12 W.J. Hardy, *Hertfordshire County Sessions Roles, 1581-1698*, Hertfordshire County Council, 1905.

13 'Goody' is a shortened version of 'Goodwife.'

14 Though it is worth noting that such evidence was acceptable to some, including the influential Michael Dalton in his *The Countrey Justice*, 1618.

Chapter Six

1 Whether 'Caull' refers to a person is not clear. It may be a reference to a caul, or amniotic sac, that sometimes covered babies' heads at birth. Cauls were believed to be lucky, and to have magical powers. They were for example believed to protect sailors from drowning, and advertisements for their sale appeared as late as the First World War.

2 Hertfordshire Archives and Local Studies, HAT/SR2, 100.

3 Hertfordshire Archives and Local Studies, HAT/SR10, 75/6, 82/3, 105-108.

4 The Hamonds were accused of, on 10 October 1613, bewitching 3 horses 'of the goods and chattels of Edward Parker, and the murder of Henry Chapman'. The Grand Jury returned a true Bill, but the Hamonds were acquitted.

5 I am obliged to Brendan King of Baldock Museum and Local History Society for these cases. The extracts are from the ecclesiastical consistory court records for the Archdeaconry of Huntingdon, held at the Diocesan Record Office (Lincolnshire Archives). The same

NOTES

records also contain an item concerning an offender who admitted his offence to a Cambridgeshire court: 'St Neots: Thomas Gamelyn of Staunton uses divination, incantations and necromancy all of which he having confessed before the [court?] he abjured'.
6 In 1679, 6d was worth about £2.50 at 2003 values.

Chapter Seven

1 William Drage, *Physical Experiments Being a Plain Description Of the Causes, Signes and Cures of most Diseases incident to the body of Man. To which is added a Discourse on Diseases proceeding from Witchcraft*, 1668.
2 Doctor Woodhouse of Berkhamsted was also involved in the case of the Baldwin children described later.
3 Nicholas Culpeper, 1616-1654, best known for his book *The English Physitian: or an Astrologo-Physical Discourse of the Vulgar Herbs of this Nation*, 1652, commonly referred to as *Culpeper's Herbal*. The book was immediately popular, and was reprinted many times. 'Misselto' is 'under the Dominion of the Sun,' and when hung around the neck it 'remedies Witchcraft.' Culpeper also recommends it for a number of other conditions, including epilepsy.
4 Cacodemon: an evil spirit or devil. From the Greek, evil genius.
5 Possibly the possession of the nuns of Loudun (1630) or more likely those of Louviers (1647).
6 Bittersweet: also known as Woody Nightshade.
7 Exact meaning uncertain: a 'pleasing to Mercury?'
8 Amerson: probably Amersham, a few miles south of Gaddesden, over the Buckinghamshire border.
9 Presumably the classical languages, Greek and Latin.
10 Hannah Crump (1661) and James Barrow (1664) are described in *The Lord's Arm Stretched Out in an Answer of Prayer* by John Barrow, 1664, but this is a much larger work than that described by Drage. *The Doctrine of Transubstantion and the English Protestant Dispossession of Demons*, Kathleen R. Sands, History, no. 85, The Historical Association, 2000.
11 'Not a people but a mind, not birth but spirit; virtue ennobles and Reason differentiates men from beasts and between them, of the creed of the Emperors Emilian & Claudius. Glory to God, and peace to Man.'
12 W.B. Gerish, *Hertfordshire Folklore*.
13 In order to hold the meeting an application had to be made to the St Albans Quarter Sessions held on April 27 under the Toleration Act, passed by the first Parliament of William and Mary. Unfortunately the Quarter Sessions Rolls for St Albans for the years preceding 1784 are lost.
14 Hertfordshire Archives and Local Studies, D/Egr/76.
15 Hertfordshire Archives and Local Studies, D/Egr/59.
16 Hertfordshire Archives and Local Studies, D/Egr/55.

Chapter Eight

1 'Much of nature, more of fiction, of demons nothing.'
2 Reginald Hine gives a brief biography of Bragge in *Hitchin Worthies*, George Allen & Unwin Ltd., 1932, p.126-30. There are a number of references to Bragge in the same author's *History of Hitchin*.
3 A few additional details are drawn from the contemporary *The Gentleman's Magazine*, reprinted in *Hertfordshire 1731-1800 as Recorded in The Gentleman's Magazine*, edited by Arthur Jones, Hertfordshire Publications, 1993, and *Jane Wenham of Walkern* by Anne How, *Hertfordshire Past and Present*, 3rd Edition, issue 1 (Spring 2003). Ms. How's article provides valuable background research into the case.
4 Most of the quotations in account are from Bragge.
5 Chauncy is best known in Hertfordshire for his *Historical Antiquities of Hertfordshire* of 1700.
6 Gardiner was a Fellow of King's College, Cambridge.
7 Arthur was Sir Henry Chauncy's youngest son. The entry in the Ardeley parish records for Arthur's burial describes him as 'crafty' and 'wicked.' Anne How, *Jane Wenham of Walkern*, *Hertfordshire Past & Present*, 3rd Edition, issue 1 (Spring 2003).
8 This was an attempt to break the spell by drawing blood. The practice was known as 'scoring above the breath,' or 'laying on the Ten Commandments' (the ten fingers).
9 It should be remembered that in the same year as the Wenham case Lord Chief Justice Parker declared that if 'the Party lose her life by it [swimming of witches], all that are the Cause of it are guilty of Wilful Murther.'
10 According to W.B. Gerish, Thomas Adams met a violent end; he was murdered by a highwayman on his way home from Hertford Market in 1728.
11 See Part I, witch bottles.
12 In 1711 Jonathan Swift described Justice Powell 'an old fellow with grey hairs, was the merriest old gentleman I ever saw, spoke pleasant things, and laughed and chuckled till he cried again.' *Journal to Stella*, Letter 26.
13 According to *The Gentleman's Magazine*, it was

'an apartment over the stables.'

14 Gilston is in south-eastern Hertfordshire, only a little more than a mile from a village appropriately named High Wych.

15 The addition of the extra cases is presumably to boost sales. The first, Florence Newton, was one of the few instances of witchcraft recorded in Ireland. The story was also used by Joseph Glanvill in his *Saducismus Triumphatus of 1681*. The Bury St Edmunds case must be *A Tryal of Witches at the assizes held at Bury St Edmunds for the County of Suffolk; on the tenth day of March, 1664*.

16 Rictor Norton, *Early Eighteenth-Century Newspaper Reports: A Sourcebook*, 18 November 2001; updated 8 May 2003, http://www.infopt.demon.co.uk/grub/grub.htm I am grateful to Dr Norton for permission to reproduce these items.

17 Francis Hutchinson, *An Historical Essay Concerning Witchcraft*, p. 194.

18 *Hertfordshire 1731-1800 as Recorded in The Gentleman's Magazine*, Arthur Jones, Ed., Hertfordshire Publications, 1993.

19 Presumably Bragge's booklet.

20 Joseph Glanvill, author of *Some Philosphical Considerations Touching Witches and Witchcraft*, 1666, and *Saducismus Triumphatus*, 1681.

21 A written instruction from a justice of the peace to a gaoler commanding him to keep under lock and key a person charged with an offence.

22 This tactic is reminiscent of the *Malleus Maleficarum*, Part III Question 14, where its authors recommend promising a suspect her life if she will confess, only to break the promise after she has done so.

Chapter Nine

1 Further cases may come to light from a search of Hertfordshire newspapers, a method pioneered by Owen Davies of the University of Hertfordshire. A preliminary scan by the author of the *Hertford Mercury* up to the year 1826 was unsuccessful however.

2 Paul Muskett reviews the evidence in this case in a fascinating article entitled A Late Instance of English Witchcraft, published in *Hertfordshire's Past*, Spring 2000.

3 There were errors in the initial report in *The Gentleman's Magazine*. Both Osbornes were said to be over seventy years of age, and both where reported to have been killed.

4 The Jacobite Rebellion, led by Charles Edward Stuart, the Young Pretender, whose bloody defeat at Culloden on 16th April 1746 ended the revolt.

5 A copy of the paper handed to Dell survives at Hertfordshire Archives and Local Studies, D/EP/F272. The unusual spelling given here is taken from that document.

6 In a series of letters at Hertfordshire Archives and Local Studies the first reference to murder is not until 1 August; and in that letter, from Howard Johnson to Earl Cowper, the writer expresses the hope that the action taken will stop this sort of riotous assembly for fifty years or more. There has, he says, to be an example in living memory of the common people, them 'knowing little or nothing of History.'

7 Letter from Howard Johnson to Earl Cowper, 1 August 1751. Hertfordshire Archives and Local Studies, D/EP/F272.

Chapter Ten

1 The British Library holds a copy of the original, ref. E.475.(23).

2 The Whore of Babylon was a derogatory name for the Catholic Church. It originates from the Book of Revelations of St John the Divine.

Chapter Eleven

1 Personal communication, Don Smith, the Mill House, Purwell Mill.

2 Brian maintains a database of ritual hoards, witch bottles and similar finds. Readers are invited to send details of any examples they might come across to the author, or to Brian Hoggard at his web site at www.folkmagic.co.uk. Please do not wash out containers, as analysis of their contents can reveal a great deal.

3 Ralph Merrifield, *The Archaeology of Ritual and Magic*, p.133

4 E. & M. A. Radford, *Encyclopaedia of Superstitions* (ed. Christina Hole), Hutchinsons & Co, 1974.

5 I am grateful to Bryn and Julie Lerwill for permission to examine and photograph their finds.

6 Some of this hoard has been lost. What remains is now kept at Hitchin Museum.

7 John Aubrey, *Remaines of Gentilisme and Judaisme*, Quoted in E. & M.A. Radford's *Encyclopaedia of Superstitions*.

8 Glanders was the name given to a highly infectious bacterial disease affecting horses. It causes ulcers and inflammation in the animal's mucous membranes.

9 Doris Jones-Baker, *The Folklore of Hertfordshire*.

10 There are a number of superstitions concerning puddingstone. It was believed to grow in fields, causing damage to ploughshares; and under the name of 'woe stone' it was thought to cause disasters such as floods. David Curry,

Hertfordshire Puddingstone, Museum of St Albans leaflet.
11 Examples in Hertfordshire are the churches of St John the Baptist, Cottered; St Mary's, Brent Pelham; St Mary's, Stocking Pelham; and St Nicholas, Great Munden. The church of St John the Baptist at Aldenham has puddingstone in the tower and two of its buttresses.
12 *Hertfordshire Puddingstone*, David Curry, undated.
13 A website for Hertsmere implies that the parish is that of St John the Baptist at Aldenham, but there the parish register does not contain the reference, and the bishop's transcripts for that year are missing. If anyone knows where this quotation originates, I would be most interested. Unfortunately Mr Curry has moved and I have been unable to trace him.
14 Pun intended.
15 The plague of 1349 is recalled in an example at Ashwell. There is also a fine graffito of the old St Paul's Cathedral in London before its destruction by fire in 1666.
16 Brian Hoggard, *The Archaeology of Folk Magic*, White Dragon Magazine, Beltane, 1999, pp 17-20.
17 Doris Jones-Baker, *The Folklore of Hertfordshire*.

Chapter Twelve

1 This account is an amalgamation of information from the following sources: *The Folklore of Hertfordshire*, Doris Jones-Baker; *Maypoles, Martyrs and Mayhem*, Quentin Cooper & Paul Sullivan; and *The Mystery of the Witch of Datchworth*, Betty Puttick, article in *Hertfordshire Countryside*, Winter 1964.
2 Strutt died in 1802. The book was edited by Sir Walter Scott, who also wrote the last chapter.
3 Sources for this example are 'The Legend of Sally Rainbow', an article by Eileen Burns, published in *Hertfordshire Countryside*, April 1978; and Doris Jones-Baker, *The Folklore of Hertfordshire*.
4 To my embarrassment I must confess that I did not make a note of the source when I recorded this story some years ago, before I began researching this book. Nor can I recall where it came from.
5 Reginald Hine, *History of Hitchin*, vol. 2. Hine's reference is Cal. S.P.D., 1581-90, p.404.
6 I am grateful to Gillian Spraggs, author of *Outlaws and Highwaymen*, Pimlico, 2001, from which this item is taken.
7 Perhaps a magnetic compass.
8 Rictor Norton, *Early Eighteenth-Century Newspaper Reports: A Sourcebook*, 18 November 2001; updated 8 May 2003, http://www.infopt.demon.co.uk/grub/grub.htm I am grateful to Dr Norton for permission to reproduce this item.

Chapter Thirteen

1 See for example Johanna Leper and Thomas Gamelyn, mentioned earlier.
2 Owen Davies has done great work in the field of post-1736 cases, and his *Witchcraft, Magic and Culture 1736-1951* is highly recommended, as are his books on cunning folk (see bibliography). The concept of searching for cases of assault upon, or libel against, witchcraft suspects is ingenious. I have made a cursory scan of the *Hertford Mercury* up to the mid 1820s without success, but there are other newspapers and more years to cover. And I may have missed some.

Appendix A

1 C.L. Ewen, in *Witch Hunting and Witch Trials*, estimated that about 77 per cent of records for the whole of the Home Circuit survive.
2 They appear under the reference HAT SR. Helen Browne appears in HAT/SR 1, and Elizabeth Lane under HAT/SR 10.
3 Trespass at this time meant any wrong-doing of any sort, as in the Christian prayer, 'Forgive us our trespasses'. In the case of Mercy Hill, we do not know therefore which statute she was sentenced under, and hence what her punishment was. It might have been anything from the pillory to the hangman's noose.

Appendix B

1 In 1599 Alice Fulwood was indicted for bewitching Marion, or Mary, Harwood. Marion's age was given at the inquest into her death on 12 Feb 1600 before Denis Hynde, coroner; she was sixteen years old. Alice Fulwood was acquitted at the next assizes.

INDEX

INDEX OF PERSONS

Adams, Thomas, Junior 140, 143, 213
Addams, Mary 192, 197
Adownes, George 189, 190, 212
Adownes, Hugh 103, 190
Adownes, John 103
Adownes, Robert 103
Adownes, Sarah 103, 189, 190, 194
Adownes, Thomas 103
Adownes, William 103
Aelsi, father of Wulfstan 21
Agnes, wife of Odo 23
Agrippa, Cornelius 30, 206
Aldridge, Thomas 130, 133, 134
Alfred the Great 21
Allen, John 156
Altham, Sir James 41, 207
Anderson, George 103
Andrewes, Thomas 103
Andrews, Henry 73, 210
Androwe (Andrew), Helen 103
Anne, Queen 146
Archer, Henry 160
Arnold, George 190
Ashelyn, Frances, 191
Assar, Sara 95, 188
Asser, George 155
Asser, Mary 155
Aubrey, John 60, 64, 67, 107, 175, 209, 210, 212, 214
Augustalis 17
Augustine, St 20
Aylott, Susan 140

Bailey, Goodwife 155-6, 193
Baker, Elizabeth 190
Baker, J. 136, 146
Balden, Elizabeth 192
Balden, Hugh 188
Baldwin, (family) 117, 130-134

Barley, John 189
Barnard, Richard 24
Barrow, James 126, 213
Baxter, Richard 86
Beauman, Henry 11
Beaumont, Luke 108
Becket, St Thomas 23, 210
Bellarmine, Cardinal Roberto 61
Bennet, Elizabeth 80
Benyon, Michael 171-2
Bernard, Richard 41, 68, 85, 210
Bigge, John 112
Bird, Anne 110
Bishopp, Margaret 104, 191
Bishoppe, William 104
Blagrave, Joseph 63, 209
Bland, Richard 99, 189
Bockett, Alice 188
Bodin, Jean 30, 34, 80, 90, 206
Boguet, Henri 30, 34 206
Bolingbroke, Roger 40
Bonner, Margaret 186
Boones, Joyce 208
Botele, Henry junior 103
Bouchier, Rev Edward 162
Bragge, Francis 135-154 passim, 213, 214
Braie, Henry 104, 191
Braine, Roger 189
Bramfield, William 187
Bray, Agnes 104
Bretton, Helen 115
Bright, Sarah 208
Bromley, Sir Edward 41, 207
Bromley, Thomas 188
Browne, Elizabeth 192
Browne, Ellen, or Helen 185, 186, 187
Browne, William 188, 195, 197
Burby, Margaret 191
Burgen, Oliver 112

Burgis (or Burgess), Mary 50, 97-8, 185, 186-7
Burridge, Thomas 134
Burvile, James 143
Bushe, Mary 185, 187
Butterfield, John 157, 158, 162
By-chance (or Bychance), Mary, 106, 108
Byett, William 80

Cade, William 11
Calles, Hellen 179
Camp, Andrew 155-6, 193
Canute 21
Carpenter, Solomon 103
Carter, Richard 133
Cate, Anne 208
Catlyn, Francis 191
Catusminianus 17
Chapman, Henry 190
Chapman, John 109, 137, 143, 156
Charles I 77, 204
Charles II 48, 209
Chauncy, Arthur 139, 142, 143, 149, 152, 154, 213
Chauncy, Sir Henry 135, 137, 138, 139, 140, 142, 148, 153, 156, 205, 207, 208, 213
Cheare, Alice 189
Chester, Sir Robert 104
Clark, Agnes 187
Clark, Elizabeth 208
Clark, John 186
Clark, Sampson 106
Clark, Susan 187
Clarke, Ellen 208
Clarke, Jane 86
Clarke, Sir Robert 98
Cleaver, Mr 106
Cobham, Eleanor 40

INDEX

Cock, Robert 188
Cocke, William 191
Cocker, Mary 180-1
Colley, Thomas 56, 157, 160-2
Colsey, Elizabeth 43
Combes, Francis 189
Comitianus 17
Cooper, Agnes 114
Cooper, Anne 208
Copis, Walter 114
Cordal, George 103
Cotta, John 64, 209
Cotterell, Margaret 192
Cowle, Alice 186
Cowper, Earl 146, 214
Cowper, Lady Sarah 146, 214
Cranmer, Thomas 43
Crewe, Sir Randolph (or Ranulph) 77, 104, 210-1
Croke, Sir John 12
Crowtch (or Crutch), Thomas 185, 197
Crowtch (or Crutch), Alice 185, 188
Crump, Hannah 127, 213
Culpeper, Nicholas 121, 213
Curll, F. 135

Dalton, Michael 10, 41, 85, 204, 207, 208, 210, 212
Danne, Joan 186
Darling, Thomas 79, 80
Darrell, John 79-80, 211
Davis Serjeant John 103
Davy, Elizabeth 103
de Lancre, Pierre 30, 90, 206
Dee, John 69, 71
Dell, Annis 98-100
Dell, George 98-100
Dell, William 158
Dellew, Margaret 187
Denmark, Anne of 46
Dewxburie, Katherine 188
Diana 22, 29
Dicconson, Frances 77, 78
Dickenson, Robert 112
Dickinson, Rivers 115
Dixon, Alice 208
Docwra, Thomas 111, 113
Domingo, James 115-6, 215
Domingo, Sarah 115, 193
Downeham, Richard 104
Downes, *see* Adownes
Dowse, Elizabeth 104
Drage, William 63, 64, 78, 85, 117-8, 125, 128, 202, 204, 209, 210, 211, 212, 213
Dewe, Richard 104
Duncan, Gelie 46
Duncan, Helen 84, 211
Dworkin, Andrea 38, 207

Eames, Alice 187, 189
Eastoff (alias East), John 160, 161
Edmonds, Joan 185, 187
Edward I 23
Edward the Confessor 209
Edward the Elder 21
Edward VI 43, 69
Elizabeth I 7, 43, 44, 46, 69, 95, 108, 180, 212
Ellis, Dorothy 52, 208
Ellis, Robert 208
Ellis, Sarah 89
Ellis, William 19, 205
England, Susan 109-10, 192
Ewen, Cecil L'estrange 7, 50, 95, 205, 207, 208, 109, 215
Exsupereus 17
Eye, Witch of, *see* Jourdemayne, Marjery

Fian, John 46, 208
Field, Elizabeth 143
Firebrand, William 99
Fitch, Susan 104
Fitch, Thomas 104
Follye, Elizabeth 114
Foreman, Simon 74
Foster, Dr John 160
Francis, Earl of Bothwell 46
Free, Alice 108-9, 193
Frisbye, Richard 191
Frost, Robert 113
Fulwood, Alice 188, 215

Gage, Matilda 38, 207
Gaiena 23
Gamelyn, Thomas 212
Gardiner, Agnes 109-10, 192
Gardiner, Christopher 109
Gardiner, Mrs 138-9, 143, 149-53 passim
Gardiner, Rev. Godfrey 138-9, 143, 144, 153, 154, 213
Gardner, Gerald 38
Garnier, Gilles 33
Garrett, Joan 187
Gates, John 187
Gaule, the Rev. John 53, 55, 57, 62, 85, 86, 208, 209, 210, 211
Gerish, W. B. 7, 107, 210, 212, 213

Germanilla 17
Gibson, Ellen 96
Gifford, or Gyfford, George 41, 85, 207
Gilston, Matthew 137, 139, 143
Glanvill, Joseph 83, 85, 153, 211, 214
Gleane, Lyon 190
Godfrey, Elizabeth 155
Godfrey, Philip 103
Godfrey, Richard 155
Gold, Anne 110
Gold, Edward 110
Gold, John 110
Gold, Thomas, junior 110, 192
Gold, Thomas, senior 110
Gooderidge, Alse 79
Goodfellow, Robin 51, 208
Goodwin, Elizabeth 208
Gothe, Mr 112
Gotobed, John 52
Grave, George 97, 98
Grave, or Grace, Thomas 188
Green, Sebastian 158
Green, William 145, 151
Gregory I 20
Gregory, Robert 160
Grew, Margery 208
Grilland, Paul (Grillandus) 34, 208
Grindley, John 115
Grubb, Simon 188
Guazzo, Francesco Maria 30, 32, 35, 90, 205, 206
Gunnill, Clement 191
Guthrum 21
Gybbons, Roger 99, 189
Gynne, Henry 186

Haggy, Mother 41, 179-80
Hale, Sir Matthew 42
Hale, William 43
Halfehead, William 192
Hall, Goodman 118, 119, 120, 122
Hall, Goodwife 123, 125
Hall, Mary 117-25, 128, 130
Halliwell, J. O. 73
Hamond, Agnes 114, 190, 195
Hamond, Thomas 190
Hamont, Mary 187
Hantler, Thomas 188
Harding (or Harden), Thomas 68, 111-3, 193
Harod (or Harwood), Goodwife 118, 120, 122

Harrison, Anne 41, 47, 59, 98-102
Harrison, Hugh 103
Harrison, Johane 41, 47, 59, 98-102
Hartlay, Edmund 79, 211
Harvey, John 186
Harvey, Richard 140
Harvey, Thomas 143, 150
Harwood, Marion 188, 197, 215
Hatyn, Sarah 208
Havers, Alice 188
Hawkes, Margery 187
Haynes (or Heynes), Joseph 115-6, 193
Heare, Elizabeth 208
Heather, Thomas 42, 186, 207
Henry V 91
Henry VI 40
Henry VIII 42, 210
Hill, John 97
Hill, Mercy 188, 189, 215
Hill, Susan 97, 186
Hills, Thomas 189
Hind, "Captain" James 181-2
Hine, Reginald 180, 210, 213, 215
Hitch, Thomas 52
Hockett, Mary 208
Hockley, John 115
Hoggard, Brian 8, 173, 178, 209, 214, 215
Holdsworth, Peter 115
Hole, Christina 205, 206, 208, 209, 211, 214
Holmes, Lady Anne 192
Holt, Sir John 86
Hood, Robin 24
Hopkins, Matthew 51, 52-5, 183, 184
Hopton, Francis 160, 161
Houghton, Sir Robert 104
Howe, John 11
Hullett, Margaret 104, 191, 195
Hullett, Richard 104, 195
Humphrey, Agnes 11
Humphrey (or Humfrey), Elizabeth 11, 12, 190
Hurst, Abraham 109
Hutchinson, Francis 86, 146, 211, 214
Hutten, Agnes 191

Ingroom, Margaret 116, 193
Ingroom, Thomas 116, 193
Innocent VIII, Pope 25
Institoris, Heinrich 25, 27, 29, 33, 206

Ireland, Mary (or Mercy) 95, 188
Ireland, Robert 95
Ireland, Susan 96
Ireland, Thomas 143

James I (VI of Scotland) 7, 46, 56, 58, 59, 77, 95, 179, 207, 208, 209
James, Anthony 98, 99
James, Elizabeth 99-100
Jenkinson, Richard 186
Jewel, Bishop John 43
Joanes, Easter 116, 193, 210
Johnson, Howard 214
Jones, Rebecca 208
Jones-Baker, Doris 175, 205, 209, 214, 215
Jonson, Ben 85
Jourdemayne, Marjery 40
Jovina 17

Keep, Robert 162
Kelly, Edward 69-71
Kempe, Ursley 80
Kent, John 109
Kidd, John 114
King, Margery 187
King, Thomas 187
Kinge, John 104
Kinge, William 112
Knightly, Rev John 113, 156
Knott, or Knot, Elizabeth 104-8
Kramer, Henry see Institoris, Heinrich

Laman, or Lamen (family) 106
Landish, Margaret 208
Lane (or Laine), Elizabeth 59, 68, 113-4, 156, 185, 193, 195
Lane, Woolmer 190
Langton, Walter 23
Lea, Thomas 103
Leach, Anne 208
Leper, Johanna 114-5, 215
Levack, Brian 38, 207
Lewis, Alexander 189
Ley, Margaret 51
Lilley, Anne 114
Lilley, Grace 114
Lilley, Richard 114
Lilly, William 105, 166, 212
Litchfield, Prudence 108, 192
Litchfield, William 108, 192
Lowes, John 86
Luke, Sir John 103
Macfarlane, Alan 7, 207, 208, 210

Magnus, Olaus 31, 34, 36
Man, Anne 108, 192
Man (or Mann), Marion 187, 193
Marlowe, Christopher 84
Marsh, Francis 105, 107
Marshall, William 187
Mary I 43
Massey, Rosina 180
Mayer, Mr 106
Mayes, Joan 108
Mayor, John 160
Melton, John 72, 210
Meriweather, Joanna 43
Merrifield, Ralph 7, 205, 209, 211, 214
Messenger, Joan 191
Michaell, Henry 104
Mills, Jone (or Joan) 156
Mills, Richard 156
Milton, Richard 192
Molland, Alice 86
Montague, Serjeant Henry 103
Moone, Margaret 208
Moore, Hannah Maria 82, 84
Morduck, Sarah 86
More, George 80
Morris, Agnes 186
Moyses, or Mayster, James 187
Moyses, Thomas 104, 187
Munke, Elizabeth 190
Munn, Joseph 133
Murray, Margaret 91-2, 205, 211
Mychell, Barnard 185, 188

Nashe, Alice 104, 191
Nashe, Elizabeth 11
Navarre, Joan of 91
Newell, Joan 179
Newell, John 179
Newland, Joice 189
Nicholas, Mary 87
Nicholls, Daniel 158
Nider, Johan 25
Noble, Elizabeth 97, 186, 197
Noble, Thomas 97, 197
Noble, William 98, 186
Noone, Joseph 109
North, Roger 50, 208
Norwood, Thomas 109

Ollivere, Anne 189
Ollivere, Grace 188
Osborne, John 56, 157-62, 214
Osborne, Ruth 56, 87, 157-62, 214
Osland, John 104

INDEX

Osmond, Henry 103
Oswell, George 24

Palmer, John 52, 104-8, 208, 212
Palmer, widdow 108
Parker, Doctor 131
Parker, Edward 190, 212
Parker, Lord Chief Justice Sir Thomas 87, 213
Parnell, Matthew 156, 193
Parrat, Elizabeth 191
Parrat, John 191
Parsons, Catherine 61
Pattin, Robert 191
Payne, Thomas 113
Peacock, Cuthbert 24
Peacock, Elizabeth 191, 196
Pearls, Goodwife 106
Peckham, Archbishop of 23
Peddleton, Bernard 11
Peirse, John 99, 189
Pemberton, John 137
Penifather, Christopher 187
Pennyfather, Mary 111-2
Perkins, William 85, 210
Peter, Stubb 33
Phillips, Mary 52
Phipp, John 24
Plumer, Colonel 145, 146
Plumer, Thomas 192
Poope, Elizabeth 191
Porter, Thomas 24
Powell, Sir John 143
Prentis, Joan 45
Price, Benjamin 160
Puckering, Sir John 98
Puddeford, Elizabeth 110

Radford, E. & M. A. 174, 211, 214
Rainbow, Sally 180, 215
Randolph, John 211
Raye, Elizabeth 11-12, 184, 190
Raye, Margery 11-12, 184, 190
Raye, Ralph 11-12, 184
Raye, Tobias 11, 184
Redcap, Mother 61, 209
Redman, of Amersom (Amersham) 124, 125
Remy, Nicholas 30
Revells, Doctor 115
Reynolds, Richard 106, 108
Richard III 206
Rid, Samuel 74
Robinson, Edmund 77-8, 211
Rockwell, Martha 109

Roper, Margaret 79
Rudolph II, Emperor of Bohemia, 71, 210
Rumbold, John 99, 189
Rustat, Frances 109, 193
Rustat, Samuel 109

Sadleir, Thomas 180
Salmon, John, senior 106
Salmon, Joseph 106, 108
Salmon, Judeth 106, 108
Salter, Marie 52
Salter, Thomas 52
Samm, Edward 109
Sampson, Agnes 46
Sanders, Mr 124
Scot, Reginald 30, 47, 57, 60, 68, 80-2, 85, 92, 107, 204, 206, 208, 209, 211
Scrope, Ralph 89
Sely, John 187
Severinus 17
Sewell, Audrey 190
Sewell, Joan 186
Sewell, William 186
Shakespeare, William 84, 164, 208, 211
Shatbolt, Robert 113, 114
Shatbolte, Joan 113
Shermantine, Henry 11
Sibley, or Sibly, Ebenezer, 70, 210
Sixtus V, Pope 71
Skelton, John 185, 186
Skepp, Thomas 191
Slowden (or Slowen), Alice 188
Smith, Agnes 189, 190
Smith, Anne 106, 191
Smith, Emma 87
Smith, John 109
Smith, Sarah 109
Smythe, John (1) 77, 211
Smythe, John (2) 113
Snowe, Robert 186
Somers, William 79-80
Sothwell, Thomas 40
Sparke, Alice 186
Spede, Richard 113, 114, 195
Spencer, John 187
Spencer, Marcy (or Mercy) 109, 192
Sprenger, Jacob 25, 27, 29, 30, 33, 92, 206
Squier, Adam 77, 110
Squire, Rev Mr 47
Stammers, Samuel 87
Standly, Stephen 11

Starchie, Nicholas 79
Stearne, John 52, 53, 208
Steele, Robert 50, 208
Stokes, Alice 98-102, 189
Stokes, Christian 98-102, 189
Strate, Goodwife 112
Street, Anne 135, 137, 145, 152, 154
Stretton, Jane 128-30
Stretton, Thomas 128-30 passim
Strutt, Joseph 180, 215
Strutt, Rev 140, 142-4 passim, 153, 154
Stuart, Charles Edward 214
Summers, Montague 92, 205, 212
Sutton, Agnes 190
Sutton, John 103
Swift, Jonathan 213
Symmonds, Richard 160, 161
Sympson, John 186

Tacita 18
Tankerville, George 43
Taylor, Mary 188
Tenngler, Ulrich 30
Theodore, Archbishop of Canterbury 20, 212
Thompkins, John 158
Thorne, Anne 135-54 passim
Thybault, John 73
Tilbury, Gervase of 34
Tockfield, Isaac 134
Townsend, Amey 156-7
Tretia Maria 18
Turlogg, Elizabeth 188
Turpin, Dick 188
Twygg, Alice 188

Umbles, William 160, 161, 162

Vaughan, Joan 188, 189
Velvinna 17
Vilbia 17

Wakefield, Jane 99, 189
Walby, William 187
Walker, Henry 109
Walker, John 103
Wallis, John 109
Walmesley, Sir Thomas 12
Walters (alias Waters), John 160
Ward, Mary 110
Ward, Mary Ann 89
Warren, Susanna 189
Watson, John 187
Wattes, Agnes 188

Webb, Ellen 191, 196
Webster, John (1) 57, 84, 85, 209, 211
Webster, John (2) 211
Wells, Thomas 188
Wenham, Edward 137, 140
Wenham, Jane 41, 58, 86, 109, 135-54, 156, 192
West, Anne 208
Weston, William 79
Weyer, Johan 30, 47, 211
Walleys, Edward 104
Whillocke, Joane 155, 156, 193
White, Joan 187, 193
Whitenbury, Edward 191

Whittenbury, Agnes 189, 194
Wiles, Mary 208
Wilkenson (or Wylkenson), Michael 113, 114
William I 22-3
Willowbye, Ralph 188
Winch, Sir Humphrey 77, 210
Witch of Eye, see Jourdemayne, Marjery
Wodd, Miles 191
Wood, Henry 114
Wood, John 129
Wood, Susan 116, 193, 210
Woodhouse, Doctor 118-24 passim, 130, 131, 213

Worcester, Henry 160, 161
Worcester, John 160
Wrangle, Thomas 191
Wright, David 134
Wright, Elizabeth 79
Wright, Isaiah 150
Wright, John 99
Wright, Katherine 79
Wright, Uriah 143
Wycliffe, John 59

Young (alias Leigh), Charles 160, 161, 162
Young, Goodwife 118, 120
Aldbury 160

INDEX OF PLACES: HERTFORDSHIRE

Anstey 174
Ardley 108, 192, 195
Ashwell 108, 174, 175, 176, 178, 189, 190, 191, 192, 195, 196, 215
Aspenden 114, 185, 186, 190, 195
Aston 189, 195

Baldock 17, 174, 205, 212
Barkway 104, 187, 191, 195, 196
Barley 188, 189, 191, 195
Barnett 179, 188
Bengeo 97, 185, 186-7, 191, 195, 196
Bennington 109, 191, 192, 195
Berkhamsted (Barkhamsted etc.) 11, 107, 110, 118, 123, 124, 184, 190, 191, 192, 196, 213
Bishop's Hatfield, *see Hatfield*
Bishop's Stortford 43, 46, 115
Bramfield 180
Brent Pelham 182, 214
Broxbourne 155, 193
Buntingford 185, 186, 187, 188, 195, 197
Bushey 187, 193, 195

Caddington 103, 196
Cheshunt 188, 189, 190, 192, 195
Chipping Barnett 188, 195
Codicote 112, 113
Cottered 191, 214

Datchworth 24, 215

Eastwick 190, 195
Flamstead 103, 185, 186, 189, 190, 195, 196

Gaddesdens, the 19, 20, 118, 128, 187, 188, 189, 195, 213
Gilston 145, 146, 213
Gravely 178
Gubblecote Brook 158
Gubblecote Cross 161

Halls Green, Weston 174
Harpenden 103, 205
Hatfield 20, 99, 100, 181, 185, 187, 190
Hemel Hempstead 158
Hertford, or Hartford, 11, 20, 46, 49, 50, 75, 96, 98, 99, 103, 104, 108, 116, 118, 130, 136, 143, 145, 148, 155, 156, 157, 160, 161, 162, 164, 171, 184, 185, 186, 188, 195, 196, 207, 208, 210, 213, 214
Hertingfordbury 146, 147

Hitchin 19, 24, 63, 67, 78, 85, 106, 108, 113, 114, 117, 134, 137, 174, 180, 186, 190, 195, 209, 210, 213, 214, 215
Hoddesdon 42, 112, 186, 191, 195, 207
Hormeads, the 174

Ickleford 111, 114, 115, 193

Kings Walden 112, 113
Knebworth 192, 195

Long Marston 157, 158
Markyate 103, 134

Marston Mere 160, 161
Mundens, the 95, 188, 192, 195, 214
Munder's Hill 137

Newnham 196
Northchurch (Littleheath) 11
North Mimms (Water End) 174
Norton 105, 106
Offley 134

Purwell 173, 214
Queen Hoo Hall 174, 180

Redbourn 171
Royston 41, 47, 59, 73, 98-102, 189

St Ippolyts (Hippollettes) 111, 112

St Albans 8, 41, 43, 46, 49, 52, 98, 104, 105, 108, 118, 156, 161, 163-6, 167, 179, 189
Sarratt 117
Stapleford 98, 186, 187
Stevenage 109, 186, 195
Stondon 25, 156, 193
Stanstead (Stansted) 187, 185

Temple Dinsley 180
Tewin 174
Therfield 16, 186, 195
Tring 56, 87, 130, 134, 158, 160, 161, 185, 188, 195

Ver (River) 180

INDEX

Walkern 41, 58, 86, 135-54 passim, 187, 192, 195
Walsworth 59, 63, 113, 114, 156, 174, 193
Ware 102, 115, 128, 129, 188, 195
Weston 106, 108, 112, 174-5
Wheathampstead 103, 177, 191, 195
Wilston Green 160, 161
Wymondleys, the 137, 173

INDEX OF PLACES: NON-HERTFORDSHIRE

Abbots Bromley 91, 178

Ban de la Roche 39
Bath 17, 18
Bedburg 33, 206
Bedfordshire 10, 53, 103, 175, 209
Bexhill 58

Bremen 27
Braynford 179
Bury St Edmunds 86, 207, 214

Cambridge 101
Cambridgeshire 10, 16, 19, 23, 52, 53, 61, 112, 113, 212
Chelmsford 45, 52, 69
Chesham 160
Clacton-on-Sea 80
Chester 43
Cleworth 79
Cologne 27, 30, 206
Cornhill 40
Coventry 23

Dann, Basel 27
Dole, Lyons 33
Dunstable 105, 107, 128, 134

Egypt 74
Ely 208
Ely, Isle of 23
Essex 7, 10, 49, 50, 52, 69, 80, 87, 146, 175, 179, 183, 192, 196, 208, 209, 210, 211, 212
Euphrates (River) 18
Exeter 86

Finland 38
Flag Fen, Peterborough 16
France 30, 39, 123, 205, 206

Gamlingay 112, 113
Germany 25, 30, 33, 37, 87, 124, 206, 207
Gloucestershire 89

Great Giddings 19
Great Shelford 23
Great Stoughton 53
Great Wigston 86
Guilden Morden 113, 156

Highgate 112
Horseheath 61
Huntingdonshire 52, 53, 114, 212

Iceland 38
Isle of Man 38
Italy 30
Ivinghoe 160

Jerusalem 66

Kent 49, 80, 212

Lambeth 74
Lancaster 41, 77, 207
Lapland 58
Leadenhall 40
Leamington 82
Leicester 77, 86
Leighton Buzzard 158, 160
Lincoln's Inn 69, 89
Lindow End 15
Liverpool 51
London 8, 18, 20, 21, 47, 55, 64, 80, 98, 99, 115, 128, 135, 136, 137, 156, 164, 193, 206, 208, 210, 211, 215
Loudun 213
Louviers 213
Lyons 33, 208

Mainz 27
Manningtree 52
Middlesex 43, 175
Monmouth 87

Norfolk 23, 24, 52
Normandy 38
North Berwick 46, 48
Northamptonshire 21, 53, 158, 209
Oakley 58, 209

Oxford 77, 161, 209

Peckham 23
Pendle Forest 77, 207
Pitstone 160
Plymouth 84
Pompeii 18
Portugal 18
Prague 71

Rome 22, 23, 36, 172

St Osyth (St Oses) 80, 211
Salisbury 43
Salzburg 27
Scotland 46, 48, 51, 78, 183, 206, 208
Sible Hedingham 87
Somerset 19, 77
Southwark 126, 127
Spain 30
Star Carr 14, 16
Staunton 212
Stowmarket 53
Strasbourg 30
Stretham 52
Studham 103
Suffolk 52, 57, 207, 209, 214
Surrey 42, 49, 212
Sussex 49, 212
Switzerland 30

Thames (River) 16
Tréves 27
Trois Frères 14, 15, 16
Venice 206

Warwick 127
Wells 60
Wilton Place, Dymock 89
Wiltshire 74
Winslow 158
Whenham 52

INDEX OF SUBJECTS

accomplices 25, 40, 44, 48, 81, 212
acquittals 23, 29, 42, 46, 50, 80, 86, 96, 98, 103, 104, 108, 109, 110, 185, 186-92 passim, 194, 212, 215
Agnus Dei 67, 199, 210
ague 59, 60, 86, 102, 124, 125, 132, 199
alchemy 69-72, 77, 199
almanacs 72, 73-4, 85, 199
Anglo-Saxons 14, 19, 21, 205, 208
Assize Courts 7, 11, 12, 41, 42, 49, 50, 52, 53, 77, 79, 86, 95-9 passim, 102, 103, 108, 109, 113, 114, 143, 145, 157, 160, 161, 183, 184, 185, 186, 193, 197, 199, 201, 204, 207, 208, 210, 212, 214, 215
astrology 67, 69, 72, 73, 76, 88, 89, 107, 124, 125, 199, 209, 210, 212, 213

barrows 14, 16, 42
Bellarmine jars 61
benefit of clergy 43, 44, 48, 207
bleeding corpses 58-9
Borough and Liberty Courts 49, 208
Bronze Age 15-16
broomsticks 9, 180
cannibalism 200

Canon Episcopi 21, 29, 34, 93
casualties 38-9, 183, 197, 198
Cathars 90, 93
Catholicism 66, 67, 91, 92, 171, 214
cats 46, 51, 52, 55, 63, 79, 81, 106, 109, 118, 142, 143, 144, 145, 148, 152, 173, 174, 180, 192
cattle 27, 47, 52, 60-61, 64, 80, 100, 101, 124, 150, 187, 186, 187, 188, 189, 192, 198
celestial alignments 15
Celts 19
Charms, *see curses, spells and charms*
Christian Church, attitudes of 9, 20, 21, 22, 31, 44, 59, 66, 79, 80, 90, 91, 93, 184
Christian Church, strength of belief in 24, 89
church bells 67, 177, 178
Civil War 84, 90, 108, 184, 212
conjurers and jugglers 68, 79, 80-1, 82, 84, 124, 199, 210
corpses, use of 31, 32, 47, 70, 88, 200, 209
crop circles 87, 167
cunning folk 13, 31, 33, 49, 61, 64, 65-9, 87, 88, 91, 93, 105, 107, 111-6, 126, 179, 199, 201
curses, spells and charms 10, 14, 16-18, 19, 21, 27, 43, 44, 59, 60-3, 64-6, 68, 77, 86, 87, 88, 89, 100, 111, 113, 139, 142, 152, 158, 181-2, 199, 200, 201, 213

dagaz 18
daisywheels 177, 178
Deermen, *see Abbots Bromley*
demons and devils 13, 14, 20, 21, 22, 23, 27, 29, 30, 31, 32, 33, 34, 35, 40, 41, 44, 45, 48, 50, 51, 52, 53, 56, 59, 62, 66, 67, 68, 71, 77, 79, 82, 84, 85, 87, 88, 90, 93, 101, 105, 107, 117, 118-25, 126, 128, 129, 133, 134, 142, 143, 144, 148, 149, 150, 151, 152, 163-72, 177, 184, 192, 199, 200, 201, 212, 213,
desiccated animals 173-4
divination, diviners 14, 20, 21, 46, 68, 74, 76, 77, 82, 87, 88, 111, 115-6, 180, 181, 193, 199, 201, 210, 212
doctors and physicians 30, 35, 63, 64, 67, 69, 78, 117, 118-28 passim, 130, 131, 136, 164, 209, 213
doom paintings 23, 205
dreams 76, 180-1, 210

Ecclesiastical Courts 49, 184, 199, 200, 208, 212
ergot 15, 90, 205
evidence 10, 11, 29, 30, 41-2, 52-9, 77, 85, 86, 98, 100, 101, 103, 104, 108, 109, 110, 113, 114, 115, 143, 154, 205, 212
execution, methods of 15, 33, 37, 43, 45, 207
exorcism 33, 66, 67, 79-80, 92, 148, 150, 151, 200

familiars 41, 45, 51-2, 53, 54, 57, 77, 80, 94, 100, 105, 106, 107, 112, 118-25, 126, 127, 128, 129, 142, 152, 173, 200, 201, 207
flight 21, 22, 29, 41, 42, 87, 93, 125, 179-80
flying ointments 31, 32, 88
folk medicine 20, 65, 67, 68, 88, 115
fortune telling, *see divining*
fraud 49, 53, 68, 69, 71, 74, 76-84, 88, 115, 184, 193
Fraudulent Mediums Act 1952 49

Gaol Delivery Rolls 98, 103, 208
gaols 44, 46, 53, 84, 95, 98, 108, 116, 135, 143, 160, 181, 194
Gospel of St John 59, 79
graffiti and good luck marks 177-8,
Grand Jury 11, 41, 50, 87, 96, 98, 103, 104, 109, 114, 143, 161, 183, 190, 192, 200, 201, 204, 210, 212
Gypsies 67, 72, 74-5, 116, 181

hagstones 177, 200
Hell 23, 82, 122, 166, 168, 199
hoards, ritual, and spiritual middens 62-3, 173-5, 209, 214
hobby horses 177, 211
Holy Water and Host, Holy Oil 67, 210
Home Circuit 49, 50, 95, 185, 194, 212, 215
horned god 14, 15, 91-2, 204
horseshoes 62, 64

image magic 21, 40, 46, 69, 88-9, 101, 130, 200
imps, *see demons and devils*
incubi 27, 200
Inquisition 27, 30-1, 90, 200, 206
interrogatories 25
Iron Age 15

INDEX

Jews 90
jugglers, *see conjurers*

killing of offerings 15-6, 17-8
King's Bench 86
King's Evil 134, 209
Knights Templar 90, 93

lepers 90
Lindow man 15, 205
Lord's Prayer 58, 140, 142, 146, 149
love magic 31, 65, 111, 200, 209
lycanthropy and shapeshifting 33-4, 36, 55, 106, 127, 158, 201

Macbeth 84
magic squares 18-9, 66
magicians 13, 14, 19, 21, 23, 69, 71, 91, 148, 201
Malleus Maleficarum 25-30, 33, 40, 58, 64, 80, 90, 92, 93, 203
mandrake root 78-9
Midland Circuit 50
midwives 27, 35, 90
necromancy, nigromancy etc. 84, 115, 200, 212

ordeal, trial by, 9, 23, 56, 58, 86, 87, 106, 107, 140, 156-62 passim, 201, 205, 213
penitentials 20, 200, 205
Petty Jury 12, 42, 98, 103, 104, 144, 204
poisoning 23, 72, 81, 90, 91, 148, 150, 189, 201, 212, 213
possession 66, 67, 79, 85, 91-2, 113, 117-34, 200
prickers & pricking 56, 57, 78, 142, 149, 200
prophecy 46, 180
Protestantism 22, 43, 79, 91, 92
puddingstone 64, 175, 177
Puritanism 52, 86

Quarter Sessions 7, 49, 75, 95, 96, 108, 111, 113, 115, 116, 185, 193, 200, 213

Reformation 91, 167, 205, 207
relics 20, 66-7, 92
Roman Law 25, 40, 200

Romans 16-9, 66, 71, 89

sabbat 22, 31, 32, 40, 87, 88, 91, 200, 206
sacrifice 15, 20, 21, 63, 87, 173
sanctuary 43, 44, 48, 207
Satan, *see demons and devils*
scepticism 22, 30, 42, 47, 85, 195, 204, 211
scratching 59, 87, 100, 101, 102, 124, 140, 148, 153, 155-6, 157, 200, 201, 213
scoring above the breath, *see scratching*
sorcery 14, 18, 23, 40, 41, 43, 47, 48
sources, reliability of 95-6
spells, *see curses, spells and charms*
stone circles 14, 15
succubi 27, 201
suicide 119, 134, 145

Ten Commandments, laying on of, *see scratching*
toads 20, 46, 51, 52, 53, 107, 109, 129, 192
torture 10, 25, 28, 29, 33, 46, 57, 58, 90, 93, 94, 183, 200, 201, 204, 207, 208
treasure hunting 42, 43, 44, 47
unofficial action 56-8, 155-62, 184 (see also ordeal and scratching)
walking, *see unofficial action and torture*
watching, *see unofficial action and torture*
weighing against the Bible, *see unofficial action and torture*
werewolves, *see lycanthropy*
Wild Hunt 22, 93
wise men and women, see *cunning folk*
witch bottles 61-2, 142-3, 150, 152, 178, 201
witch hunts, causes of 31, 90-4, 183-4, 200
witch's marks 53, 56-7, 79, 105, 107, 140, 150, 200, 201
witch's teats 53, 56-7, 105, 107, 140, 201
Witchcraft Act, 1542 42-3, 44, 184
Witchcraft Act, 1563 13, 44, 46, 48, 98
Witchcraft Act, 1580 46
Witchcraft Act, 1604 47-8, 86, 144
Witchcraft Act, 1736 48-9, 82, 84, 184
witchcraft and witches, concepts of 9, 13-4, 21, 30, 31-33 passim, 89, 90, 93-4, 107
witchcraft and witches, reality of 88-89 see also *cunning folk*
witchcraft, as a pagan survival 9, 91-2
witchcraft, as heresy 10, 27, 29, 30, 40, 43, 90, 199, 200
witchcraft, development of 13-24
witchcraft, diabolic pact 13-4, 23, 40, 87, 93, 94, 105, 107, 142, 206, 212
witchcraft, motives behind prosecutions for 77, 78, 79, 80, 91-3 *passim*, 196-7
witchcraft, statistics of 38-9, 49-51, 62-3, 90, 93, 183-5 passim, 194-8
witches, and the law 13, 25, 33, 41-49, 90, 184 see also Witchcraft Acts
witches, confessions of 10, 25, 27, 29, 33, 41, 43, 44, 46, 51, 52, 57-8, 59, 77, 79, 80, 86, 89, 90, 100, 105, 106, 107, 112, 115, 142, 143, 153, 201
witches, decline in belief 84-7
witches, defences against and detection of 21, 55-9, 59-64, 65, 173, 177, 199, 200 see also ordeal, unofficial action, witch marks and teats, witch bottles, etc.
witches, punishment of 12, 21, 23, 27, 29, 31, 33, 37, 40, 42-8 passim, 50, 85, 88, 98, 103, 180, 184, 204, 215
witches, sex of 8, 14, 27, 34, 35, 38, 197
witches, sexual behaviour of 27, 31, 32, 93, 200
Witchfinder General, *see Hopkins, Matthew*
witchfinders 53, 55, 67, 78, 200, 201
wizards 14, 21, 40, 78, 124, 130, 201

If you are interested in purchasing
other books published by Tempus, or in case you have
difficulty finding any Tempus books in your local bookshop,
you can also place orders directly through our website

www.tempus-publishing.com

or from

BOOKPOST
Freepost, PO Box 29,
Douglas, Isle of Man
IM99 1BQ
Tel 01624 836000
email bookshop@enterprise.net